AQUINAS

OUTSTANDING CHRISTIAN THINKERS

Series Editor: Brian Davies OP, Professor of Philosophy at Fordham University, New York.

Cappadocians
Anthony Meredith SJ

Hans Urs von Balthasar
John O'Donnell SJ

Augustine
Mary T. Clark RSCJ

Teresa of Avila
Archbishop Rowan Williams

Catherine of Siena
Giuliana Cavallini OP

Bultmann
David Fergusson

Kierkegaard
Julia Watkin

Karl Barth
John Webster

Lonergan
Frederick Rowe SJ

Aquinas
Brian Davies OP

Reinhold Neibuhr
Kenneth Durkin

Paul Tillich
John Heywood Thomas

Venerable Bede
Benedicta Ward SLG

Karl Rahner
William V. Dych SJ

Apostolic Fathers
Simon Tugwell OP

Anselm
G. R. Evans

Denys the Areopagite
Andrew Louth

Newman
Avery Cardinal Dulles SJ

AQUINAS

Brian Davies OP

continuum
LONDON • NEW YORK

CONTINUUM
The Tower Building, 11 York Road, London SE1 7NX
370 Lexington Avenue, New York NY 10017-6503

www.continuumbooks.com

First published 2002

British Library Cataloguing-in-Publication Data
A catalogue record for this book is available from the British Library.

ISBN: 0-8264-5085-7 (paperback)
0-8264-5084-9 (hardback)

Typeset by Kenneth Burnley, Wirral, Cheshire
Printed and bound in Great Britain by Biddles Ltd, Guildford and King's Lynn

Contents

For Victor Austin and Brian Leftow

*And in memory of Herbert McCabe OP
(1926–2001)*

Editorial Foreword

St Anselm of Canterbury (1033–1109) once described himself as someone with faith seeking understanding. In words addressed to God he says 'I long to understand in some degree thy truth, which my heart believes and loves. For I do not seek to understand that I may believe, but believe in order to understand.'

This is what Christians have always inevitably said, either explicitly or implicitly. Christianity rests on faith, but it also has content. It teaches and proclaims a distinctive and challenging view of reality. It naturally encouarges reflection. It is something to think about; something about which one might even have second thoughts.

But what have the greatest Christian thinkers said? And is it worth saying? Does it engage with modern problems? Does it provide us with a vision to live by? Does it make sense? Can it be preached? Is it believable?

The Outstanding Christian Thinkers series is offered to readers with questions like these in mind. It aims to provide clear, authoritative and critical accounts of outstanding Christian writers, from New Testament times to the present. It ranges across the full spectrum of Christian thought to include Catholic and Protestant thinkers, thinkers from East and West, thinkers ancient, medieval and modern.

The series draws on the best scholarship currently available, so it will interest all with a professional concern for the history of Christian ideas. But contributors also write for general readers who have little or no previous knowledge of the subjects to be dealt with. Its volumes should therefore prove helpful at a popular as well as an academic level. For the most part they are devoted to a single thinker, but occasionally the subject is a movement or school of thought.

BRIAN DAVIES OP

Preface

If anyone deserves to be called an outstanding Christian thinker, then Aquinas is such a person. As well as being highly respected by generations of Christians, he has also been valued by philosophers with no special religious affiliation. Many of the recent ones rank him together with figures such as Plato, Descartes, Locke, Hume, and Wittgenstein.

But those approaching Aquinas for the first time have problems to face. His writings are extensive, and the secondary literature on him is enormous. Studies of Aquinas are also often highly academic in style and frequently written in languages other than English.

In this book, I aim to provide a brief but comprehensive overview of Aquinas for English-speaking readers who want quickly to learn something about him without wading through many volumes. In doing so I assume no previous knowledge of Aquinas, and I try to keep technical matters to a minimum, though I include a solid and up-to-date bibliography and a chronology of Aquinas's writings.

Some scholars will doubtless wish to take issue with some of my readings of Aquinas. Where scholarly debate on aspects of his teaching is especially lively, I indicate so in my text. But I do not linger to argue in detail when it comes to matters of exegesis. Readers who wish to learn more about discussions concerning the interpretation of Aquinas will find plenty to help them in works cited in the Bibliography.

Accounts of Aquinas's writings have often given the impression that he was primarily a philosopher. I believe that this way of presenting him is wrong. The mistake is understandable since Aquinas had a lot to say on what are commonly thought to be philosophical matters. But he was first and foremost a great theologian. He was also an exceptional *Christian* thinker. In what follows, therefore, I focus on Aquinas the Christian as well as on Aquinas the philosopher. Philosopher though he was, Aquinas took God to be the beginning and end of all things. He also believed in Christ as the definitive revelation of God who gave us a believable message of hope. As well as tracing Aquinas's philosophical thinking, this book is also designed briefly to explain how all that is so.

Aquinas wrote in Latin (another obstacle facing those embarking on a study of him). Many of his writings are available in English and, where the translation is not misleading, I quote from available English editions, though sometimes with modifications. Quotations from the Bible are from the RSV edition except when they occur in quotations from Aquinas. In my own text, and in extracts from Aquinas, I have tried to avoid gender specific reference to God. Occasionally, however, I have used 'he'/'his' simply to avoid awkwardness in wording.

Some of my friends and colleagues were kind enough to read through earlier drafts of this book and to offer comments on them. I am especially indebted to Christopher Arroyo, Victor Austin, Michael Baur, James Claffey, Christopher Cullen, Ariane Economos, Peter Groves, Brian Leftow, Gyula Klima, Hilde and James Nelson, and Sara Penella.

BRIAN DAVIES
Fordham University, New York

Bibliography

1. PRIMARY SOURCES

The most authoritative listing of Aquinas's works in English is I. T. Eschmann, 'A Catalogue of St Thomas's Works: Bibliographical Notes', in E. Gilson, *The Christian Philosophy of St Thomas Aquinas* (New York: Random House, 1956). It is supplemented by 'A Brief Catalogue of Authentic Works', in James A. Weisheipl, *Friar Thomas D'Aquino* (Oxford: Basil Blackwell, 1974; republished with Corrigenda and Addenda, Washington, DC: The Catholic University of America Press, 1983).

The definitive edition of Aquinas's writings is currently being published by the Leonine Commission, established by Pope Leo XIII in 1880, which has now produced volumes containing Aquinas's most important works (*Sancti Thomae Aquinatis Doctoris Angelici. Opera Omnia. Iussu Leonis XIII*, Rome: Vatican Polyglot Press, 1882–). Publications of Aquinas's writings prior to the Leonine edition include the Parma edition (*Opera Omnia*, Parma: Fiaccadori, 1852–73) and the Vivès edition (*Opera Omnia*, Paris: Vivès, 1871–82). Most of Aquinas's writings have also been published in manual size by the Casa Marietti (Torino-Rome). Students of Aquinas should also consult R. Busa, *Index Thomisticus* (Stuttgart-Bad Cannstatt: Frommann-Holzboog, 1974–80), which provides a text of Aquinas's writings and a useful, if somewhat unwieldy, way to search for terms used by him.

A substantial amount of Aquinas's writings still remains untranslated into English. There are, however, some currently available English editions of a number of his more important works.

To date, the best English edition of the *Summa theologiae* (with notes and commentaries) is the Blackfriars edition (61 vols, Latin and English with notes and introductions, London: Eyre & Spottiswoode; and New York: McGraw-Hill Book Company, 1964–80). Unfortunately, however, this translation is sometimes unreliable. For a more literal rendering of the text, see *St Thomas Aquinas Summa Theologica* (translated by the Fathers of the English Dominican Province, originally published by Burns, Oates and Washbourne in London in 1911 and now available from Christian Classics, Westminster, Maryland, 1981). This edition may be found on the Internet at: http://www.newadvent.org/summa. A searchable concordance to it can be found on the Internet at: http://www.gocart.org/summa.html. Also worth consulting is Timothy McDermott (ed.), *St Thomas Aquinas,* Summa Theologiae: *A Concise Translation* (London: Eyre & Spottiswoode, 1989).

For a reliable translation of the *Summa contra Gentiles*, see *On the Truth of the Catholic Faith*, translated by Anton Pegis, James F. Anderson, Vernon J. Bourke and Charles J. O'Neil (New York: Doubleday, 1955–57, reprinted as *Summa Contra Gentiles*, Notre Dame, IN, and London: University of Notre Dame Press, 1975). An annotated translation of the *Summa contra Gentiles* (by Joseph Rickaby, with some abridgements) is available on the Internet at: http://www.nd/departments/maritain/etext/gc.html.

Other English translations of Aquinas's writings include:

(a) Disputed Questions

Truth (*Quaestiones disputatae De veritate*), translated by Robert W. Mulligan, J. V. McGlynn, and R. W. Schmidt (3 vols, Chicago, IL: Henry Regnery Company, 1952–54).

On the Power of God (*Quaestiones disputatae De potentia*), translated by the English Dominican Fathers (3 vols, London: Burns, Oates and Washbourne, 1932–34).

The Soul (*Quaestio disputata De anima*), translated by J. H. Robb (Milwaukee, WI: Marquette University Press, 1984).

On Spiritual Creatures (*Quaestio disputata De spiritualibus creaturis*), translated by M. C. Fitzpatrick and J. J. Wellmuth (Milwaukee, WI: Marquette University Press, 1949).

On Evil (*Quaestiones disputatae De Malo*), translated by Richard Regan (New York and Oxford: Oxford University Press, 2001).

Disputed Questions on Virtue (*Quaestio disputata De virtutibus in communi* and *Quaestio disputata De virtutibus cardinalibus*), translated by Ralph McInerny (South Bend, IN: St Augustine's Press, 1999).

On Charity (*Quaestio disputata De caritate*), translated by Lottie H. Kendzierski (Milwaukee, WI: Marquette University Press, 1984).

Quodlibetal Questions 1 and 2, translated by Sandra Edwards (Toronto: Pontifical Institute of Medieval Studies, 1983).

(b) Commentaries on Scripture

The Literal Exposition on Job (*Expositio super Job as litteram*), translated by Anthony Damico (Atlanta, GA: Scholars Press, 1989).

Commentary on the Gospel of John (*Lectura super Ioannem*), translated by James A. Weisheipl and F. R. Larcher (2 vols, Albany, NY: Magi Books, 1980; and Petersham, MA: St Bede's Publications, 1998).

Commentary on Saint Paul's First Letter to the Thessalonians and the Letter to the Philippians, translated by F. R. Larcher and Michael Duffy (Albany, NY: Magi Books, 1969).

Commentary on Saint Paul's Epistle to the Ephesians, translated by Matthew L. Lamb (Albany, NY: Magi Books, 1966).
Commentary on Saint Paul's Epistle to the Galatians, translated by F. R. Larcher (Albany, NY: Magi Books, 1966).

(c) Commentaries on Aristotle

A Commentary on Aristotle's De anima (*Sententia Libri De anima*), translated by Robert Pasnau (New Haven, CT, and London: Yale University Press, 1999).
Commentary on Aristotle's Physics (*Sententia super Physicam*), translated by R. Blackwell (New Haven, CT: Yale University Press, 1963).
On Interpretation (*Expositio Libri Peri hermenias*), translated by Jean T. Oesterle (Milwaukee, WI: Marquette University Press, 1962).
Commentary on the Posterior Analytics *of Aristotle* (*Expositio Libri Posteriorum*), translated by F. R. Larcher (Albany, NY: Magi Books, 1970).
Commentary on Aristotle's Nicomachean Ethics (*Sententia Libri Ethicorum*), translated by C. I. Litzinger (2 vols, Notre Dame, IN: University of Notre Dame Press, 1964).
Commentary on Aristotle's Metaphysics (*Sententia super Metaphysicam*), translated by John P. Rowan (Notre Dame, IN: University of Notre Dame Press, 1995).

(d) Other Commentaries

Saint Thomas Aquinas, Faith, Reason, and Theology. Questions I-IV of his Commentary on the De Trinitate *of Boethius* (*Expositio super librum Boethii De trinitate*), translated by A. Maurer (Toronto: Pontifical Institute of Medieval Studies, 1987).
Saint Thomas Aquinas, The Divisions and Methods of the Sciences. Questions V and VI of his Commentary on the De Trinitate *of Boethius* (*Expositio super librum Boethii De trinitate*), translated by A. Maurer (Toronto: Pontifical Institute of Medieval Studies, 1986).
Saint Thomas Aquinas, An Exposition of the 'On the Hebdomads' of Boethius, Introduction and translation by Janice L. Schultz and Edward A. Synan (Washington, DC: The Catholic University of America Press, 2001).
Commentary on the Book of Causes (*Expositio super librum De causis*), translated by Vincent A. Guagliardo, Charles R. Hess and Richard C. Taylor (Washington, DC: The Catholic University of America Press, 1996).

(e) Other Writings

On Being and Essence (*De ente et essentia*), translated by Joseph Bobik (Notre Dame, IN: University of Notre Dame Press, 1965).
Aquinas on Matter and Form and the Elements (translations of *De principiis naturae* and *De mixtione elementorum*), translated by Joseph Bobik (Notre Dame, IN: University of Notre Dame Press, 1998).
On There Being Only One Intellect (*De unitate intellectus contra Averroistas*),

translated by Ralph McInerny in *Aquinas Against the Averroists* (West Lafayette, IN: Purdue University Press, 1993).

Compendium of Theology (*Compendium theologie*), translated by Cyril Vollert (St Louis, MO, and London: B. Herder Book Company, 1949).

The Sermon Conferences of St Thomas Aquinas on the Apostles' Creed (*Collationes in Symbolorum Apostolorum*), translated by Nicholas Ayo (Notre Dame, IN: University of Notre Dame Press, 1988).

Readers might like to note that Thérese Bonin maintains an updated website listing currently available English translations of Aquinas at: http://www.home.duq.edu/~bonin/thomasbibliography.html.

The Thomas Institute in Utrecht also lists translations into English of Aquinas and provides one of the most helpful of Internet research sites for students of Aquinas. It can be found at: http://www.ktu.nl/thomas/

2. USEFUL SELECTIONS FROM AQUINAS IN ENGLISH

Steven E. Baldner and William E. Carroll, *Aquinas on Creation* (Toronto: Pontifical Institute of Medieval Studies, 1997).

Mary T. Clark, *An Aquinas Reader* (revised edition, New York: Fordham University Press, 2000).

Timothy McDermott (ed.), *Aquinas: Selected Philosophical Writings* (Oxford and New York: Oxford University Press, 1993).

Ralph McInerny, *Thomas Aquinas: Selected Writings* (Harmondsworth: Penguin Books, 1998).

Christopher Martin (ed.), *The Philosophy of Thomas Aquinas* (London: Routledge, 1988).

Anton C. Pegis (ed.), *Introduction to St Thomas Aquinas* (New York: The Modern Library, 1945).

3. BIBLIOGRAPHICAL WORKS

Vernon J. Bourke, *Thomistic Bibliography: 1920–1940, The Modern Schoolman*, 1921.

Richard Ingardia, *Thomas Aquinas: International Bibliography 1977–1990* (Bowling Green, OH: The Philosophy Documentation Center, 1993).

P. Mandonnet and J. Destrez, *Bibliographie Thomiste*, 2nd edition revised by M.-D. Chenu (Paris: Vrin, 1960).

Terry L. Miethe and Vernon J. Bourke, *Thomistic Bibliography, 1940–1978* (Westport, CT: Greenwood Press, 1980).

The *Bulletin Thomiste* (1940–1965), continued in *Rassegna di Letteratura Tomistica* (1966–), receives all Thomistic publications and is a useful research tool with respect to Thomistic bibliography.

4. GENERAL STUDIES AND INTRODUCTIONS TO AQUINAS

Jan Aertsen, *Nature and Creature: Thomas Aquinas's Way of Thought* (Leiden: E. J. Brill, 1988).

G. E. M. Anscombe and P. T. Geach, *Three Philosophers* (Oxford: Basil Blackwell, 1961).

Robert Barron, *Thomas Aquinas: Spiritual Master* (New York: The Crossroad Publishing Company, 1996).

M. D. Chenu, *Towards Understanding Saint Thomas* (trs. A. M. Landry and D. Hughes, Chicago: Henry Regnery Company, 1964).

M. D. Chenu, *St Thomas D'Aquin et la théologie* (Paris: Éditions du Seuil, 1959).

G. K. Chesterton, *St Thomas Aquinas* (London: Hodder and Stoughton Ltd, 1943).

F. C. Copleston, *Aquinas* (Harmondsworth: Penguin Books, 1955).

Brian Davies, *The Thought of Thomas Aquinas* (Oxford: Clarendon Press, 1992).

Leo J. Elders, *The Philosophical Theology of St Thomas Aquinas* (Leiden: E. J. Brill, 1990).

Etienne Gilson, *The Christian Philosophy of St Thomas Aquinas* (London: Victor Gollancz Ltd, 1961).

John Inglis, *On Aquinas* (Belmont, CA: Wadsworth, 2002).

Anthony Kenny, *Aquinas* (Oxford: Oxford University Press, 1980).

Norman Kretzmann and Eleonore Stump, *The Cambridge Companion to Aquinas* (Cambridge: Cambridge University Press, 1993).

Ralph McInerny, *St Thomas Aquinas* (Notre Dame, IN, and London: University of Notre Dame Press, 1982).

Ralph McInerny, *A First Glance at St Thomas Aquinas: A Handbook for Peeping Thomists* (Notre Dame, IN, and London: University of Notre Dame Press, 1990).

Thomas F. O'Meara, *Thomas Aquinas Theologian* (Notre Dame, IN, and London: University of Notre Dame Press, 1997).

Josef Pieper, *Guide to Thomas Aquinas* (translated by R. and C. Winston, Notre Dame, IN: University of Notre Dame Press, 1987).

Peter A. Redpath, *A Simplified Introduction to the Wisdom of St Thomas* (Washington, DC: University Press of America, 1980).

Francis Selman, *St Thomas Aquinas: Teacher of Truth* (Edinburgh: T. & T. Clark, 1994).

John F. Wippel, *The Metaphysical Thought of Thomas Aquinas* (Washington, DC: The Catholic University of America Press, 2000).

5. MATERIAL FOR STUDYING THE LIFE OF AQUINAS

A. Ferrua (ed.), *Thomae Aquinatis vitae fontes praecipuae* (Alba: Ed. Dominicane, 1968).

Kenelm Foster (ed.), *The Life of Thomas Aquinas* (London: Longmans, Green and Co.; and Baltimore: Helicon Press, 1959).

Jean-Pierre Torrell, *Saint Thomas Aquinas: The Person and His Work* (Washington, DC: The Catholic University of America Press, 1996).

Simon Tugwell (ed.), *Albert and Thomas – Selected Writings* (New York, Mahwah, and London: Paulist Press, 1988).

James A. Weisheipl, *Friar Thomas D'Aquino* (Oxford: Basil Blackwell, 1974; republished with Corrigenda and Addenda, Washington, DC: The Catholic University of America Press, 1983).

6. OTHER RELEVANT READING ON ASPECTS OF AQUINAS'S WRITINGS

Jan A. Aertsen, 'The Convertibility of Being and Good in St Thomas Aquinas', *The New Scholasticism* 59 (1985).

Jan A. Aertsen, 'The Philosophical Importance of the Doctrine of the Transcendentals in Thomas Aquinas', *Revue Internationale de Philosophie* 52 (1998).

Marc Aillet, *Lire la Bible avec S. Thomas: le passage de la littera à la res dans la Somme théologique* (Fribourg: Éditions Universitaires Fribourg Suisse, 1993).

E. J. Ashworth, 'Signification and Modes of Signifying in Thirteenth Century Logic: A preface to Aquinas on Analogy', *Medieval Philosophy and Theology* I (1991).

E. J. Ashworth, 'Analogy and Equivocation in Thirteenth-Century Logic: Aquinas in Context', *Medieval Studies* 54 (1992).

Stéphane-Marie Barbellion, *Les 'preuves' de l'existence de Dieu: Pour une relecture des cinq voies de saint Thomas d'Aquin* (Paris: Les Éditions du Cerf, 1999).

Otto Bird, 'How to Read an Article in the *Summa*', *The New Scholasticism* XXVII (1953).

Oliva Blanchette, *The Perfection of the Universe According to Aquinas: A Theological Cosmology* (University Park, PA: The Pennsylvania State University Press, 1992).

Vivian Boland, *Ideas in God according to Saint Thomas Aquinas: Sources and Synthesis* (Leiden, New York, Köln: E.J. Brill, 1996).

John Bowlin, *Contingency and Fortune in Aquinas's Ethics* (Cambridge: Cambridge University Press, 1999).

Leonard E. Boyle, *The Setting of the* Summa Theologiae *of Saint Thomas* (The Etienne Gilson Series, 5, Toronto: Pontifical Institute of Medieval Studies, 1982).

Patterson Brown, 'St Thomas: Doctrine of Necessary Being', *The Philosophical Review* LXXIII (1964).

David Burrell, *Aquinas, God and Action* (Notre Dame, IN: University of Notre Dame Press, 1979).

David Burrell, *Knowing the Unknowable God* (Notre Dame, IN: University of Notre Dame Press, 1986).

David Burrell, *Freedom and Creation in Three Traditions* (Notre Dame, IN: University of Notre Dame Press, 1993).

Daniel A. Callus, *The Condemnation of St Thomas at Oxford* (The Aquinas Society of London Aquinas Paper No. 5, London, 1955).

Romanus Cessario, *The Godly Image: Christ and Salvation in Catholic Thought from Anselm to Aquinas* (Petersham, MA: St Bede's Publications, 1990).

W. N. Clarke, 'What Is Most and Least Relevant in the Metaphysics of St Thomas Today?', *International Philosophical Quarterly* 14 (1974).

W. N. Clarke, 'St Thomas' Essence–Existence Doctrine', *The New Scholasticism* XLVIII (1974).

Yves Congar, *Thomas d'Aquin: sa vision de théologie et de l'Eglise* (London: Variorum Reprints, 1984).

Michel Corbin, *Le Chemin de la Théologie chez Thomas D'Aquin* (Paris:

Beauchesne, 1974).

William Lane Craig, 'Aquinas on God's Knowledge of Future Contingents', *The Thomist* 54 (1990).

Michael Bertram Crowe, 'Peter of Ireland: Aquinas's Teacher of the ARTES LIBERALES' in *Arts Liberaux et Philosophie au Moyen Age* (Paris, 1969).

Brian Davies, 'Classical Theism and the Doctrine of Divine Simplicity', in Brian Davies (ed.), *Language, Meaning and God* (London: Geoffrey Chapman, 1987).

Brian Davies, 'The Mystery of God: Aquinas and McCabe', *New Blackfriars* 77 (1996).

Brian Davies, 'Aquinas, God, and Being', *The Monist* 80 (1997).

Brian Davies (ed.), *Thomas Aquinas: Contemporary Philosophical Perspectives* (New York and Oxford: Oxford University Press, 2002).

Michael J. Dodds, *The Unchanging God of Love: A Study of the Teaching of St Thomas Aquinas on Divine Immutability in View of Certain Contemporary Criticism of this Doctrine* (Fribourg: Éditions Universitaires Fribourg Suisse, 1986).

James C. Doig, *Aquinas on Metaphysics* (The Hague: Martinus Nijhoff, 1972).

James C. Doig, *Aquinas's Philosophical Commentary on the* Ethics*: A Historical Perspective* (Dordrecht/Boston/London: Kluwer Academic Publishers, 2001).

Alan Donagan, 'Thomas Aquinas on Human Action', in N. Kretzmann, A. Kenny, and J. Pinborg (eds), *The Cambridge History of Later Medieval Philosophy* (Cambridge: Cambridge University Press, 1982).

Dominique Dubarle, *L'Ontologie de Thomas D'Aquin* (Paris: Les Éditions du Cerf, 1996).

Umberto Eco, *The Aesthetics of Thomas Aquinas* (London: Radius, 1988).

Léon Elders, *Autour de Saint Thomas D'Aquin: receuil d'études sur sa pensée philosophique et théologique* (2 vols, Paris: Fac-éditions; and Brugge: Uitgeverji Tabor, 1987).

Leo J. Elders, *The Metaphysics of Being of St Thomas Aquinas in a Historical Perspective* (Leiden, New York, Köln: E. J. Brill, 1993).

C. Fabro, *Participation et causalité selon Saint Thomas d'Aquin* (Louvain: Publications Universitaires de Louvain, 1961).

John Finnis, *Aquinas* (Oxford: Oxford University Press, 1998).

Robert J. Fogelin, 'A Reading of Aquinas's Five Ways', *American Philosophical Quarterly* 27 (1990).

David Gallagher, 'Free Choice and Free Judgment in Thomas Aquinas', *Archiv für Geschichte der Philosophie* 76 (1994).

David Gallagher (ed.), *Thomas Aquinas and His Legacy* (Washington, DC: The Catholic University of America Press, 1994).

R. A. Gauthier, *Somme Contre Les Gentils: Introduction* (Paris: Éditions Universitaires, 1993).

Peter Geach, *God and the Soul* (London: Routledge & Kegan Paul, 1969).

Louis-Bertrand Geiger, *Penser avec Thomas d'Aquin* (Fribourg: Éditions Universitaires Fribourg Suisse; and Paris: Les Éditions du Cerf, 2000).

Thomas Gilby, *The Political Thought of Thomas Aquinas* (Chicago, IL: University of Chicago Press, 1958).

BIBLIOGRAPHY

Etienne Gilson, *Being and Some Philosophers* (2nd edition, Toronto: Pontifical Institute of Medieval Studies, 1952).

Harm J. M. Goris, *Free Creatures of an Eternal God: Thomas Aquinas on God's Infallible Foreknowledge and Irresistible Will* (Leuven: Peeters, 1996).

John J. Haldane, 'Aquinas on Sense-Perception', *The Philosophical Review* 92 (1983).

Douglas C. Hall, *The Trinity: An Analysis of St Thomas Aquinas's* Expositio *of the* De Trinitate *of Boethius* (Leiden, New York, Köln: E. J. Brill, 1992).

W. J. Hankey, *God in Himself: Aquinas's Doctrine of God as expounded in the* Summa Theologiae (Oxford: Oxford University Press, 1987).

R. J. Henle, *Saint Thomas and Platonism* (The Hague: Martinus Nijhoff, 1956).

Thomas S. Hibbs, *Dialectic and Narrative in Aquinas* (Notre Dame, IN: University of Notre Dame Press, 1995).

J. N. Hillgarth, *Who Read Aquinas?* (The Etienne Gilson Series 13, Toronto: Pontifical Institute of Medieval Studies, 1992).

John Jenkins, 'Expositions of the Text: Aquinas's Aristotelian Commentaries', *Medieval Philosophy and Theology* 5 (1996).

John Jenkins, *Knowledge and Faith in Thomas Aquinas* (Cambridge: Cambridge University Press, 1997).

Mark Jordan, 'The Intelligibility of the World and the Divine Ideas in Aquinas', *The Review of Metaphysics* 38 (1984).

Mark Jordan, *Ordering Wisdom: The Hierarchy of Philosophical Discourses in Aquinas* (Notre Dame, IN: University of Notre Dame Press, 1986).

Mark Jordan, *The Alleged Aristotelianism of Thomas Aquinas* (The Etienne Gilson Series 15, Toronto: Pontifical Institute of Medieval Studies, 1992).

James F. Keenan, *Goodness and Rightness in Thomas Aquinas's* Summa Theologiae (Washington, DC: Georgetown University Press, 1992).

Anthony Kenny (ed.), *Aquinas: A Collection of Critical Essays* (London and Melbourne: Macmillan, 1969).

Anthony Kenny, *The Five Ways* (London: Routledge & Kegan Paul, 1969).

Anthony Kenny, *Aquinas on Mind* (London and New York: Routledge, 1993).

Bonnie Kent, 'Transitory Vice: Thomas Aquinas on Incontinence', *Journal of the History of Philosophy* 27 (1989).

Fergus Kerr, 'Aquinas After Marion', *New Blackfriars* 76 (1995).

Gyula Klima, 'The Semantic Principles Underlying Saint Thomas Aquinas's Metaphysics of Being', *Medieval Philosophy and Theology* 5 (1996).

John F. X. Knasas, 'Aquinas: Prayer to An Immutable God', *The New Scholasticism* LVII (1983).

Kenneth J. Konyndyk, 'Aquinas on Faith and Science', *Faith and Philosophy* 12 (1995).

Norman Kretzmann, 'Goodness, Knowledge, and Indeterminacy in the Philosophy of St Thomas Aquinas', *Journal of Philosophy* LXXX (1983).

Norman Kretzmann, *The Metaphysics of Theism* (Oxford: Clarendon Press, 1997).

Norman Kretzmann, *The Metaphysics of Creation* (Oxford: Clarendon Press, 1999).

Brian Leftow, 'Aquinas on Time and Eternity', *American Catholic Philosophical Quarterly* 64 (1990).

Brian Leftow, 'Souls Dipped in Dust', in Kevin Corcoran (ed.), *Soul, Body, and*

Survival (Ithaca and London: Cornell University Press, 2001).

Anthony J. Lisska, *Aquinas's Theory of Natural Law: An Analytic Reconstruction* (Oxford: Clarendon Press, 1996).

Paul Lockey (ed.), *Studies in Thomistic Theology* (Houston, TX: Center for Thomistic Studies, 1995).

Bernard Lonergan, *Verbum: Word and Idea in Aquinas*, ed. D. B. Burrell (Notre Dame, IN: University of Notre Dame Press, 1967).

Scott MacDonald, 'Aquinas's Parasitic Cosmological Argument', *Medieval Philosophy and Theology* I (1991).

Scott MacDonald, 'Ultimate Ends in Practical Reasoning: Aquinas's Aristotelian Moral Psychology and Anscombe's Fallacy', *The Philosophical Review* 100 (1991).

Scott MacDonald, 'Aquinas's Libertarian Account of Free Choice', *Revue Internationale de Philosophie* 52 (1998).

Scott MacDonald and Eleonore Stump (eds), *Aquinas's Moral Theory: Essays in Honor of Norman Kretzmann* (Ithaca and London: Cornell University Press, 1999).

Scott MacDonald, 'Practical Reasoning and Reasons-Explanations: Aquinas's Account of Reason's Role in Action', in Scott MacDonald and Eleonore Stump (eds), *Aquinas's Moral Theory: Essays in Honor of Norman Kretzmann* (Ithaca and London: Cornell University Press, 1999).

Herbert McCabe, *God Matters* (London: Geoffrey Chapman, 1987).

Herbert McCabe, 'The Logic of Mysticism', in Martin Warner (ed.), *Religion and Philosophy* (Royal Institute of Philosophy Supplement 31, Cambridge: Cambridge University Press, 1992).

Herbert McCabe, 'Aquinas on the Trinity', *New Blackfriars* 80 (1999).

Ralph McInerny, *Ethica Thomistica: The Moral Philosophy of Thomas Aquinas* (Washington, DC: The Catholic University of America Press, 1982),

Ralph McInerny, *Being and Predication* (Washington, DC: The Catholic University of America Press, 1986).

Ralph McInerny, *Boethius and Aquinas* (Washington, DC: The Catholic University of America Press, 1990).

Ralph McInerny, *Aquinas on Human Action: A Theory of Practice* (Washington, DC: The Catholic University of America Press, 1992).

Ralph McInerny, *Aquinas and Analogy* (Washington, DC: The Catholic University of America Press, 1996).

Stephen Makin, 'Aquinas, Natural Tendencies and Natural Kinds', *The New Scholasticism* LXIII (1989).

C. F. J. Martin, *Thomas Aquinas: God and Explanations* (Edinburgh: Edinburgh University Press, 1997).

Patrick Masterson, 'Aquinas' Notion of God Today', *Irish Theological Quarterly* 44 (1977).

Armand Maurer, *Being and Knowing: Studies in Thomas Aquinas and Later Medieval Philosophers* (Toronto: Pontifical Institute of Medieval Studies, 1990).

D. Juvenal Merriell, *To the Image of the Trinity: A Study in the Development of Aquinas' Teaching* (Toronto: Pontifical Institute of Medieval Studies, 1990).

B. Mondin, *St Thomas Aquinas's Philosophy in the Commentary on the Sentences*

(The Hague: Martinus Nijhoff, 1975).

Fran O'Rourke, *Pseudo-Dionysius and the Metaphysics of Aquinas* (Leiden, New York, Köln: E. J. Brill, 1992).

Joseph Owens, *St Thomas Aquinas on the Existence of God, Collected Papers of Joseph Owens,* edited by John R. Catan (Albany, NY: State University of New York Press, 1980).

Robert Pasnau, *Theories of Cognition in the Later Middle Ages* (Cambridge: Cambridge University Press, 1997).

Robert Pasnau, 'Aquinas on Thought's Linguistic Nature', *The Monist* 80 (1997).

A. Patfoort, *Thomas d'Aquin, les Clés d'une Théologie* (Paris: FAC-éditions, 1983).

Anton Charles Pegis, *St Thomas and the Problem of the Soul in the Thirteenth Century* (Toronto: Pontifical Institute of Medieval Studies, 1934).

Terence Penelhum, 'The Analysis of Faith in St Thomas Aquinas', *Religious Studies* 13 (1977).

Per Erik Person, *Sacra Doctrina: Reason and Revelation in Aquinas* (Oxford: Basil Blackwell, 1970).

Otto Hermann Pesch, *Thomas von Aquin: Grenze und Grösse mittelalterlicher Theologie* (Mainz-Weisenau: Matthias-Grünewald-Verlag Gmb, 1988: French translation [*Thomas d'Aquin: Limites et grandeur de la théologie médiévale*], Paris: Les Éditions du Cerf, 1994).

Josef Pieper, *The Silence of Saint Thomas* (translated by John Murray and Daniel O'Connor, Chicago: Henry Regnery Company, 1965).

Carlos-Josaphat Pinto de Oliveira (ed.), Ordo Sapientiae et Amoris*: image et message de Saint Thomas D'Aquin à travers les récentes études historiques, herméneutiques et doctrinales* (Fribourg: Éditions Universitaires Fribourg Suisse, 1993).

J. van der Ploeg, 'The Place of Holy Scripture in the Theology of St Thomas', *The Thomist* 10 (1947).

Walter H. Principe, *Thomas Aquinas' Spirituality* (The Etienne Gilson Series, 7, Toronto: Pontifical Institute of Medieval Studies, 1984).

Hilary Putnam, 'Thoughts Addressed to an Analytical Thomist', *The Monist* 80 (1997).

E. S. Radcliffe, 'Kenny's Aquinas on Dispositions for Human Acts', *The New Scholasticism* LVIII (Autumn, 1984).

Peter A. Redpath, *The Moral Wisdom of St Thomas: An Introduction* (Lanham, New York and London: University Press of America, 1983).

James P. Reilly Jr, *Saint Thomas on Law* (The Etienne Gilson Series 12, Toronto: Pontifical Institute of Medieval Studies, 1990).

Thomas F. Ryan, *Thomas Aquinas as Reader of the Psalms* (Notre Dame, IN: University of Notre Dame Press, 2000).

R. W. Schmidt, *The Domain of Logic according to Saint Thomas Aquinas* (The Hague: Martinus Nijhoff, 1966).

Henk J. M. Schoot, *Christ the 'Name' of God: Thomas Aquinas on Naming Christ* (Leuven: Peeters, 1993).

Henk J. M. Schoot (ed.), *Tibi Soli Peccavi: Thomas Aquinas on Guilt and Forgiveness* (Leuven: Peeters, 1996).

Laurent Sentis, *Saint Thomas D'Aquin et le Mal: Foi Chrétienne et Théodicée*

(Paris: Beauchesne, 1992).

Paul E. Sigmund, *St Thomas Aquinas on Politics and Ethics* (New York: W. W. Norton, 1988).

Edward Sillem, *Ways of Thinking About God: Thomas Aquinas and Some Recent Problems* (London: Darton, Longman & Todd, 1961).

Luc-Thomas Somme, *Fils Adoptifs de Dieu par Jésus Christ* (Paris: Vrin, 1997).

Fernand van Steenberghen, *Le Problème de l'Existence de Dieu dans les Ecrits de S. Thomas D'Aquin* (Louvain-La-Neuve: Éditions de l'Institut Supérieur de Philosophie, 1980).

Fernand van Steenberghen, *Thomas Aquinas and Radical Aristotelianism* (Washington, DC: The Catholic University of America Press, 1980).

Neil Stubbens, 'Naming God: Maimonides and Aquinas', *The Thomist* 54 (1990).

Eleonore Stump, 'Atonement According to Aquinas' in Thomas V. Morris (ed.), *Philosophy and the Christian Faith* (Notre Dame, IN: University of Notre Dame Press, 1988).

Eleonore Stump, 'Faith and Goodness', in Godfrey Vesey (ed.), *The Philosophy in Christianity* (Cambridge: Cambridge University Press, 1989).

Eleonore Stump, 'Atonement and Justification', in Ronald J. Feenstra and Cornelius Plantinga Jr (eds), *Trinity, Incarnation and Atonement* (Notre Dame, IN: University of Notre Dame Press, 1989).

Eleonore Stump, 'Intellect, Will and the Principle of Alternate Possibilities', in M. Beaty (ed.), *Christian Theism and the Problems of Philosophy* (Notre Dame, IN: University of Notre Dame Press, 1990).

Eleonore Stump, 'Aquinas on the Foundations of Knowledge', *Canadian Journal of Philosophy*, supplementary volume 7 (1992).

Eleonore Stump, 'Aquinas's Account of the Mechanisms of Intellective Cognition', *Revue Internationale de Philosophie* 52 (1998).

Eleonore Stump, 'Aquinas on the Mechanisms of Cognition: Sense and Phantasia', in Sten Ebbesen and Russell L. Friedman, *Medieval Analyses in Language and Cognition* (Copenhagen: The Royal Danish Academy of Sciences and Letters, 1999).

Stephen Theron, 'Esse', *The New Scholasticism* LIII (1979).

J. L. H. Thomas, 'The Identity of Being and Essence in God', *The Heythrop Journal* XXVII (1986).

Jean-Pierre Torrell, *Saint Thomas d'Aquin, Maître Spirituel* (Fribourg: Éditions Universitaires Fribourg Suisse; and Paris: Les Éditions du Cerf, 1996).

Jean-Pierre Torrell, *La Somme de Théologie de Saint Thomas d'Aquin* (Paris: Les Éditions du Cerf, 1998).

Jean-Pierre Torrell, *Récherches Thomasiennes* (Paris: Vrin, 2000).

Simon Tugwell, 'Prayer, Humpty Dumpty and Thomas Aquinas', in Brian Davies (ed.), *Language, Meaning and God* (London: Geoffrey Chapman, 1987).

Wilhelmus G. B. M. Valkenberg, *Words of the Living God: Place and Function of Holy Scripture in the Theology of St Thomas Aquinas* (Leuven: Peeters, 2000).

Rudi A. te Velde, *Participation and Substantiality in Thomas Aquinas* (Leiden, New York, Köln: E. J. Brill, 1995).

Lubor Velecky, *Aquinas' Five Arguments in the Summa Theologiae Ia 2,3* (Kampen: Kok Pharos Publishing House, 1994),

Arvin Vos, *Aquinas, Calvin and Contemporary Protestant Thought* (Washington, DC: Christian University Press, 1985).

Joseph P. Wawrykow, *God's Grace and Human Action: 'Merit' in the Theology of Thomas Aquinas* (Notre Dame, IN: University of Notre Dame Press, 1995).

Édouard-Henri Wéber, *Le Christ selon Saint Thomas D'Aquin* (Paris: Desclée, 1988).

James A. Weisheipl, *Thomas D'Aquino and Albert His Teacher* (Toronto: Pontifical Institute of Medieval Studies, 1980).

Daniel Westberg, *Right Practical Reason: Aristotle, Action, and Prudence in Aquinas* (Oxford: Clarendon Press, 1994).

Victor White, *God the Unknown* (London: The Harvill Press, 1956).

Victor White, *Holy Teaching: The Idea of Theology According to St Thomas Aquinas* (The Aquinas Society of London Aquinas Paper No. 33, London, 1958).

A. N. Williams, T*he Ground of Union: Deification in Aquinas and Palamas* (New York and Oxford: Oxford University Press, 1999).

C. J. F. Williams, *What is Existence?* (Oxford: Clarendon Press, 1981).

C. J .F. Williams, *Being, Identity, and Truth* (Oxford: Clarendon Press, 1992).

C. J. F. Williams, 'Being', in Philip L. Quinn and Charles Taliaferro (eds), *A Companion to the Philosophy of Religion* (Oxford: Basil Blackwell, 1997).

John F. Wippel, *Metaphysical Themes in Thomas Aquinas* (Washington: The Catholic University of America Press, 1984).

John F. Wippel, 'Thomas Aquinas and Participation', in J. F. Wippel (ed.), *Studies in Medieval Philosophy* (Washington, DC: The Catholic University of America Press, 1987).

John F. Wippel, 'Substance in Aquinas's Metaphysics', *Proceedings of the American Catholic Philosophical Association* 61 (1987).

John F. Wippel, 'Truth in Thomas Aquinas' (Part I and Part II), *Review of Metaphysics* 43 (1989).

John F. Wippel, *Thomas Aquinas on the Divine Ideas* (The Etienne Gilson Series 16, Toronto: Pontifical Institute of Medieval Studies, 1993).

John F. Wippel, 'Thomas Aquinas on Demonstrating God's Omnipotence', *Revue Internationale de Philosophie* 52 (1998).

John F. Wippel, *The Metaphysical Thought of Thomas Aquinas* (Washington, DC: The Catholic University of America Press, 2000).

J. B. M. Wissink (ed.), *The Eternity of the World in the Thought of Thomas Aquinas and his Contemporaries* (Leiden/New York/Kobenhavn/Köln: E. J. Brill, 1990).

Abbreviations

AC   *Sermon Conferences on the Apostles' Creed (Collationes Credo in Deum)*

CE   *Commentary on St Paul's Letter to the Ephesians*

CJ   *Commentary on the Gospel of John*

CT   *Compendium of Theology (Compendium theologiae)*

DA   *Commentary on Aristotle's* De Anima *(Sententia Libri De anima)*

DE   *On Being and Essence (De ente et essentia)*

DM   *On Evil (Quaestiones disputatae De Malo)*

DN   *Commentary on Dionysius's* The Divine Names *(Expositio super Dionysium De divinis nominibus)*

DP   *On the Power of God (Quaestiones disputatae De potentia)*

DT   *Commentary on Boethius's* De Trinitate *(Expositio super librum Boethii De trinitate)*

DV   *On Truth (Quaestiones disputatae De veritate)*

EC   *Commentary on St Paul's First Letter to the Corinthians*

IP   *Commentary on Aristotle's* Physics *(Sententia super Physicam)*

PH   *Commentary on Aristotle's* Peri Hermeneias *(Expositio Libri Peri hermeneias)*

SG   *Summa contra Gentiles*

SL   *Commentary on the* Sentences *of Peter Lombard*

ST   *Summa theologiae*

1

Introducing Aquinas

If you want to place Aquinas historically, think of him as living for about fifty years almost exactly in the middle of the thirteenth century. He was born in what we now call Italy and at a time when the politics of that region were dominated by serious conflict between papal and imperial parties. His exact year of birth is a matter of scholarly controversy, but we can safely place it between 1224 and 1226. His family were local gentry, and his birthplace was probably the castle of Roccasecca, midway between Rome and Naples. His father was known as 'Lord Landulph d'Aquino'. His mother, of noble Neapolitan background, was called Theodora. His own baptismal name was Thomas.

EARLY YEARS

In 1230 or 1231 Aquinas's parents sent him to the Benedictine abbey of Monte Cassino, where he lived and studied for about eight years. Since money could then make an abbot, they may have hoped that he would eventually succeed to high office at Monte Cassino. But military conflict between the Emperor Frederick II and Pope Gregory IX made it a centre of imperial–papal rivalry while Aquinas was there. Frederick's troops occupied the abbey early in 1239, and, by July of that year, Landulph and Theodora, then supporting the imperial cause (in 1254 they switched to the papal one), removed him from Monte Cassino and dispatched him to study at the university (or *studium generale*) recently founded by Frederick in Naples. Here, in the course of a general foundation in the so-called liberal arts, he was almost certainly introduced to the study of Aristotle (384–322 BC), who more or less singlehandedly invented what

1

we now think of as science, logic, and the philosophy of language. Also at this time, most probably, he was introduced to thinkers such as the Arabic philosopher Averroes (1126–98) and the Jewish philosopher Maimonides (1135–1204), both of whom came to influence him in particular ways. Early accounts of Aquinas's life mention one 'Master Peter of Ireland' as someone he encountered in his time at Naples. So Aquinas, we may say, also had Irish roots.

Though he was not a Benedictine monk when he went to study in Naples, we have no reason to suppose that Aquinas and his family were not still anticipating a Benedictine future for him. In Naples, however, Aquinas encountered the Dominican Order of Friars (the Order of Preachers) founded by St Dominic Guzman (c. 1170–1221), which he joined some time between 1242 and 1244. We have no special historical evidence to explain why he chose to become a Dominican, but his writings testify to a deep commitment to the Order's ideals of poverty, teaching, and preaching. And he evidently entered it with a strong, personal resolve, for he firmly resisted his family's attempts to remove him from it (like many of their contemporaries, they took it to be somewhat unrespectable). In an effort to dissuade him from remaining with the Dominicans, his mother tried to track him down first in Naples and then in Rome. Having failed to catch up with him, she arranged for him to be detained by his brothers and subsequently held for around two years in the family homes at Montesangiovanni and Rocasecca.

Aquinas enjoyed a fair degree of liberty during this period. He had access to books and to members of the Dominican Order. And he acted as a tutor to his sisters. He was not seriously a prisoner. Yet he was still being prevented from pursuing a Dominican vocation. By the middle of 1246, however, he was back with the Dominicans and subsequently spent a short time of study in Paris, where he transcribed some lectures of another Dominican, St Albert the Great (c. 1199–1280). He then moved to Cologne, where he continued to work under Albert and was probably ordained to the priesthood. Aquinas clearly showed himself to be a gifted student, and by 1256 he was again in Paris. Now, however, his role was that of teacher rather than student.

TEACHER AND AUTHOR

First of all, he lectured on the Bible and on the *Sentences* of Peter Lombard (c. 1095–1160), a doctrinal distillation of Scripture and the teaching of the early Christian Fathers written in the 1140s. By the time of Aquinas, it was a standard university textbook, and many teachers lectured and wrote commentaries on it. It is not at all surprising that Aquinas should have had to teach with respect to it. But in 1256 he was able to broaden his horizons. In that year he became a Master in Theology and, as well as continuing to lecture on the Bible, he was able to preside over what were called 'Quodlibetal Questions' or 'Quod-libetal Disputations' (*Quaestiones Quodlibetales*) and 'Disputed Questions' or 'Ordinary Disputes' (*Quaestiones Disputatae*). The former were public university debates conducted in Paris during Lent and Advent. 'Disputed Questions' resembled them by being very much a feature of university life in Aquinas's time, but (unlike 'Quodlibetal Questions') they also took place in non-university contexts such as study houses of religious orders. Scholars disagree about the precise nature and conduct of 'Disputed Questions' during the time of Aquinas, but there is no doubt that their primary aim was to get people to think clearly and in the most rigorous way possible. Like the 'Quodlibetal Questions' (though more focused and more under the control of the presiding Master), they were very much an exercise in disciplined thinking and argument. At their core was a question, or a series of questions, often ranging widely in subject matter and raised without special reference to any one text or author. The purpose of posing the questions was to arrive at solutions to them in the light of a detailed discussion chiefly comprising objections and replies to the theses propounded. In universities such as Paris, disputations were organized and presided over by a Master, whose job was to provide an authoritative verdict on the preceding debate. During the course of his teaching career, Aquinas presided over a number of such disputations. And their way of proceeding can be seen at work in much that he writes.

During his first teaching spell in Paris (commonly known as his 'first Parisian regency'), Aquinas began to produce the earliest of the works for which he is best known today. Even before arriving to teach in Paris he may have completed his commentary on the book of Isaiah and his treatise *De principiis naturae*. From the time he began teaching, however, we can firmly date his commentary on the *Sentences* of Lombard, his Disputed Question *De veritate*, the work known as *De ente et essentia*, a commentary on Boethius's *De trinitate*, and a defence of the mendicant orders – *Contra impugnantes Dei cultum et religionem*. During his first Parisian regency Aquinas also began his *Summa contra Gentiles*.

A *summa* ('summary') was an extended treatment of intellectual matters set out in an orderly and comprehensive manner. It was a standard literary genre for medieval writers working in a variety of fields (not only theology and philosophy) from around the early twelfth century. Discussing the purpose of the *Summa contra Gentiles* (not a title given to it by him; we do not know what he called it), Aquinas says that he aims 'by the way of reason to pursue those things about God which human reason is able to investigate' (SG I, 9). A similar, though perhaps broader, intention can be detected in his *Summa theologiae* (again, not Aquinas's title), which he began around 1265–68 but which remained unfinished at the time of his death. Commonly and rightly deemed to be his greatest achievement, this work contains three long treatises (or 'Parts') ranging over a very large range of topics including the existence and nature of God, the notion of creation, the nature and abilities of angels, human nature and its powers, the concept of human happiness, the characteristics of human action, the goal of human living, human virtues and vices, the life and work of Christ, and the meaning and significance of the Christian sacraments.

Aquinas's medieval biographers seem little interested in sorting out the details of his career from around 1256. They focus instead on his character and status as saint, teacher, and author. We can, however, be sure that he vacated his teaching position at Paris before 1260, that he lived and taught for a time at Orvieto in Italy, that in 1265 he was assigned by the Dominicans to establish a house of studies (or *studium*) for the Order in Rome (at the priory of Santa Sabina), and that he was reassigned to teach at Paris in 1268. And he was solidly writing throughout all this time. At Orvieto, for instance, he worked on the *Catena aurea* (a continuous commentary on the four gospels composed of quotations from the Church fathers), the *Contra errores graecorum* (devoted to Greek Orthodox theology), an edition of a liturgy for the newly created feast of Corpus Christi, and a commentary on the Old Testament book of Job. In Rome he began the *Summa theologiae* and also worked on his disputed question *De potentia*, his theological synthesis known as the *Compendium theologiae*, the political treatise *De regno*, and a commentary on Aristotle's *De anima*. Having returned to Paris in or around 1268, Aquinas's output included more of the *Summa theologiae*, a disputed question *De virtutibus*, the *De aeternitati mundi* (on the question 'Did the world have a beginning?'), and the *De unitate intellectus* (a critique of what Averroes taught on the nature of the human intellect). He also began commenting on the gospels of Matthew and John, and on Aristotle's *Physics*, *Nichomachean Ethics*, and *Metaphysics*.

Some time in 1272 Aquinas left Paris once again. In that year the Dominicans of his home province deputed him to establish a theological study house in a place of his choosing and with staff selected by him. He opted for Naples, where he continued to teach and write. He carried on, for instance, with the *Summa theologiae* (now into its third part). He also probably lectured on St Paul's letter to the Romans, and he may have lectured on the Psalms. During Lent 1273 he preached to the people of Naples (his sermons were subsequently reworked to appear as commentaries on the Apostles' Creed, the Lord's Prayer, and the 'Hail Mary'). But Aquinas was now reaching the end of his life. In December 1273 he abandoned his usual routine and neither wrote nor dictated anything else. What brought him to this state is very much a matter of conjecture. A plausible explanation commonly given nowadays is that he suffered a stroke or a physical and emotional breakdown caused by overwork.

Early in 1274 Aquinas left Naples for Lyons since he had been instructed to attend the second Council of Lyons to advise on matters of ecumenical theology (on which he was an expert). He became seriously ill *en route* and lodged for a while with his niece at the castle of Maenza, where he is reported to have said: 'If the Lord is coming for me, I had better be found in a religious house than in a castle.' So he was taken to the Cistercian abbey of Fossanova, where he died in a guest-room a week or two later. The cause of his death is another matter for speculation. One account tells us that, on the journey to Lyons, Aquinas struck his head against a tree that had fallen across the road and that this left him half-stunned and hardly able to stand. On the basis of this report, it has been suggested that he died of a brain haemorrhage. But we really do not know what, in the end, took him to his grave. We do, however, know that his remains now lie in the Jacobins church in Toulouse. And they are very much worth visiting, not because Aquinas is there (as, so we shall see in Chapter 11, Aquinas himself would have agreed), but because the Jacobins church is one of the most beautiful buildings in Europe.

THE IMPACT OF AQUINAS

Aquinas was the greatest European philosopher of the thirteenth century. Many would say that he was the greatest of all medieval thinkers, whether philosophical or otherwise. Yet his appeal and reputation have waxed and waned. In the period immediately following his death he had relatively few admirers willing to promulgate his teaching: and there were many anxious to censure it. In 1277 ideas thought to be his were ecclesiastically condemned in Paris and Oxford. From 1278 General Chapters of the Dominican Order insisted that his writings be respected and defended within the Order. He was canonized by Pope John XXII in 1323 (his feast day is 28 January), and his influence subsequently increased. Yet his thinking never commanded anything like universal agreement in the Middle Ages. And, though his impact on Roman Catholic teaching has been strong from the fifteenth century to the present (in 1567 Pope Pius V declared him a Doctor of the Church), his work was largely ignored by the best known Western philosophers from the time of René Descartes (1596–1650) to the middle of the twentieth century. Descartes himself sometimes mentions Aquinas with respect, yet his most famous writings show little serious debt to Aquinas's major emphases. And some notable modern philosophical figures have been positively dismissive of Aquinas. According to Bertrand Russell (1872–1970), for instance:

There is little of the true philosophical spirit in Aquinas. He does not, like the Platonic Socrates, set out to follow wherever the argument may lead . . . Before he begins to philosophize, he already knows the truth; it is declared in the Catholic faith . . . The findings of arguments for a conclusion given in advance is not philosophy, but special pleading. (*A History of Western Philosophy*, New York, 1945, p. 463)

Russell's opinion of Aquinas is still not uncommon, but it is now fair to say that it is increasingly under attack. For in the last few decades Aquinas has been more and more studied by professional philosophers, many of whom have come to view him as one of the most perceptive thinkers of all time. Hence, for example, a 1990 editorial comment in the journal *Philosophy* asserts that 'St Thomas Aquinas is a genius whose claim to that accolade is barely debatable'. Then again, according to Anthony Kenny, one of the most distinguished of contemporary analytical philosophers: 'Aquinas is . . . one of the dozen greatest philosophers of the western world . . . His metaphysics, his philosophical theology, his philosophy of mind, and his moral philosophy, entitle him to rank with Plato and Aristotle, with Descartes and Leibniz, with Locke and Hume and Kant' (*Aquinas: A Collection of Critical Essays*, Notre Dame, 1976, p. 1). Kenny views Aquinas as having something positive and valuable to contribute to contemporary discussions of key philosophical issues; and so do many others. The respect which Aquinas now commonly commands is evident from the large number of publications concerning him (articles and many substantial volumes) which appear almost daily. Translations of Aquinas into English have been increasingly emerging for a number of years. Russell was a philosophical genius, but it is now widely recognized that Aquinas was as well.

What has brought about this revival of respect? In Roman Catholic circles a major cause was Pope Leo XIII's encyclical *Aeterni Patris* (1879), which presented Aquinas as an effective antidote to erroneous ideas and methodologies. The encyclical prompted the study of Aquinas in centres of religious education. It also inspired several generations of Catholic scholars to work on Aquinas and to recommend his principles. And its contents were effectively reiterated by the Second Vatican Council. But why has Aquinas come much more into vogue beyond an explicitly confessional context?

One reason lies in the fact that we are now much more informed about the mind of Aquinas than were people in the early years of the twentieth century. Since the time of *Aeterni Patris* (and especially since the 1920s) an enormous amount of careful critical work has been done on Aquinas's writings. This has allowed them to be properly viewed in their historical context and with attention to what they have to say in detail (as opposed to what it might be thought that they have to say from a reading of a paraphrase or manual abridgement). And this, in turn, has led people increasingly to realize that Aquinas was a complex and subtle thinker, one whose thought developed, one whose thought was decidedly less rigid and simplistic than, for example, some of his eighteenth-, nineteenth-, and early twentieth-century critics supposed.

Another reason for the renewal of interest in Aquinas lies in the growth of twentieth-century analytical philosophy. Analytical philosophers have always placed a premium on logical rigour and detailed attention to linguistic usage. Yet concern with such matters is very much a feature of Aquinas's writings (as it is with medieval philosophers in general). Analytical philosophy finds natural conversational companions in thinkers such as Aquinas; and analytical philosophers have come to realize as much. Some of them have also been led to a respect for Aquinas owing to the work of Ludwig Wittgenstein (1889–1951). For many twentieth-century analytical philosophers, Wittgenstein brilliantly showed that European philosophy from the time of Descartes was riddled with a large number of confusions and positive errors. Were these confusions and errors absent in earlier writers? Several contemporary thinkers (Kenny is a significant example) have concluded that they were, and, in particular, that they were notably absent from the writings of Aquinas, and that Aquinas is therefore someone with whom it is currently worth engaging.

But is he? One cannot begin to answer the question without knowing something about the details of his thinking. So let us now turn to some of those.

2

The Cast of a Mind

Aquinas will strike many contemporary readers as somewhat off-putting. As well as writing in Latin, and in prose which does not exactly sparkle, he frequently uses technical terms which are not in vogue today and which need to be explained. And he often alludes to authors of which most people now have never even heard. In addition, he often deals with questions which would not now be taken very seriously. Should Christ have been born in winter? (cf. ST 3a, 35,8). Did the star which appeared at his birth belong to the heavenly system, or was it specially created? (cf. ST 3a, 36,7). Do inferior angels speak to superior ones? (cf. ST Ia, 107,2). Aquinas raises all these questions. And they are not silly ones (especially when viewed in the context of Aquinas's writings). But they hardly reflect the major concerns of most people in the twenty-first century.

Then again, Aquinas has nothing to say on a number of topics which engage people currently interested in religious studies. For example (and inevitably), he offers no discussion of issues which have arisen only in the course of the last fifty years or so – such as the problem of Christian environmental ethics and questions raised by modern religious pluralism. And he has little to say on the subject of women. He talks about them, and, with an eye on the Virgin Mary, he is happy to concede that they can be highly graced. But modern feminists will recoil from some of his observations. Should woman have been created in the beginning? Yes, replies Aquinas, but only to help man in the work of procreation. Women, he suggests, are naturally defective. They are 'by nature subordinate to man, because the power of rational discernment is by nature stronger in man' (ST Ia, 92,1). They 'seldom keep a firm grip on things' (ST 2a2ae, 156,1), and they must be especially sober since 'they are not tough enough to withstand their longings' (ST 2a2ae, 149,4).

Or consider Aquinas on the topic of heretics. In the *Summa theologiae* Aquinas discusses heretics as part of his treatment of faith, and he has some rather unsettling things to say about them. They should, he asserts, be executed. The Church, he agrees, is on the side of mercy. Yet, he insists, 'since forgers and other malefactors are summarily condemned to death by the civil authorities, with much more reason may heretics as soon as they are convicted of heresy be not only excommunicated but also justly be put to death' (ST 2a2ae, 11,3).

This is not the stuff of which modern theology is made. And Aquinas's philosophical interests and commitments are also somewhat different from those of many recent thinkers. A lot of philosophers since the seventeenth century have been much preoccupied with questions concerning the possibility of knowledge. They have typically asked questions like 'Can we know anything?' or 'Is there a world distinct from our ideas?' But Aquinas, though he has views about knowledge, has no great concern with such issues. Nor, unlike some contemporary philosophers, is he remotely attracted to the view that truth is an illusion or something we believe in because of social conditioning and the like. Aquinas is a robust realist prepared to say that, as we might put it, there is indeed such a thing as Truth with a capital 'T'. He certainly cannot be roped in as an ally for contemporary 'modernists' and 'postmodernists'.

So, in many ways, it might be said that Aquinas is not our contemporary. In many ways he belongs firmly to the Middle Ages. Yet fashions have a way of coming round again, and much that we find in Aquinas evidently engages a number of our contemporaries. Hence, for example, though his prose might seem dull, it also displays the clarity and conciseness currently prized by practitioners of analytical philosophy. And though some of his questions may seem dated, others are at the forefront of current theological and philosophical inquiry. Aquinas has a major interest in the question of God's existence and nature, which is now just as high on the theological and philosophical agenda as it was in his day. And his approach to human knowledge and understanding can be viewed as uncannily like that to be found in some major twentieth-century philosophers. It is also worth mentioning that Aquinas is now very much a partner in discussion when it comes to recent moral philosophy and theology. Since (roughly) the time of Immanuel Kant (1724–1804), treatises on ethics have been dominated by a concern with concepts such as duty and obligation. In recent years, however, there has been a serious revival of interest in what is now commonly called 'virtue ethics'. Yet, as is now well recognized, 'virtue ethics' lies at the heart of Aquinas's moral thinking.

PHILOSOPHER OR THEOLOGIAN OR WHAT?

So, for these reasons and for others, perhaps Aquinas should not be taken to be all that off-putting. But how is he to be characterized as a thinker? In the last chapter we saw that Aquinas has had an influence in both theological and philosophical circles. But what exactly is he? Is he primarily a theologian? Is he primarily a philosopher? Is he a philosopher who sometimes incorporated theological teachings into his writings? Is he some kind of hybrid philosopher-theologian? A number of his readers have, with good reason, taken these questions very seriously, and the result has been a range of often conflicting portraits.

According to some people, Aquinas is a theologian through and through: he is definitely no philosopher. And there is a lot to be said in favour of this conclusion. As we have seen, Aquinas functioned as a Master of Theology in Paris. And theological concerns are right to the foreground in many of his writings: this is evident from his biblical commentaries, but it can also be seen from a reading of many of his other works. For example, the first topic raised in the *Summa theologiae* is what Aquinas calls 'sacred teaching' (*sacra doctrina*). And he clearly wishes to stress both that this is his chief concern in the discussions which follow and that it comprises the revealed content of Christian faith, understood as truth which cannot be arrived at merely by philosophical argument. One sometimes encounters the idea that Christian doctrine is rational in the sense that it is grounded on philosophical demonstrations which any thinking person ought to accept. But such is not Aquinas's view. He thinks that rational arguments in defence of Christian doctrine cannot claim to be probative. For him, Christian doctrine is primarily taught by God. Hence the need for sacred *teaching* (*sacra doctrina*).

Another fact to be reckoned with is that Aquinas spent much of his professional life expounding and commenting on the Bible. For him, as for the other professors at Paris in his day, the Bible was (quite literally, though subject to various interpretations) the word of God and, therefore, something in the light of which other teaching was to be judged. And he thought that it is here that *sacra doctrina* is to be found. For him, *sacra doctrina* ('sacred teaching') and *sacra scriptura* ('sacred scripture', i.e. the Bible) are virtually synonymous since their content is the same. In Aquinas's view, access to revelation is given in the words of canonical scripture, especially in the teachings of Christ contained there. Christ, says Aquinas, is 'the first and original teacher of the faith' (ST 3a, 7,7; cf. ST 3a, 11,6), who, being God, knows divine truth without benefit of revelation. With him come the prophets and apostles (including the evangelists). And from all of them, and from nothing else, comes the matter of revelation. *Sacra doctrina* (the chief concern of the *Summa theologiae*, which can be justly described as a sophisticated and systematic commentary on the Bible) is, for Aquinas, the content of Scripture. It is also the content of the Christian creeds since, in Aquinas's view, these basically amount to a restatement of what is in Scripture – a pocket Bible, so to speak. The Old and New Testaments need to be studied with care, Aquinas argues, since 'the truth of faith is contained in Holy Writ diffusely, under various modes of expression, and sometimes obscurely, so that, in order to gather the truth of faith from Holy Writ, one needs long study and practice' (ST 2a2ae, 1,9). The creeds are needed to make the truth of faith quickly accessible to everyone. But they add nothing to what is already contained in Scripture: they merely summarize or highlight with a view to the needs of those who hear them.

Teachings such as these clearly mark Aquinas out as a theologian. And Aquinas never called himself a philosopher. In his writings 'philosophers' always fall short of the true and proper 'wisdom' to be found in Christian revelation. 'Philosophers', for Aquinas, are pagans. Yet there is still a case for thinking of Aquinas as a philosopher, as long as we bear in mind the points just noted. For, though his chief preoccupations are manifestly theological, Aquinas frequently turns to them in ways that are philosophical in a fairly obvious sense. If a philosopher is a person who is not primarily a Christian believer, and if philosophers only write with little or no religious commitment, then Aquinas is no philosopher. But if we take philosophers to be people prepared to try to think clearly without necessarily invoking religious doctrines as premises in their arguments, Aquinas is unquestionably a philosopher.

There are committed Christians universally regarded as remarkable philosophers. Examples include Descartes, the so-called 'father' of modern philosophy, John Locke, the founder of the British philosophical empiricist tradition (1632–1704), and Gottfried Wilhelm Leibniz, one of the great European 'rationalists' (1646–1716). And Aquinas should be grouped with people like these. He robustly defends the powers of what he calls 'natural reason'. He writes about logic, the world of nature, human cognition, human action, metaphysics, ethics, and other topics, without relying on theological premises alone. He also offers commentaries on philosophical texts written by non-Christians – commentaries which respect these texts as attempts to understand how things are or ought to be without recourse to religious authority.

Religious authors write in very different ways. Some proceed with no sense of what a rigorous argument looks like. Some work on the assumption that there are really no serious philosophical questions to be asked about the meaning of religious beliefs or the grounds on which they are held. Some suppose that non-religious thinkers have little to offer. Some avoid discussing questions which have preoccupied philosophers. Yet Aquinas does not write in any of these ways. Even his most explicitly theological writings display high standards of argumentative rigour. They are also full of probing and intelligent questions concerning the significance and truth of both religious and other claims.

The truth of the matter is that Aquinas is both a theologian and a philosopher. And the extent to which he is one or the other is not easily quantifiable. His writings constantly combine theological commitment and philosophical acumen. And the range of his intellectual interests are significantly indicated by the authors to whom he is indebted. Are they theological? Are they philosophical? The answer is that they are both, though some of them are as hard to classify with an eye on the terms 'theology' and 'philosophy' as is Aquinas himself.

AQUINAS AND HIS PREDECESSORS

One of the major influences on Aquinas is clearly an austerely philosophical one. For Aristotle, whose impact on Aquinas can be seen in almost everything he wrote, was evidently a philosopher. Aquinas, indeed, calls him 'the philosopher'. Yet we should not simply suppose that Aquinas's debt to Aristotle means that we should unequivocally call him an 'Aristotelian' or a disciple of Aristotle. His commentaries on Aristotle comprise only a tenth of his literary output (less than half the space devoted by Aquinas to interpretation of Scripture). And his thinking is notably different from Aristotle's in a number of ways. According to Aquinas, the most important reality is God the Creator, and the most important authority is Christ. Yet (contrary to what Aquinas himself says) Aristotle makes no reference to what Aquinas means by 'God' considered as Creator. And (of course) Aristotle knows nothing of Christianity.

Aristotle is not the sole secular philosopher on whom Aquinas draws. He is extremely sympathetic to Aristotle's major teachings. Yet much that he has to say echoes ideas and ways of talking to be found in thinkers of a Platonic rather than Aristotelian orientation: Plato himself (c. 424–347 BC), and also thinkers like Porphyry (c. 232–c. 305) and Proclus (410–85). But it is not only secular philosophers who contribute to what we now know as the thinking of Aquinas. He is evidently indebted to authors with clearly religious backgrounds. A notable example is

Maimonides, whose teaching on the unknowability of God is remarkably close to that of Aquinas. Another is the Islamic philosopher Avicenna (980–1037), whose views on the notions of essence and existence are remarkably akin to some of Aquinas's most central teachings. Above all, Aquinas invokes and appeals to Christian authors. St Ambrose of Milan (c. 339–97), St Anselm of Canterbury (c. 1033–1109), St Augustine of Hippo (354–430), the Venerable Bede (c. 673–735), St Bernard of Clairvaux (1090–1153), Boethius (c. 480–c. 524), St John Damascene (c. 655–c. 750), John Cassian (c. 360–after 430), St John Chrysostum (c. 347–407), St Cyprian (d. 258), St Cyril of Alexandria (d. 444), St Gregory of Nazianzus (329/330–389/390), St Gregory of Nyssa (c. 330–c. 395), Pope St Gregory I (c. 540–604), St Hilary of Poitiers (c. 315–367/8), St Jerome (c. 345–420), Pope St Leo I (d. 461), Peter Lombard (c. 1100–60): all of these, and others to be compared with them, are frequently referred to by Aquinas. And all of them are mentioned as authorities to take seriously. This is not to say that Aquinas views them as beyond criticism (he is, for example, highly critical of some of St Augustine's ideas). But figures such as these are very much part of what Aquinas profoundly respected. They helped to shape his thinking every bit as much as did people such as Aristotle.

At the outset, therefore, readers should recognize that Aquinas is not easily characterized with an eye to terms such as 'theology', 'philosophy', 'theologian', and 'philosopher'. I always prefer to say that he is simply a 'Christian thinker'. His cast of mind is both Christian and reflective, as we shall now begin to see in more detail.

3

Building-Blocks

All of us think with respect to basic ideas or concepts which we use as we seek to say how things seem to us. We might call them the building-blocks of our intellectual systems. We often fail to notice them as we go about our business and explain our points of view. Yet they are always there, and it helps to be aware of them, though some of them, on reflection, might seem muddled or confused.

Aquinas has such building-blocks. He uses them throughout his writings, and his readers need to know this from the start. He borrows a number of them from Aristotle, but others are very much of his own making. They may be basically thought of as constituting his most general view of the world, his fundamental answer to the question: 'What is there around us?'

THINGS AND THINGS

One obvious answer to this question is 'things', for the world is surely made up of these. And that is what Aquinas thinks. But 'thing', of course, is not the name of anything. To be told that there are things is not to be told what there is. And Aquinas agrees with that view as well. He thinks, for example, that there at least two kinds of things.

Consider dogs. And then think about computers. Are these both things? In an obvious sense they are since we can single them out and talk about them. We can refer to them by the subject terms of sentences. We can say 'The dog is in the yard' and 'The computer is in the library'. But dogs are naturally occurring units while computers are only collections assembled by technology. Dogs exist as independent wholes, regardless of human contrivance; and their parts belong to the units they are. A dog's leg is, for example, nothing but the leg of a particular dog, and removed from the dog it is no longer even a leg. We can produce new kinds of dogs by inter-breeding and the like (cf. ST Ia, 73,2). But dogs are *given*, not made. They are discrete items in their own right. As Aquinas would say, they are *entia per se* (beings on their own account).

On the other hand, we assemble computers from bits which already exist as what they are, and we do not think they turn into something completely different by becoming parts of computers. They are not parts of computers in the sense that a dog's legs are parts of a dog. When it comes to computers, the bits are prior to the whole. But, while we can dismember a dog by taking the bits apart, we cannot assemble a dog simply by adding the bits together. A computer, however, is secondary. It is simply an assemblage of already existing things that have been placed into contact with each other. The units in this case are the bits, and the computer is only a quasi-unit by courtesy of our construction, culture, and language. Or, as Aquinas would observe today, a computer is an *ens per accidens* (a thing which exists by *coincidence*, something made up from what already has, so to speak, a life or way of being *of its own*). He would also say that the most striking difference between dogs and computers is that dogs are alive, while computers are not.

For Aquinas, the most obvious examples of *entia per se* are living things. But what does he take to be the difference between these and other things? His primary thought is that living things are genuine 'automo-biles' while non-living things are not. In his view, something alive (something having a soul (*anima*)) is *self-moving*. Or, as he explains: 'those things alone are in the proper sense living which move themselves with one or another kind of movement' (ST Ia, 18,1). Most people do not think that cars are alive. Most people draw a sharp distinction between cars and, say, cockroaches. Is this blind prejudice, analogous to racism? Why should *these* automobiles (cars) be arbitrarily excluded from the realm of living things? Aquinas would say that the 'automobiles' we call cars depend for their movements on something outside themselves. For example, they need us to get their ignitions started. And, Aquinas thinks, it is not at all like this with cockroaches. These, he holds, genuinely move themselves. These, he thinks, have *souls* (are *animate* as opposed to *inanimate*), just like you and me (not to mention such things as cabbages and lemon trees).

SUBSTANCES AND ACCIDENTS

For Aquinas, then, there are natural units, and there are things we think of as units though they are really a mix of independent things. And, in his view, living things are obvious examples of the former. But he also thinks that there are units other than living things, things which he calls 'substances' (*substantiae*), which include living things but which also include many non-living ones. In his *Categories*, Aristotle refers to 'what neither is asserted of nor exists in a subject' (Ch. 2). He has in mind nameable objects or individuals. We do not ascribe Jimness to Jim ('Jim is Jimness' means nothing). We single Jim out (by his name or some other expression), and we talk *about* him (we say that he is the husband of Mary or that he won the Lottery last week, and so on). Aristotle would have said that 'Jim' here names a substance, a distinct individual. And Aquinas follows Aristotle's usage. So he speaks of there being substances, by which he means distinct and self-contained units, whether living or not. Hence, for example, he calls stones substances. And he uses the same word when talking of anything which can be reasonably taken to be a distinct entity. For Aquinas, people and other animals are substances – so are any other things which are not themselves parts of some greater natural whole.

When speaking of substances, Aquinas typically has in mind things which make up the world as in principle open to our investigation. Substances, for him, are the basic constituents of the natural world. So he thinks that they have 'natures' (or, as he sometimes says, 'essences'). On his account, each substance is the kind of thing it is and not something of a different kind. And, with this thought in mind, he assumes that there is a job to be done which springs from the way things are. For, much in the spirit of Aristotle, Aquinas holds that, as well as seeking to change the world, we also need to understand it. To put the point another way, he thinks that we need to do science, that we need to discover just what makes this kind of thing to be *this* kind of thing and not *that* kind of thing.

And yet, as he frequently observes, a thing may be more than just a thing of some kind. Take, for example, my cat Smokey. He is certainly something of a kind, for he is a cat. Or, as Aquinas would say, he is something whose nature or essence is feline. But, as I write, Smokey is grey, asleep, and lying on my bed, none of which attributes (or whatever you want to call them) are part and parcel of what it takes for a cat simply to exist. Smokey will still be a cat if his fur turns from grey to white. And he will be just as much a cat when awake and in my kitchen. Smokey, so we may say, is one thing essentially and a whole lot of other things which are not to be captured in an account of what he essentially is.

To highlight the difference which we seem to need to note here, Aquinas distinguishes between 'substances' on the one hand and 'accidents' on the other. For him, a naturally occurring unit is a thing of some kind (a particular substance). But, he reasons, we can describe substances in ways which tell us not what they are essentially but, rather, what they happen to be at some time or other: what they *are* but might cease to be without ceasing to be what they *essentially* are.

Consider Smokey again. We might say that he is a cat. And, so long as he is alive, that is what he always is. If Smokey ceased to be a cat, then Smokey would cease to exist. But we might also say of Smokey that he is running, sleeping, or eating. Or we might say that he weighs eight pounds, that he is playful, that he is friendly, that he prefers meat to fish, that he is now in the bedroom and now in the kitchen: and so on. To say such things of him is not to refer to what he is essentially or by nature. It is to note truths about him which can cease to be such without him ceasing to be a cat. And this is what Aquinas has in mind in his use of the word 'accident'. For him, accidents are what we latch on to in things as we say what they are without stating what they are essentially. They are, if you like, features or aspects or attributes of things, but not essential ones, not ones which the things in question need simply in order to exist as the kinds of things they are.

Corresponding to this distinction between substance and accident is another to which Aquinas often appeals: one between what he calls 'substantial form' and 'accidental form'. A form, for Aquinas, is what we have in mind when we ask or answer questions where the focus is on the question 'What?' What is a cat? According to zoologists, there is an answer to that question (even if it still needs refining). Here Aquinas would say that the answer tells us about the form of cats. But what of Smokey? Well, in addition to being a cat, he is, as I say, grey. Here also Aquinas would say that we have an answer which hones in on form. Yet there is a significant difference between Smokey being a cat and Smokey being grey. A cat is what it is so long as it is alive (so long as it exists as a cat). But it can lose its greyness while still enjoying perfect health. So we need to mark a difference between form as constituting the *essence* or *nature* of a substance and form as constituting what a substance is *only in passing*. And this difference is what Aquinas has in mind as he distinguishes between 'substantial form' and 'accidental form'.

On his account, Smokey is a cat because he has the substantial form of a cat, which all cats have. And he is grey accidentally (he has the form of greyness only accidentally). Going along with this distinction between substantial and accidental forms, Aquinas also discriminates between what he calls 'substantial change' and 'accidental change'. Smokey can gain weight, and this will be a change in him. But what if he is run over by a car? 'Change', we might think, is hardly the word to capture what would have happened to him on this horrendous account. At any rate, it will not be a change *in* him. For, strictly speaking, a dead cat is not a cat which has undergone change. It is not a cat at all (just as beef is not a cow). When we point to the corpse of a cat, we are pointing to what used to be a cat but is now one no longer. Or, as Aquinas suggests, we are pointing to the result of a *substantial* and not an *accidental* change.

Notice, of course, that all of what I have just been reporting as the teaching of Aquinas depends on accepting the idea of 'natural units' as distinct from quasi-units assembled from them. Yet we do, in fact, accept this idea in the ways that we think and talk. We speak as though we were familiar with natural units. Although we talk metaphorically of the 'life' of a city, we do not think that a city is literally alive precisely because we do not think that a city is a natural unit. We can treat it for many purposes as though it were such. But we are well aware that it is fundamentally a coming together of all kinds of things that exist in their own right prior to being parts of the city.

One might even say that it is part of our sanity that we recognize that there are natural units and quasi-units, that some of the things we name by single nouns or noun phrases are aggregates and that others are natural units. It is part of our sanity that we recognize a cat as a single unit extending from the tip of its nose to the tip of its tail. People who would just as often think of it or see it as two units, one extending from the nose to the middle and the other from the middle to the tail, would (should we not say?) be going mad. They would not be able to live a successful human life among cats. I do not, of course, mean that we cannot reclassify the world in ways that cut across its natural units in order to make jokes or brilliant imaginative constructions. But all such ways of proceeding are parasitic on our normal perceptions and normal ways of talking about things. I also do not mean that our so-called commonsense way of talking of the world is always a reliable clue to what its natural units are. After all, a large part of the physical sciences consists in analysis of what we *treat* as natural units into the *real* units of which they are composed. Nevertheless, if we did not start with a commonsense approximate framework, there would be nothing for scientific analysis to work on and no basis in common speech for the technical language it has to use. And this is very much the thinking which lies behind what

Aquinas says on *entia* (things) *per se* and *per accidens*, and on what he has to offer in his talk about substances, accidents, and concepts related to them (substantial and accidental form, and substantial and accidental change).

FORM AND MATTER

Yet, when speaking of form, Aquinas often introduces another term of which I have so far said nothing. This is the term 'matter' (or 'prime matter' (*materia prima*)). And, for Aquinas, matter matters. Why? Because, he argues, it is what we depend on in order to distinguish between things, in order to individuate between things sharing a nature. Forms, he thinks, allow us to talk in general terms. They allow us to refer, say, to cats or to being grey. But what about *this* grey cat? On Aquinas's account, our ability to identify a particular cat has nothing to do with form. And this, for him, is where matter comes in.

Let us now give Smokey a companion; and let us call him Ginger. Let us also consider the following question: why is Smokey not Ginger? Or, to frame the question another way, what accounts for the fact that Smokey and Ginger are two cats and not one cat?

It should be immediately obvious that we cannot answer this question by appealing to what Aquinas has in mind when he speaks of substantial form. Smokey and Ginger cannot be different just because Smokey is a cat and Ginger is a cat. They share their feline nature, so it cannot serve to individuate them or to help us to distinguish between them.

But what about what Aquinas means by 'accidental forms'? Could these serve to make Smokey and Ginger two cats and not one cat? The suggestion is appealing since we commonly discriminate between things of the same kind precisely by means of their different but non-essential properties or features. 'Which is John and which is Bill?' An intelligible answer might run along the lines: 'John is the tall one with the dark hair, and Bill is the short, bald one.' Yet, when you come to think about it, such an answer cannot capture what makes two things of a kind to be two things and not one thing; for it already presupposes that we are dealing with a one and an other. John and Bill cannot come to possess the non-essential (or accidental) features we ascribe to them if they are not already distinct to start with. No accidental predicate, like 'being dark-haired' or 'being bald', can provide an account of what makes something to be this individual thing and not that individual thing. And two individuals can agree in all their common characteristics and yet still be two distinct entities, as is the case with 'identical copies' (which, of course, are not actually numerically identical).

There have been thinkers who have not accepted this point. They have insisted that, if X is not identical with Y, then there must be something that can be predicated of X and not of Y. Some have even spoken of there being a law called 'the identity of indiscernables' ('If you can predicate of Y everything that you can predicate of X, and vice versa, then Y is identical with X'). But Aquinas takes a different view. According to him, and apart from the case of identity statements of the form 'Mary is Mary' or 'The Morning Star is the Evening Star', predicative expressions (like 'is dark-haired' or 'is bald') describe rather than name or refer (they are, as Aquinas says, 'taken formally' (*tenetur formaliter*) rather than 'taken materially' (*tenetur materialiter*)). And descriptions, he thinks, can be shared (as being the individual that one is cannot). Any number of cats can be grey. Any number of men can be tall, dark, short, and bald. But no cat but Smokey can be Smokey. So Aquinas's conclusion is that identity or non-identity (whether Smokey and Ginger are identical, or whether John and Bill are) is not a matter of what we say about them but of what it is we are talking about. It is not a matter of whether what we say about Smokey is the same as what we say about Ginger. It is not a matter of whether what we say about John is the same as what we say about Bill. It is a matter of whether what we say about Smokey is also about Ginger, or whether what we say about John is also about Bill.

For Aquinas, what makes it that two things of a kind are distinct individuals sharing a nature is not anything that we can say or understand about them. For him, 'This is one and that is the other' neither describes nor attributes any meaningful feature. The meaning of a word is, in Aquinas's view, never an individual thing (not even when it comes to proper names, like 'Smokey', which can be assigned to different individuals and which do not perish when their bearers do). For him, therefore, in order to know about or to try to understand an individual, we need more than a mind: we need a body and its sensual awareness. If we did not have bodies, we might, Aquinas thinks, know a great deal of pure mathematics; but we would not be able to lay hold on what it was *about*.

For Aquinas, we lay hold of individuality within a kind by means of our senses, by being able to point at or to rub up against things at a physical level. If a cat walks behind the sofa and a cat emerges at the other end, how do we know it is the same cat? Aquinas would say: 'Not by anything we know about either cat.' He thinks that we could take many elaborate notes about the beast that disappeared behind the sofa. He also thinks that we could suppose that the one that emerges has exactly the same description. But he does not think that any of this would show that it was the same cat. His view is that our only way to be quite sure that a cat is the same cat is to track it not with our minds but with our senses.

Or, as Aquinas puts it, *matter* is the *principle of individuation* when it comes to things belonging to kinds. In his view, for instance, being a cat, being an *individual* cat, is not just having the cat-nature (substantial form) plus a whole lot of accidental features; it is also being this cat and not that, where 'this' and 'that' are not additional bits of *description* but, so we might say, the music that accompanies the bodily dance we call 'pointing'. Or, we might also say, Aquinas's conclusion is that, as well as having intelligible or understandable forms, things can have an unintelligible factor (matter) with which we can only acquaint ourselves at the bodily level.

EXISTING THINGS

At this point, however, we need to be a little more discriminating when it comes to the word 'thing'. Earlier on I offered 'things' as a translation of Aquinas's *entia*. And the translation is justifiable. *Entia* is the plural of *ens*, and *ens* can readily be translated as 'thing'. But 'thing' is an unhelpful word. We use it all the time, of course. Yet what if I were to ask you to place this book down and to count the things around you? Where would you begin? Where would you end? Look at your hand. Is that one thing? Or is it six (because of your fingers and your palm)? Or is it eleven (because of your fingers and your fingernails)? And so on. It makes perfect sense to say that, if I try to count the things around me, there is no objectively right total answer.

Another problem with 'thing' is that many things are not on a level with each other. We speak about numbers. And we speak about trees. Are numbers nothing? Surely not. So numbers are something. Perhaps they are things? But are they things in the sense that trees are? And consider such expressions as: 'I've just thought of something', 'There's something you have not considered', and 'The things we aim for now are . . .'.

Yet Aquinas has something fairly precise in mind when he uses the word *ens* (both when speaking of an *ens per se* and when speaking of an *ens per accidens*). An *ens* for him is not just anything which might, in common English, be referred to as a 'thing' (if you see what I mean). He takes an *ens* to be something having what he calls *esse*. So now we need to turn to what he means by that term.

4

Being and Existence

Aquinas's thinking is dominated by the notion of being or existence. His early work *De ente et essentia* is much concerned with it; so are many of his subsequent works. And this is not surprising. In the last chapter I said that Aquinas is concerned to ask 'What is there around us?', and I added that an obvious answer to this question is 'Things'. But an equally obvious answer is 'Things which exist.' For existence seems unavoidable. There *being* things would seem to be the most primary fact of which we are aware. And it seems natural to say that things have to be existing things. Aquinas, at any rate, finds it natural to say this. So he also likes to ask 'What does it mean to say that something exists?' And he is much interested in what might be implied by the fact that something exists. In this sense, his thinking is thoroughly 'existentialist'.

BEING, FORM, AND *ESSE*

To understand this 'existentialist' aspect of Aquinas, we can start by noting what he says when he writes about the word *ens* (being). Specifically, we can note that, according to him, it can be thought of as used in at least two ways. Or, as Aquinas puts it:

> There are two proper uses of the term 'being': firstly, generally for whatever falls into one of Aristotle's ten basic categories of thing, and secondly, for whatever makes a proposition true. These differ: in the second sense, anything we can express in an affirmative proposition, however unreal, is said to be: in this sense, lacks and absences are, since we say that absences are opposed to presences, and blindness exists in an eye. But, in the first sense, only what is real is, so that in

this sense blindness and such are not beings. (DE 1; cf. ST Ia, 48,2, SG III, 8–9, and DM 1,1)

What does Aquinas have in mind in making this distinction? He is basically discriminating between sentences which tell us something about a distinct individual and sentences which look or sound as though they are doing this, but which, in fact, are not. If I say that Roger is blind, I am telling you something about a particular thing which exists in its own right. But I am not doing this if I say that blindness exists. There are, of course, people and animals who cannot see. So it is true that blindness exists. But 'blindness' is not the name of any individual thing with an existence of its own (as Roger is). And that is what Aquinas wants to say. On his account, 'being-talk' can tell us something about an individual (e.g. 'Roger is blind'), or it can tell us something true without telling us something about any individual (as in 'Blindness exists', which is true, not because there is something which can be called 'blindness', but because some people and animals cannot see).

Does Aquinas think that a being (an *ens*) in the first sense is something with the property or attribute of existing? Some have thought that anything rightly called a being is something which has a property or attribute properly called 'existence' or 'being'. But this is not Aquinas's view. When he says that 'being' can be understood with respect to what falls under Aristotle's ten categories, he does not mean that 'existing' or 'being' can serve to tell us anything significant about a thing. For Aquinas, one way of distinguishing between individuals is in terms of genus and species. So we can say, for instance, that Roger is a man and that Smokey is a cat. According to Aquinas, however, 'is a being' cannot serve to help us to distinguish between things, and it does not tell us anything about anything. For, on his account, it does not signify a way of being (what something is). Roger may indeed be a man, and Smokey may indeed be a cat; but, for Aquinas, there is nothing which can be characterized simply by saying that it *is*. Following Aristotle, he agrees that there is no such class of things as things which simply *are*. 'Being', for Aquinas, is not a generic term (cf. SG 1a, 24–26 and ST 3a, 77,1). As we have seen, on his account, genuine individuals are whatever they are by virtue of what he calls 'form'. And 'existence' or 'being', Aquinas holds, is not a form.

So, what does Aquinas think we are saying when we say that something exists? English employs the word 'being' to refer to something which exists (as in 'a being'). But it also uses the word as a kind of adjective (as equivalent to 'existent' or 'existing'). Latin is rather more generous with its options. In Latin, one can distinguish between *ens* (meaning 'a being') and *esse* (meaning 'act of being' or '(particular) existence'). A speaker of Latin would naturally say that any *ens* has *esse*: and Aquinas follows this usage. He speaks of there being X, Y, and Z (each an *ens*). He also speaks of X, Y, and Z as having *esse* (as being or existing). We shall not, however, grasp what he means by such talk unless we are clear as to what he means by *esse*, a notion which, for him, is more fundamental than that of *ens*.

Perhaps the best way to understand what Aquinas means by *esse* is to start by focusing on fictional narrative. Suppose I am telling a story about Fred the happy unicorn. We shall assume I am telling the story to a group of children who are enchanted with Fred from their book-reading and from television-viewing. With this scenario in mind, an interesting thing to note is that I can, in a sense, be wrong in what I say about Fred. Suppose I observe that he has no horn on his forehead. Any sensible child will rightly correct me. 'But Fred is a unicorn and unicorns have horns on their foreheads', the child will say. And rightly so. Of course unicorns have horns on their foreheads. The fact can be quickly verified. Just consult a decent dictionary. So I need to be careful to get things right as I tell my tale of Fred, otherwise my audience will abandon me.

On the other hand, however, dictionaries which confirm that unicorns have horns will also tell us that unicorns are mythical animals, and mythical animals do not exist. So it is actually not the case that unicorns have horns. But, in that case, how can I be wrong when telling my story of Fred the happy unicorn?

The answer, of course, is that I can be wrong since I can offend against what people can rightly take to be the meaning of certain words. The word 'unicorn', for instance, is not a piece of gibberish. It is there in the dictionaries, and one can entertain people with stories about unicorns. One can even, after a fashion, make mistakes about them, even though they do not exist (though the mistakes, strictly speaking, would not be about unicorns; they would be mistakes concerning how people have spoken of them).

Now suppose we ask what a unicorn is. Our answer will have to be based on some literary detective work. We shall start, perhaps, with a standard dictionary, then we shall move from there to other writings in which 'unicorn' occurs. And, if we are persistent, we shall, from our reading, have lots to say about unicorns. Yet there are, of course, no unicorns: and there never have been any. That is why I say that our answer to the question 'What is a unicorn?' will need to be settled on literary grounds. In trying to answer it, we are seeking to learn what people mean by the word 'unicorn'. We are seeking a kind of nominal definition.

Knowing what a unicorn is simply amounts to knowing the meaning of a word.

Aquinas, we should now note, is perfectly aware of the fact that answers to questions of the form 'What is X?' may have to be settled simply with respect to what words mean. He also agrees that knowing what things are on the basis of word meanings is compatible with the things in question not really existing. For him, however, we might know what something is in a way that goes beyond learning what a dictionary tells us that a word means: we might actually develop a scientific understanding of things and, in this way, be able to say what they are.

There are no unicorns, but there are lots of cats (Smokey is a wonderful example). And though we shall never be able to study Fred the happy unicorn (or any of his fellow mythical unicorns), we can certainly get our hands on Smokey and his fellows. And, as in fact has happened, on this basis we can develop an understanding of cats, a grasp of what they are. Or, as Aquinas would say, we can begin to explain what it is to be a cat. We can begin to explain what cats *actually are*, something we cannot do with respect to unicorns and the like since they are not anything in actuality.

For Aquinas, then, there is a difference between 'A unicorn has a horn on its forehead' and anything that a scientist might come up with as an account of what cats are. And it is this difference which Aquinas has chiefly in mind when he speaks of things having *esse*. Translators of Aquinas have rendered him as saying that creatures 'have being'. And we need not quarrel with the translators. The expression *habere esse* recurs in Aquinas, and I do not know how to translate it except by writing 'to have being' (or 'to have to be' which is clumsy and unintelligible without a lot of explanation). But such a translation could easily suggest that 'being', for Aquinas, is a property which something *has*; as, for example, redness is a property of most British post boxes. Yet that is not at all what he thinks. His idea is that in truly knowing what, for example, a cat (as opposed to a unicorn) is, we are latching onto the fact that cats have *esse*. And his view is that we lay hold on the *esse* of things not by *understanding words* but by using them to latch on to what is actually there. For Aquinas, the real existence of things is not a form which things have (whether substantial or accidental): it is captured by our capacity to speak truly of what is there to be described (this 'being there' marking the difference between that which has *esse*, or is existent, and that which has not, or is non-existent). A number of Aquinas's commentators have suggested his teaching on being and existence is hard to understand, that it is intelligible only at some esoteric or mystical level. But it is actually rather straightforward. For him, we lay hold on the *esse* of things by living in the world and by truly saying what things actually are. We lay hold on *esse* (the difference between existence and non-existence) by being natural scientists exploring our environment and talking about it as we try to understand it. We lay hold on it by speaking truly of things that are actually there to be spoken about.

So Aquinas concludes that the existence of, say, Smokey is reportable by saying what Smokey is. 'No entity without identity', so some philosophers have said. Or, as Aquinas puts it, existence is given by form (ST Ia, 76,2). 'Every mode of existence', he writes, 'is determined by some form' (ST Ia, 5,5; cf. Ia, 29,2; Ia, 50,5; Ia, 75,6; Ia, 76,2; DPN 1). For him, we cannot describe something by saying that, for example, as well as being feline, intelligent, and so on, it *also* exists. According to Aquinas, we can make sense of statements like 'Smokey exists' (*Smokey est*) only on the understanding that they tell us what something is substantially (what something needs to be in order to exist at all). So *Smokey est*, said truly of Smokey the cat, means, for Aquinas, 'Smokey is a cat'. Hence, for example, Aquinas maintains that names like 'Socrates' or 'Plato' signify human nature as ascribable to certain individuals (*Hoc nomen 'Socrates' vel 'Plato' significat naturam humanam secundum quod est in hac materia* (PH I,9)). On Aquinas's account, saying *Socrates est* or *Plato est* is not to inform people of a property of existence had by Socrates and Plato. And it is certainly not to inform them of what they are but might cease to be while still hanging around: it is to assert that their humanity is actual.

ESSE AND GOD

Yet pedestrian and matter of fact as Aquinas's teaching on *esse* might seem to be, it is, for him, something which ought to strike us as a starting point for thinking to take us way beyond Socrates and Plato (not to mention Smokey). Indeed, he suggests, the fact that things have *esse* is our chief reason for saying that God exists. Why? Because he believes that Smokey, and everything else having *esse*, ought to lead us to ask a question. What sort of question? Basically, one of the form 'How come?'

When we ask 'How come?', the objects of our concern are fairly specifiable for the most part. We may, for example, wonder how it comes to be that some local phenomenon obtains. How come my cousin Mary? How come there are mountains east of Paris?

Sometimes, however, the range of our inquiry may be wider. Someone might explain why there are mountains east of Paris. But we might then wonder why there should be *any mountains*, whether east of Paris or anywhere else. And we might wonder how there come to be *any people*, whatever their names.

And, if these questions are answered, we might deepen the range of our inquiry. Mountains and people are there for reasons to be documented and explored by physicists, geologists, biologists, chemists, astronomers, and so on. They will tell us how it comes to be, not that this and that individual is there, but why things of certain kinds are there. And, in telling us this, they will be invoking levels of explanation which run deeper and deeper.

In doing so, however, they will always presume a background of things, a world or universe in the light of which explanation is possible. The mountains east of Paris are explicable on geological and other grounds. People are explicable in genetic and other terms. And, if we ask why geology is possible and why genetics is possible, we shall again be looking for things of a kind behaving in certain ways.

But we might further deepen the level of our inquiry. For we might ask, not 'What in the world accounts for this, that, or the other?', but 'Why any world at all?' How come the whole familiar business of asking and answering 'How come?' ?

The point to stress now is that this, for Aquinas, is a crucial question. For him, the question 'How come any world or universe?' is a serious one to which there must be an answer. And he gives the name 'God' to whatever the answer is. God, for Aquinas, is the reason why there is any universe at all, the reason why there is something rather than *nothing*. God, he says, is the source of the *esse* of things, the fact that things are more than the meanings of words. At the end of his *Tractatus Logico-Philosophicus*, Wittgenstein writes: 'Not *how* the world is, is the mystical, but *that* it is' (*Tractatus* 6.44). For Wittgenstein, *how the world is* is a scientific matter with scientific answers (even if we do not have all the answers as yet). But, he insists, even when the scientific answers are in, we are still left with the *thatness* of the world, the fact *that* it is. As he puts it: 'We feel that even if *all possible* scientific questions be answered, the problems of life have still not been touched at all' (*Tractatus* 6.52). And Aquinas is of a similar mind. He holds that we can explore the world and develop an account of what things in it are. But he also thinks that we are then left with a decidedly non-scientific question. How come that there is any world at all?

And why does Aquinas consider it necessary to ask this question? Because he believes that, except in the case of something the very nature of which is to exist, we can always ask of what exists 'How come it exists?' And we can assume that this question is not answered simply by describing the thing or things in question. Aquinas's view is that unless the notion of existence is built into our understanding of what things are substantially, their existence needs accounting for in terms of something other than them. And, since he takes the objects of our experience, including ourselves (what Wittgenstein means by 'the world'), to be things which do not exist by nature, Aquinas seeks to account for them. He takes them to prompt the question 'How come?'

There is a sense in which Aquinas takes all substances which make up the world as having existence written into them. For, he says, every genuine *ens* (being, substance) has a nature or essence, from which it follows that there are no non-existing essences. In Aquinas's view, all essences are actual, and there are no substances which lack *esse*. Some contemporary philosophers speak of there being possible worlds in which things which do not actually exist yet still somehow manage to make it into being of some kind. They speak, for example, of there being a world in which I never wrote the text that you are reading. But Aquinas would have little sympathy with this way of talking. For him, there are no purely possible essences since there are no purely possible substances (things which have *esse*).

For Aquinas, what is possible for nameable individuals depends on what they actually are. What does not exist, though it might possibly exist, is nothing but what is captured by an account of what a word means (as when we say what a unicorn is). At the same time, however, Aquinas thinks that, unless something exists the nature of which it is to exist, we can still ask how it comes to exist at all. All essences may be actual, but, so Aquinas holds, everything with an essence which does not include existing (everything the existence of which can be intelligibly denied without contradiction) raises the question 'How come it exists at all?'

Is Aquinas right in thinking along these lines? Some would say 'No.' Bertrand Russell, for instance, once famously asserted that the world is just there, and that is all that there is to be said about it. Yet our understanding of what makes up the world does not include an understanding that its items have to be, just as a knowledge of what Smokey is will not guarantee that he has to exist (even if he cannot be what he actually is without existing). And if we find it necessary to ask why he exists, why should we not think the same when it comes to anything whose existence is captured by a true description of it which does not include a property (or whatever you want to call it) of being such that it could not but exist? If there is something a proper understanding of which would lead us to see that it could not but exist, then of this we could possibly say 'It is there, and that is all that there is to be said about it.' The question, however, is: Is the world of our experience (everything which can, in principle, be singled out as an object of scientific inquiry) something we cannot understand except as existing? The answer is surely 'No.' No successful scientific inquiry will ever end up telling us that the objects of its investigation *have* to be there. Scientific accounts of things tell us what they are on the supposition that they exist. They describe them against the background of a world which is simply assumed at the outset. And their descriptions abstract from the notion of existence. They do not tell us that things are thus and so and that they are, in addition, 'existent' (let alone 'necessarily existent'). In the language of Wittgenstein, they explain *how* the world is: they do not explain its being there.

Yet, can there be an *explanation* here? Despite what I have been saying so far, Aquinas, in a sense, thought not. If an explanation is something which we understand better than what is to be explained, then, in his view, there is no explanation for the fact that there is something rather than nothing. There is, for him, no explanation for things having *esse*. Why he thinks that this is so is a topic to which I shall turn in due course. For now, however, we need to follow Aquinas further in what he has to say concerning the question 'Does God exist?'

5

Approaches to God

Aquinas finds it natural to think that we can give the name 'God' to whatever accounts for there being any world at all because of the Jewish and Christian tradition to which he belongs. For this tradition speaks of God as the source of all things other than himself. For example, according to the book of Genesis: 'In the beginning God created the heavens and the earth' (1:1). According to the letter to the Hebrews, 'the world was created by the word of God, so that what is seen was made out of things which do not appear' (Hebrews 11:3). When reflecting on the significance of things having *esse*, Aquinas has a convenient and, to his readers, a familiar and obvious word to employ. But he does not think that we are right to say that God exists simply because of what we have seen him suggesting when it comes to things having *esse*. For in many places he argues for God's existence without special reference to this notion (though it always seems to be not far in the background). Yet how does he go about this? And how does what he says cohere with what we have so far seen him suggesting?

REASONING AND GOD'S EXISTENCE

To begin with, readers of Aquinas should realize that he is no rationalist when it comes to God's existence. Some have held that, if people cannot demonstrate what they affirm or if they cannot somehow strongly justify their beliefs, then they are not entitled to speak and believe as they do. The idea here is that one is not intellectually (or, maybe, even morally) entitled to believe that such and such is the case unless one can defini- tively show that it is the case or that it is probably the case. But this is not an idea which Aquinas shares (which is what I mean by saying that he is

31

not a rationalist when it comes to God's existence). In his view, all of us often have to proceed on the basis of beliefs which we embrace without being able to prove that they are true. And he sees no reason in principle why 'God exists' should not be such a belief.

Suppose I believe that your name is 'John Smith' because you tell me so at a party. Am I being evidently unreasonable? You may, of course, be lying. So my belief could be false. But, unless I have some special reason for thinking you to be unreliable, there is nothing intrinsically unreasonable in my taking what you say to be true.

Suppose you have children who come home from school and tell you that Paris is the capital of France. You ask them why they say this. They explain that their teacher told them so. Are they being evidently unreasonable in asserting that Paris is the capital of France? Surely not.

Believing on the basis of testimony (rather than on the basis of some proof or demonstration that one can produce) is not necessarily unreasonable. And neither is arguing from the basis of beliefs which one cannot or does not prove or demonstrate. All of us expand our range of beliefs by starting with ones which we do not call into question, beliefs that we employ as we develop reasons for endorsing other ones, beliefs from which we argue and that are not themselves something for which we argue as we conduct our debates. And Aquinas is very much aware of all this. According to him, one can, all things being equal, be perfectly justified in believing on the basis of testimony alone. And, he thinks, rational inquiry does not depend on proving or demonstrating everything we assert as we engage in it.

So Aquinas has no problem with people believing in God's existence even if they cannot offer anything that might be thought of as a demonstration of or a philosophical argument for the existence of God. Hence, for example, early in the *Summa theologiae* he insists that there is nothing 'to stop someone accepting on faith some truth which that person cannot demonstrate, even if that truth in itself is such that demonstration could make it evident' (ST Ia, 2,2). By 'faith', Aquinas is here thinking of something like what I have when I believe that your name is what you say it is just because you say so, or what children have when they believe what their teachers tell them.

Yet Aquinas also holds that there is a difference between *believing* and *knowing* that something is so. I believe that, when I drop a stone, it falls because of gravity: I was taught so. But I could not even begin to offer a properly scientific justification for my belief. I am no physicist, and what I say about gravity derives (as it does for most people) from what I remember being taught in school and from fragments picked up from

32

casual reading. Yet there are people who can tell us exactly why stones fall when dropped. Or, as Aquinas would say, there are people who *know* why this happens, people who *know* that stones fall because of gravity. And, so he would also say, there are people who know that God exists. Aquinas thinks that 'God exists' is a proposition which need not be taken to be true only as a matter of belief (or faith). He is not a rationalist, but he is not a fideist either. A 'fideist' typically insists that, when it comes to the question of God's existence, one's attitude must be very much one of 'mouth open and eyes shut'. Typically, fideists take it as wrong or impious to look for reasons or arguments for God's existence. Their view is that 'God exists' must always be something *from which* one reasons. It is not something for which reasons should be sought ('reasons' here meaning 'arguments or exercises in reasoning which do not begin by presupposing that there is a God'). But Aquinas thinks that there are indeed reasons for claiming that God exists which do not begin by taking God's existence for granted at the outset. His view is that 'God exists' is a true proposition open to a philosophical defence which any right thinking person ought to accept.

But what kind of defence? Aquinas's answer is: 'one which proceeds to God on the basis of creatures'. His view is that we can only know that God exists because we can cogently argue for God's existence with reference to what God has produced or caused to be. But what Aquinas means by this conclusion needs some elaboration, starting with an account of ways in which he thinks that it *cannot* be known that God exists.

DEFENCES WITH FLAWS

People seeking to show that we have good reason to say that God exists (or that God's existence is knowable) have tended to employ one of three strategies. Some have said that 'God exists' cannot be consistently denied (that 'God does not exist' is logically contradictory). Others have held that we can know of God since we are directly aware of him, since he is immediately present to us by virtue of an awareness comparable to our awareness of things such as tables and chairs, not to mention other people. And (the third strategy) some have argued that we can arrive at a knowledge of God inferentially and by a process of causal reasoning (with something or other being taken to be an effect caused by God). From what I said at the end of the last paragraph, you will realize that Aquinas favours the third of these strategies. But what has he to say against the first two?

With respect to the claim that it is contradictory to deny God's existence, Aquinas basically argues that the claim is simply false. For, where does the contradiction lie? One might argue that there is something to be said about God which entails that God exists almost as a matter of definition. One might, for instance, say that God is Truth and that 'God does not exist' is a self-defeating utterance since it cannot be true that there is no Truth. Or one might claim that God must exist since he is that than which nothing greater can be thought, from which it follows that God exists since we can conceive of something greater than something which is nothing but an idea in our mind. Yet Aquinas finds these arguments unconvincing. It is, he observes, 'self-evident that truth exists in general, but not self-evident to us that there exists a first Truth' (ST Ia, 2,1). And so he reasons:

> Someone hearing the word 'God' may very well not understand it to mean that than which nothing greater can be thought; indeed, some people have believed God to be a body. And even if the word 'God' were generally recognized to have that meaning, nothing thus defined would thereby be granted existence in the world of fact but merely as thought about. Unless one is given that something in fact exists than which nothing greater can be thought (and this nobody denying God's existence would grant), the conclusion that God in fact exists does not follow. (ST Ia, 2,1)

Aquinas's view is that, if we *know* that 'X does not exist' is contradictory, we must have a clear grasp of what X is so as to see that it cannot but exist (in something like the way in which our grasp of what 'triangle' means allows us to see that 'Some triangles are square' cannot be true). But how can we construct an argument for God's existence based on a clear grasp of what God actually is? To try to do so would already depend on assuming God's existence at the outset and would not amount to arguing for God's existence from scratch (so to speak). And, even if God does exist, can we have an understanding of what he is so as to be clear that we contradict ourselves in saying 'God does not exist'? For reasons which we shall come to later, Aquinas thinks that we cannot understand what it takes to be God (what God's essence amounts to). So his view is that we can have no good arguments for the impossibility of God not existing based on an understanding of what God is. He does not deny that God *cannot but* exist. In fact, he defends that conclusion. He says: 'The proposition "God exists" is self-evident in itself . . . since God is his own existence.' But, he adds, 'because what it is to be God is not evident to us, the proposition is not self-evident to us' (ST Ia, 2,1).

Yet, might God's existence be evident as it is evident that logical contradictions cannot express true propositions? To see that a proposition cannot be both true and false (to see, as logicians sometimes say, that 'P and not-P' cannot be true) is to see something without benefit of argument. For no argument can proceed on the assumption that a proposition can be both true and false. So we might speak of seeing that logical contradictions cannot express true propositions as a matter of knowing something directly. But we can also speak of directly knowing other truths. A famous philosopher once said that he did not like the idea of having 'inferred friends'. He was trying to suggest that our acquaintances are things of which we are aware without reference to argument or inference. So, might God be yet another example? What I have called the second common strategy for arguing for God's existence suggests that he is. Yet, as with the assertion that the truth of 'God exists' is logically inescapable, Aquinas takes a contrary line. There cannot, he thinks, be anything rightly called an awareness of God which gives us knowledge that God exists.

On the basis of his Christian faith, Aquinas holds that people can enjoy a direct knowledge of God. For he believes that they can experience a union with God after death, one in which arguments and inferences are left behind. But he does not conceive of this as being anything like a direct awareness of our friends. As we shall see, Aquinas holds that God is nothing like a terrestrial individual which we might single out and recognize in a context of some sort. In the life to come, he thinks, we know God because God becomes the means by which we know, something which comes to be in us not as object perceived but as reality received. But we are not yet in the life to come. And, with a view on this fact, Aquinas is unhappy with the notion of a direct knowledge of God invoked as a reason to believe that God exists. He believes that our cognitive apparatus is incapable of acquiring such knowledge this side of the grave.

Why does he think so? The answer lies in what we have already seen concerning his views on how we can think about things in general. According to Aquinas, we encounter individuals at a sensual level and can reflect on what they are without reference to their individuality (which cannot, for Aquinas, be captured in words). He thinks that we can, for example, bump into iguanas and (if we are lucky) come to understand what they truly are or, at least, what they need to be in order to exist at all. We can develop a science, a knowledge, of iguanas. Though he is scientifically optimistic, Aquinas does not claim that current scientific accounts of things represent the last word on them. He is generally prepared to agree that we do not know what lots of things are from a strictly scientific perspective. So contemporary readers can presume that he would be open to the suggestion that our knowledge of what things are by nature might yet be extended by further investigation. Yet, given his views about how we can make sense of encountering an individual or saying what it is from a strictly scientific viewpoint, Aquinas evidently has no option but to conclude that something which is not part of our world, something which we cannot lay hold of for purposes of scientific investigation, is not something that can intelligibly be thought of as an object with which we can be directly acquainted. We can hug and tinker with millions of cats and, as a consequence, develop a science of cats. Can we do anything equivalent when it comes to God? Aquinas thinks not. He notes the opinion that 'the awareness that God exists is implanted by nature in everyone' (ST Ia, 2,1), and he sympathizes with it. People, he concedes, are 'by nature aware of what by nature they desire, and they desire by nature a happiness which is to be found only in God' (ST Ia, 2,1). But this admission comes from the voice of Aquinas the theologian, not from Aquinas as concerned with the question 'Can we know that God exists regardless of what people who already believe that there is a God have to say?' With an eye on that question, his response is:

> The awareness that God exists is implanted in us by nature in no clear or specific way. People are naturally aware of what they naturally desire: a happiness to be found only in God. But this is not, simply speaking, to be aware of God's existence, any more than to be aware of someone approaching is to be aware of Peter, even if it is Peter approaching; many, in fact, believe the perfect good which will make us happy to be riches, or pleasure, or some other such thing. (ST Ia, 2,1)

SO WHERE NOW?

We can summarize what we have so far seen of Aquinas's approach to the question 'Can we know that God exists?' by saying that, in his view, we cannot seek to answer the question definitively with reference to an understanding of God, and we cannot seek to answer it with reference to some personal acquaintance with God which guarantees that it is God with whom we are acquainted. And it is against the background of these views that Aquinas develops his own version of what I earlier called the third strategy used to back up the claim that there is reason to hold that God exists or that God's existence is knowable. We can, he suggests, 'demonstrate that God exists from the things that he has made' (ST Ia, 2,2; cf. ST Ia, 13,8 and SG I, 10–13).

But how? We sometimes connect causes and effects in the light of what we know about the causes. Given what we know about alcohol, for instance, we might quickly be able to make sense of what is going on when we see people staggering and slurring their speech. Yet, as we have seen (and as we shall later see in more detail), Aquinas does not believe that we can understand what God is. His view is that we are in no position to look at the world and correctly say 'Oh yes, that's the sort of thing a God produces.' So he opts for another approach.

Suppose I try to push the door open: and suppose I meet resistance. I may have absolutely no idea what is on the other side of the door. Maybe it is a ton of bricks. Maybe it is an elephant. Maybe it is an elephant sitting on a ton of bricks. I just do not know. Well, most of us stuck in this situation would say: '*Something* must be producing this effect even if we have no idea as to what it can be. So, let us try to work out what it is.' And that is how Aquinas reasons as he reflects on what we can know of God just by using our natural intelligence. He thinks that we must start, not from a knowledge of God, but from a knowledge of something else. And we must try to see if it allows us to develop some kind of knowledge of God. 'There are', says Aquinas, 'two types of demonstration. One, showing "why" (*demonstratio propter quid*), follows the natural order of things among themselves, arguing from cause to effect; the other, showing "that" (*demonstratio quia*), follows the order in which we know things, arguing from effect to cause . . . Now any effect of a cause demonstrates that that cause exists, in cases where the effect is better known to us, since effects are dependent upon causes, and can only occur if the causes already exist. From effects evident to us, therefore, we can demonstrate what is not evident to us, namely that God exists' (ST Ia, 2,2).

But how are we supposed to be able to do this? As we have seen, Aquinas thinks we can get somewhere significant by reflecting on the fact that there is something rather than nothing. Yet he also thinks that there are other (albeit sometimes related) ways of reasoning to God on the basis of what we encounter. In an especially celebrated text he suggests that there are actually five of them.

6

Ways to God

According to St Paul, 'ever since the creation of the world', God's 'eternal power and deity has been clearly perceived in the things that have been made' (Romans 1:20). Aquinas thought highly of this teaching. Almost all of his major works contain defences of it, some of them intricately developed. But his best-known attempt to argue for God's existence can be found in a section of the *Summa theologiae* which amounts to only a few printed paragraphs. Found in Ia, 2,3, and commonly referred to as the 'Five Ways', this tiny fragment of Aquinas's output has received almost as much attention as the rest of his writings put together.

One might regret this fact since the degree of attention given to the Five Ways has often led to a distorted impression of their purpose and place in the *Summa theologiae* and in Aquinas's thinking as a whole. On the other hand, however, there is a case to be made for paying more than a passing glance at Ia, 2,3. The *Summa theologiae* comes with a Foreword in which Aquinas explains that 'the purpose we have set before us in this work is to convey the things which belong to the Christian religion in a style serviceable for the training of beginners'. And Aquinas means what he says here. Much of the *Summa theologiae* conveniently summarizes what he argues at greater length elsewhere. And the text of the Five Ways is one of the best illustrations of this fact. It is short, and it would be wrong to approach it as if it were Aquinas's most developed treatment of its subject matter. Yet it is a good precis of his views on how we can reason to the existence of God.

SOME FEATURES OF THE WAYS

We might start by asking what Aquinas takes the Five Ways to establish in general. A cursory reading of them might lead one to feel that the question hardly needs to be raised, since its answer is obvious: Aquinas, one might say, clearly offers the Ways as arguments for God's existence. But there is reason to resist this answer. Why? Because, as we shall see later, God's *existence*, for Aquinas, is nothing other than God's *essence*, and because (as I indicated above) Aquinas takes God's essence to be something that we do not know. In the last paragraph I spoke of him reasoning 'to the existence of God', and that is a natural way of describing what he is trying to do in the Five Ways. To be strictly faithful to his own manner of putting things, however, we should recognize that the Ways are concerned to make clear, not God's existence exactly, but that 'God exists' (that *Deus est*) is true. To know God's existence is, for Aquinas, to know what God is in himself. But, he thinks, such is not the case when it comes to 'God exists'. One can know that there is *something* stopping the door from opening without knowing *what* it is. By the same token, so Aquinas holds (both in Ia, 2,3 and elsewhere), one can know that God exists without knowing what his existence amounts to.

In fact, none of the Five Ways claims to establish the truth of anything that we could rightly call a developed doctrine of God. Their critics have sometimes attacked them for alleging to deliver more than they do. They have said that, while the Ways purport to establish that God exists, they fail to do so since people take God to be more than the Ways show him to be. Yet Aquinas's intention in the Ways is minimalist. He is not concerned to show that there is a God who is all that those who believe in him commonly take him to be. Rather, he is out to maintain that God exists under certain limited descriptions. God is often said to be one, living, eternal, loving, omnipotent, omnipresent, and omniscient. For Christians, God is also three persons. Yet whether we can know God to be any of these things is a matter that Aquinas leaves for discussion until later than ST Ia, 2,3. In that text he is explicitly concerned only with a somewhat restricted understanding of the word 'God'. More exactly, he is only concerned with 'God' considered as meaning:

1. 'a first cause of things being moved';
2. 'a first efficient cause';
3. 'a necessary being owing its existence to nothing';
4. 'a cause of things being and having goodness or perfection'; and
5. 'something beyond nature which directs things which lack awareness to goals'.

Jews, Muslims, and Christians typically say more of God than is captured by these phrases, and Aquinas knows that well. Yet he also thinks (surely rightly) that the phrases capture something which Jews, Muslims, and Christians take to be true of God, and of God *alone*. And it is this, and not a more developed theology, with which he is concerned in the Five Ways.

THE FIRST WAY

Aquinas says that his First Way is 'the most obvious'. Why? The Way starts from the fact that some things in the world undergo change (*motus*), meaning that they vary in place, quantity, and quality. So Aquinas probably thinks that it is 'most obvious' as a way to God since such variation impinges on us throughout our waking lives. For it is all around us: we see it and feel it all the time. Yet should we regard it as a brute fact, as something which 'just happens', something which is 'just there', something which raises no questions?

According to the First Way, we should not. For, Aquinas argues, anything undergoing change comes to acquire that which it has not yet got. While the train is on its way to its destination (change of place), it is not yet there. While I am on the way to becoming a slimmer Brian Davies (change of quantity), I am not yet that. And while I am starting to turn pink (change of quality), I am not yet sun-tanned. Or, as Aquinas puts it: 'It is characteristic of things in process of change that they do not yet have the perfection towards which they move, though they are able to have it.'

But how are we to account for things changing? We clearly cannot do so simply by describing what they are like before they go through their changes. For this would only tell us what they were before they changed – it would not explain how they came to change.

Might we suggest that they could be the cause of their own change? In various places Aquinas agrees that some things are self-changing. As we saw in Chapter 3, he thinks, for example, that living things are 'automobiles' since they somehow move themselves. But can living things (or any comparable examples we can mention) be *wholly* self-moving or self-changing?

Arguably not. Even such an active animal as the typical dog needs a heart to keep it going, so any movement or change which it naturally goes in for is not wholly self-caused. When a dog leaps, it is, of course, the whole dog which leaps. But it leaps because (among other things) it is empowered by its heart, which is part of the dog but not simply identifiable with it. So it is not, considered as a whole, moving or changing itself.

40

Bits of it change or move because other *bits* do. And, early on in the First Way, Aquinas expresses this thought in the form of a generalization: 'anything undergoing change must be changed by something *else*' (*omne autem quod movetur ab alio movetur*).

There is scholarly controversy as to whether Aquinas is here saying 'whatever is *changed* is changed by something else' or 'whatever is *in process of change* is changed by something else'. That is because the Latin word *movetur* can be translated either passively ('is changed') or intransitively ('is changing'). But it is clear enough what Aquinas wants to maintain at the start of his First Way.

Smokey prowls around, and he apparently does so without benefit of anything like strings attached to a puppeteer. Yet his local motion, and the other changes he undergoes, are not to be deduced from what he is essentially. You will not capture what he is by saying that he is 'Change Itself'. The modifications which he undergoes depend on what cannot be simply named 'Smokey'. His prowling depends on his heart pumping his blood. Yet his heart and his blood are but *parts* of him. And, of course, if he puts on weight or becomes sick, that will be due to something quite outside him (my feeding him, for instance, or a germ of some kind). Smokey's changes may be most of what concerns me about him, but they are not simply *him*; they are what he goes through.

And Aquinas thinks that he does so because something, not simply identifiable with him, accounts for this. Why? Because anything able to be thus and so is not actually thus and so before it becomes thus and so. And how does it come to be thus and so? One might say that it just does and that there is nothing more to be said. But Aquinas finds this answer incredible. We must, he thinks, suppose that, for example, a cold piece of wood gets to be hot because something other than it makes it to be hot. For, he presumes, the being of the wood as hot is not to be deduced from a description of the wood as cold, and thus it requires an explanation in terms of something other than the wood as cold.

Yet how many such explanations might there be? I might make a piece of wood hot by applying a flame to it. But am I the end of the story when it comes to what effects what here? Aquinas thinks not. If X is changed by Y, he argues, then Y (if it undergoes change) must itself be changed by something else 'and this last by another'. And yet, so he also reasons, 'we must stop somewhere, otherwise there will be no first cause of the change, and, as a result, no subsequent causes'. He therefore concludes that 'one is bound to arrive at some first cause of change, not itself being changed by anything'.

This line of reasoning seems to presuppose that there must be a 'first' when it comes to causes of change. Yet, so one might ask, why should that be so even if nothing undergoes change simply because of itself? Why, for example, might the melting of my ice-cream not be explicable (at least in principle) in terms of what has been going on in the world before now and with no beginning? How can we be sure that the melting of my ice-cream lacks an infinite number of causes going backward in time?

From what he says in the text of the First Way, Aquinas's answer seems to be that, if all that undergoes change depends in one way or other on something that is not wholly itself (as, for example, a cat's movements are not wholly its own but depend on bits of it moving other bits), then there could not be anything undergoing change. That is, if absolutely everything were such that its undergoing change depends on something enabling this, then there would be nothing undergoing change. So, in arguing for a first cause of change, Aquinas is not ruling out an infinitely backward temporal series of changers. He is holding that anything undergoing change at any time whatever is something the changing of which needs to be accounted for, though not in terms of itself. In other words, he is maintaining that change, as such, needs something to make it to be. And since nothing which accounts for all change as such can itself undergo change, Aquinas concludes that whatever accounts for all change must be 'some first cause of change not itself changed by anything'.

THE SECOND WAY

Aquinas says that his Second Way starts from 'efficient causation' and from the fact that efficient causes are ordered 'in series'. But what does he have in mind when saying this? Here we need to note that a cause (*causa*), for Aquinas, is basically an explanation of some kind (cf. our use of 'because'). And he thinks that there are various kinds of explanation (various kinds of 'becauses' to which one can appeal).

Why did *this* object break while *that* object did not? The explanation might lie in the materials of which the different objects are made (e.g. 'This one broke because it was made of glass; that one survived because it was made of plastic'). Here Aquinas will say that there are different 'material causes' accounting for what puzzles us.

Why did *this* animal thrive under water while *that* animal died? Here Aquinas will say that there are different 'formal causes' accounting for what we are concerned with (e.g. 'This one is a shark, and that one is a dog').

Why is John running? His answer might be 'I am trying to catch the last train home.' And, so Aquinas would say, John is here offering a 'final cause' of his behaviour, a goal or end which puts it into an intelligible context (John is running *because* he is seeking what he wants).

But, in addition to material, formal, and final causes, there are, according to Aquinas, 'efficient causes', which he thinks of as what we appeal to when we offer explanations in terms of the activity of something (or maybe of many things). With efficient causation, the focus, for Aquinas, falls on questions of the form 'What did that?', or 'What keeps that going?'

What accounts for the fact that John is dead? Well, perhaps somebody murdered him. For Aquinas, the murderer would be an *efficient cause* of John's death. Why is Mary coughing and spitting blood? Mary might be the victim of whatever produces tuberculosis. So Aquinas would say that this is the *efficient cause* of her coughing and her blood-spitting. Is there anything which keeps me alive? One answer might be 'Yes, oxygen keeps you alive.' Here Aquinas would speak of oxygen being an *efficient cause* of my survival.

He would also say that we are very much aware of such causes. And, he would add, they sometimes depend on other efficient causes. For consider the case of an egg getting boiled as it sits in the water in a container on a cooker. The ongoing states of the egg are due to the water and its temperature. The temperature of the water is due to that of the container which houses it. And the container's temperature is due to whatever is heating it. Here we have a *series* of efficient causes. And it is this kind of series of which Aquinas is thinking at the start of the Second Way. He takes it as evident that series of such a kind are there to be observed. But, he wonders, what does this fact imply?

One answer might be: 'Any given series of efficient causes is self-contained and not in need of any further explanation.' The idea here is that we might, for example, note that a cooker is heating a container which (by virtue of its temperature) is accounting for what the water in it (by virtue of its temperature) is doing to some eggs, and also that we should then say that there is nothing else calling for explanation.

Another answer might be: 'Yes, indeed, there must be some further explanation (some other efficient cause or causes) accounting for the egg in the container scenario. But there is no end to explanation here (no end when it comes to efficient causes). There is only an infinite number of explanations (an infinite number of efficient causes).'

Yet Aquinas finds neither of these answers intellectually appealing. For him, effects of efficient causes are *effects*. So they *depend* on something else. And, he reasons, if all their efficient causes are equally dependent, then there could be no effects of efficient causes to start with.

Suppose I assert that nobody can do anything, including asking for permission, without asking for permission. Can anybody act on my order? Obviously not. Why not? Because every asking for permission would require a previous asking for permission. There could be no asking for permission at all if every asking for permission depended on an asking for permission. And Aquinas thinks that, if every dependent effect depends on a series of efficient causes, none of which can do its causing without itself being dependent on yet one or more efficient causes, then there could not be a series of efficient causes. 'If you eliminate a cause,' he reasons, 'you also eliminate its effects, so that you cannot have a last cause, not an intermediate one, unless you have a first.'

So, on the basis of there being a series of efficient causes, Aquinas concludes that there must be an efficient cause which does not itself depend on another one. Notice, however, that, in the text of the Second Way, Aquinas does not rule out the possibility of there being more than one such cause. He says that we are 'forced to suppose some first cause, to which everyone gives the name "God"'. But he has no comment to make as whether 'God' is the name of more than one first cause. This is a topic to which he turns later in the *Summa theologiae*. The argument of the Second Way is chiefly concerned to maintain that there is *at least* one first cause (that there is *something* which causes efficiently without itself being efficiently caused).

Also notice that the argument of the Second Way is not what we might call a chronological one. All of us have many things on which we depend for our existence. Our parents are examples. And they, we presume, had parents of their own. And so on, back to whenever. How far back? In texts other than Ia, 2,3, Aquinas holds that we cannot prove that the world had a beginning. He also implies that there is no logical absurdity in the idea of us having a backwardly infinite series of parents. So the Second Way cannot be suggesting that there has to be a cause which is first from a chronological point of view. Rather, Aquinas's point is that, if there is a relation of dependence between causes, the series of causes in question must terminate with an uncaused cause with respect to the dependence in question. In the Second Way Aquinas begins from actual series of causes (a series there in front of us, so to speak). His point is that any such series, insofar as it is actually (at the present time) dependent, must *actually now* depend on a first cause which is not similarly dependent.

THE THIRD WAY

Aquinas begins his Third Way by noting that some things come into and pass out of being, that there are, as he puts it, things which are 'able to be or not to be', things which might be called 'contingent'. He is thinking of the fact that, for instance, people are born and eventually die. These people come to be by virtue of a world which exists before they enter it. And they exit that world as easily as they entered it.

Some philosophers have distinguished between 'contingent' beings and 'necessary' beings so as to mark a logical difference. They have suggested that we should use the word 'necessary' to mean 'what has to be as a matter of logical necessity'. And they have suggested that we should use 'contingent' as an adjective to describe what need not be the case logically speaking. In the Third Way, however, Aquinas is not thinking of necessity and contingency in these ways. He takes a contingent thing to be something like a human being who comes to birth and eventually dies. Notions of logical contingency and necessity do not enter into what he has in mind as he embarks on his Third Way. Rather (to bore you yet again with my wonderful cat), he is starting with an eye on things like Smokey, who is generated and (alas) perishable. Smokey is here today, but he was born some time ago and will be dead before too long. He is, as Aquinas would put it, 'able to be or not to be' ('contingent') since he is part of a world in which things spring up and pass away.

But are there only contingent beings in our vast and puzzling universe? Aquinas does not think so. Why not? His answer is: 'Now everything cannot be like this [sc. able to be or not to be], for a thing that need not be once was not; and if everything need not be, once upon a time there was nothing.' And what does Aquinas mean by this answer? His readers have offered different interpretations of it, but it seems most plausible to take it as making the same point as one to be found in *Summa contra Gentiles* I, 15. Here we find Aquinas saying:

> We find in the world certain beings, those namely that are subject to generation and corruption, which can be and not-be. But what can be has a cause because, since it is equally related to two contraries, namely, being and non-being, it must be owing to some cause that being accrues to it. Now, as we have proved by the reasoning of Aristotle, one cannot proceed to infinity among causes.

In other words, the Third Way is arguing that not everything can be able to be or not to be because all such things depend on something for their being there, and without something not merely able to be or not to be there would be nothing at all. In the Third Way, what Aquinas finds unbelievable is that everything is *generated*. He is asking 'How can *everything* be such that its coming into being depends on something else which has brought it about?'

Yet this is not the end of Aquinas's reasoning in the Third Way. For, having argued that not everything is able to be or not to be, he continues by wondering what can be said of what is *not* able to be or not to be, i.e. of what is *necessary* as opposed to contingent.

To start with, he says that anything not able to be or not to be 'either has its necessity caused by another, or it has not'. One might understandably take this assertion as supposing that necessity is a property which a thing might acquire by virtue of what it does or by virtue of what something else does. But Aquinas can hardly be thinking along these lines. For him, a 'necessary' being is something not able to be or not to be (something not contingent). So the 'necessity' of a necessary being cannot, for him, be a property which it might acquire (if it were there to acquire it, it would not, for Aquinas, be a necessary being). For Aquinas, necessity (in a being) is not a property which something might come to have, whether by its own agency or by that of something else. So, in saying that a necessary being 'either has its necessity caused by another, or it has not', he must be suggesting that any necessary being must either exist as what it is independently of something else or exist as what it is because something else accounts for it existing as what it is. In other words, he is evidently envisaging two possibilities: a necessary being might owe its existence to something else, or a necessary being might owe its existence to nothing else.

How might a necessary being owe its existence to something else? On Aquinas's account, a necessary being cannot be the result of a substantial change since it is ungenerated. It does not come to be from something existing before it (something able to turn into it). So, if it owes its existence to something else, a necessary being, on Aquinas's account, depends for its being on what causes it to be without a change occurring.

Let us then suppose that there are many necessary beings (Aquinas actually thought that there are many). Are they, in turn, all derived? Do they *all* depend for their being there on something else? With these questions we reach the conclusion of the Third Way. For, Aquinas says, the answer to them is 'No'. 'Just as we must stop somewhere in a series of causes,' he argues (referring back to the reasoning of the Second Way), 'so also in the series of things which must be and owe this to other things. One is forced, therefore, to suppose something which must be, and owes this to no other thing than itself.' In other words, according to the Third Way, if everything not able to be or not to be depends on something (or maybe many things) causing it to be, then there will be nothing not able to be or not to be.

So the argument of the Third Way basically boils down to this:

1. We see that there are things which come about by generation and which perish.
2. Not everything can be like this since, if everything were like this, there would be nothing now (since things which come about by generation and which perish are only there by virtue of something else).
3. So there is something which exists and does not come to be by generation and which is not perishable.
4. But, of any such thing, we can ask how it comes to exist.
5. The answer to this question can lie only in something which exists of itself and is the cause of all things other than it which are neither generated or perishable.

But is the argument cogent? One may reject (1) while in the grip of a philosophical theory according to which we can know nothing, a theory which no philosophers believe in as they go about their daily business and plan for their retirement. Most people would find (1) to be obviously true, as it surely is (and if it is not, then what do we know about anything?). And (2) is evidently true: if *absolutely everything* depends for its existence on something else, then there would not be anything. If absolutely everything would not be there but for the activity of something else, then nothing would be there since everything would then depend for its being there on something and since the something in question would be part of what we mean when we speak of *absolutely everything*.

Yet what about (4)? In the text of the Third Way, Aquinas works up to it by means of a tautology. He says: 'Not everything then is the sort that need not be; some things must be, and these may or may not owe this necessity to something else.' The tautology, of course, lies in the words 'these may or may not owe this necessity to something else', and I presume that one cannot dispute it. In that case, however, Aquinas is now already home and dry with respect to the Third Way. For if X (a necessary being) owes its necessity to nothing (if nothing accounts for it existing), then there is something which is necessary and which owes its necessity (its being there as something not able to be or not to be) to nothing. And if X owes its necessity to something else (if the existence of X derives from something other than it), then there is something which is both necessary and which owes its necessity to nothing – unless we can make sense of there being an infinite series of causes for there being anything at all, which arguably we cannot.

THE FOURTH WAY

The reasoning of Aquinas's Fourth Way is sometimes summed up along the lines: 'If things are more and less good, something must be best, and this something is God.' On this interpretation, the Fourth Way is effectively saying: 'Since there is a good and a better, there must be a best, and this "best" is God.' As we have seen, however, Aquinas thinks that argument for the truth of 'God exists' can successfully proceed only from what can fairly be thought of as God's effects. His idea is that any successful argument for 'God exists' must be one which maintains that something is rightly thought of as an effect of God (something which God has brought about or is bringing about). And the Fourth Way is no exception to this general idea of his.

To be sure, it certainly begins with an eye on the good, better, and best sequence. 'Some things', says Aquinas, 'are found to be more good, more true, more noble, and so on, and other things less.' And, he adds, 'such comparative terms describe varying degrees of approximation to a superlative; for example, things are hotter and hotter the nearer they approach to what is hottest'. But does Aquinas want to suggest that, if X is good and if Y is better than X, then there must be something comparable to X and Y which is, simply speaking, good beyond improvement? It would be odd if he did, if only because there is plainly no reason to believe that, given a number of things which are good in varying degrees, there is something else of the same kind with respect to which there could be nothing better of that kind. It would also be odd since Aquinas refers in the Fourth Way to the good, better, and best sequence (and to comparable ones) as a way of arguing that there is a God, and since (as we shall see) he does not take God to be one in a group of things of the same kind. He does not think of God as the best, or whatever, of things that can be graded together intelligibly.

In fact, the core of the Fourth Way lies in what Aquinas writes towards the end of it. Here we find him saying: 'The truest things are the things most fully in being. Now, when many things possess some property in common, the one most fully possessing it causes it in the others . . . There is something, therefore, which causes in all things their being, their goodness, and whatever other perfection they have. And this we call "God".' But what is the import of this brief passage? In order to understand it we need to note two aspects of Aquinas's thinking not so far touched on. One concerns his approach to the topic of causality. The other has to do with his view of terms such as 'true', 'being', and 'good'.

The first aspect of Aquinas's thinking which I have in mind here has often been summed up in the slogan 'Effects resemble their causes'. Yet the slogan is potentially misleading. Suppose that someone's cause of death is given as 'lung cancer'. Should we conclude that the person's corpse must *look* like a lung infected by cancer? Obviously not, and Aquinas does not think otherwise. Or suppose that the US President is killed by political activists. Does it follow that the activists must themselves be assassinated? Again, obviously not. And, once again, Aquinas does not think otherwise. He thinks that understanding causes involves understanding how it is that what they are is shown forth in what they bring about. His view is that understanding *efficient* causes (producers, or things which impact on others so as to modify them somehow) is to see that their effects express or show forth what they themselves are. According to him, efficient causes explain their effects and do so precisely because of what they are. For him, we have an explanation of some development in the world when we reach the point of saying 'Oh, I see. Of course that explains it.' And he thinks that we reach this point when we see how a cause is expressing its nature in its effect.

Suppose that Fred is staggering around. We ask 'How come?' Then we learn that he has drunk a lot of whisky, and we say 'Oh, I see. Of course that explains it.' But what do we 'see'? One might be tempted to say something like 'We see that it is not surprising that Fred should be staggering since people who drink whisky often do that.' One might say that what 'seeing' means here is that we note that what is now occurring has happened a large number of times before. But if one occurrence is puzzling (if, for example, Fred's staggering is puzzling), why should a thousand such occurrences be less puzzling? That drinking whisky is followed (or regularly followed) by staggering does not *explain* what has happened: it simply reports what we have become used to experiencing.

Until quite recent times, nobody did see the connection between staggering and drinking alcohol. To see it you need a chemical account of alcohol and a grasp of what alcohol does to the human brain. Only when you have developed this kind of understanding can you be said to *see* why drunks stagger. And what you would at last see is why it has to be the case that they do so. To see, in this sense, is to have what Aquinas would have called *scientia* (a proper, scientific knowledge). And, when he says that causes are *like their effects*, he means that seeing why effects spring from their efficient causes is seeing how the nature of the causes explains their effects and renders them necessary and, therefore, unsurprising. He means that, though, when drunk, I cannot be described as looking like alcohol, I am certainly showing forth *what alcohol is*. And in this sense, he thinks, I 'resemble' it. For him, drunken people are, when properly understood, alcohol in action or at work, alcohol expressing its nature.

Actually, Aquinas rarely and bluntly says that effects of efficient causes are 'like' them. More commonly, he says that they reflect or show forth the nature of their causes. But his general picture ought to be clear. In Aquinas's view, efficient causality is not just a matter of distinct objects merely making contact with each other. For him, it takes place as causes operate in things other than themselves. It occurs as causes *show themselves forth* in something else. Aquinas thinks that this might sometimes lead to effects looking just like their efficient causes. Mostly, however, he thinks that effects of efficient causes are like their causes insofar as they display their causes *as active*.

Yet, what of the second aspect of Aquinas's thinking relevant to understanding the Fourth Way? As with the causal matter just discussed, his view can also be represented by means of a slogan: 'Truth, Being, and Goodness basically amount to the same thing.' But what on earth can it mean to say that? Aquinas's position here is not easily summarized. For present purposes, however, perhaps we can get a sense of it with respect to some questions and some possible ways of answering them.

Suppose that Mary tells the truth. What is she doing? A first answer might run along the lines: 'Mary is saying how things are.' So we might suggest that there is a connection between truth and being. You have the truth when you know how things *are*. To know the truth is to know *what is the case*.

Mary might also be a good singer. But what is she considered as such? A first answer might run along the lines: 'Mary is someone who reaches high notes without her voice cracking' or 'Mary is someone who makes tuneful noises with her vocal organs.' So we might suggest that there is a connection between goodness and being. To be good, we might say, is to *be* in some way (to *be someone who can reach high notes without cracking* or to *be someone who can make tuneful noises*). And, of course, if it is *true* that Mary is a good singer, then, we might add, this is so because Mary *is* in some way or other. For it to be true that she is a *good* singer is intricately (almost inseparably) connected with what she actually *is*.

All of this is what Aquinas is driving at when he says that 'Truth, Being, and Goodness basically amount to the same thing.' And he is clearly presupposing it as he works towards the end of the Fourth Way. For there he is evidently thinking that whatever we latch on to as we speak *truly* about the world, whatever we can single out as *good* or as *being* (having *esse*), raises a causal question. How come it is there at all? How come it is there rather than nothing? In other words, in the Fourth Way, Aquinas is thinking as I reported him doing in Chapter 4. But to that line of thinking he is adding what I have just reported concerning his views on causation and the connection between truth, being, and goodness.

So his argument is really as follows:

1. We discover things which have degrees of perfection.
2. Such things raise the question 'How come?'
3. There must be an answer to this question.
4. Whatever it is must somehow contain in itself all the perfections we encounter in the world.
5. In fact, we can think of it as the source of all perfections and as the source of all that is good and true.

Is the argument a good one? Much obviously depends on whether or not Aquinas is right to think that there is a question posed by the fact that there is something rather than nothing. The value of the Fourth Way also evidently depends on the cogency of the view that effects show forth the nature of their causes and that to account for there being truth and goodness in the world is ultimately to account for there being a world. Such matters need more discussion than is possible here.

Yet should we not seek to account for the fact that there is something rather than nothing? And is it not clearly the case that what Aquinas means by 'efficient causes' do show themselves forth in their effects? Is it not also evidently true that there is, as Aquinas suggests, a connection between being true, being, and being good so that to ask why things are true or good is ultimately to ask why they exist at all? Perhaps the right answer to these questions is 'No'. But it is surely not obvious that 'No' is the right answer. Even readers suspicious of Aquinas's reasoning in the Fourth Way might concede as much.

THE FIFTH WAY

The first four of Aquinas's Five Ways argue that God accounts for something as an efficient cause. But the Fifth Way concentrates on another aspect of causation. I might wonder *who* killed Fred; but I might also wonder *why* that person killed him. And, according to Aquinas, I would here be looking for radically different answers. In his view, a question like 'Why did X kill Y?' is not to be answered in terms of efficient causes since it is looking for something *intended* rather than something *acting* so as to bring about some effect. We might explain John's death by referring to Paul, who murdered him. But knowing that Paul murdered John leaves us still somewhat in the dark. For why did Paul murder him? No answer to that question is going to be given by a description of Paul murdering John (by reference to an efficient cause or causes). And that is what Aquinas thinks. In his view, we can satisfy our query as to why Paul killed John only by forgetting about efficient causes and by thinking about another kind of explanation, one which involves intention.

According to Aquinas, people are paradigm examples of agents acting with intention. For we often have reasons for the ways in which we behave, and we can say why we act as we do. Yet, what are we reporting as we explain ourselves on this front? Aquinas thinks that we are alluding to goals which we have in mind. In his view (to which we shall later return), intentional behaviour is always directed to an end to be achieved, an end desired by the one whose behaviour it is, an end which is therefore perceived of as good from the viewpoint of the one whose behaviour it is. It might, from some absolute moral viewpoint, be bad for Paul to kill John. And yet, Aquinas thinks, if Paul really kills John for reasons of his own, it must be because he sees something desirable to be achieved by doing so. For Aquinas, Paul's killing John with a 'why' in mind is a matter of him seeking to pursue what (at least to him) is a good end in mind. Paul is acting with a view to a goal. He is not just doing what he does because something outside him is pushing or pulling him: he is acting for reasons of his own.

But, now, consider this question: 'Are there things in the world, other than people, that might reasonably be thought of as seeking to achieve ends or goals?' As he begins to state his Fifth Way, Aquinas suggests that there are. 'For we see', he says, 'that certain things that lack knowledge, namely, natural material substances, act for the sake of an end. And this is evident because they always or more frequently act in the same way in order to achieve what is best, and hence it is evident that they reach their goal by striving, not by chance.'

The key phrase here is 'not by chance'. Aquinas believes in chance events. As he sees it, you and I would meet by chance if we happened to bump into each other on a crowded street. I was not aiming to meet you, and you were not aiming to meet me: we had other intentions in mind as we were each doing our own thing. But we happened to bump into each other. So our meeting, as Aquinas would say, was by chance. But is it by chance that, for example, acorns regularly grow into oak trees? Or is it by chance that water usually makes crops grow?

Nobody would say that it is. It is in the nature of acorns to grow into oaks. It is in the nature of water to be able to nourish crops. Or, as Aquinas would say, acorns have a tendency (*appetitus*) to become oak trees, and water has a tendency to make crops thrive. Yet, to refer to a tendency is certainly not to refer to an efficient cause. It is to draw attention to what something is moving to, or inclined to, and it brings to mind the notion of an end or a goal or a striving towards. And the notion of an end, a goal, or a striving naturally brings to mind the notion of purpose or intention. Goal-directed activity is something which it makes sense to think of as meant and not just efficiently caused.

And yet, of course, things such as acorns and water are not thinking things. They cannot reflectively direct themselves to the ends to which they naturally incline. So, what accounts for them doing so? We cannot just say that it is their nature to do so, because it is this very nature which is now in question. So, might we suggest that they aim as they do because their nature and activity is, indeed, meant? Aquinas, at any rate, thinks that we can. 'Things that lack knowledge', he argues towards the end of the Fifth Way, 'do not strive for goals unless a being with knowledge and intelligence directs them, as, for example, an archer aims an arrow.' In other words, Aquinas thinks that goal-directed phenomena in nature would seem to imply the activity of a director beyond nature. Or, as he puts it: 'There is a being with intelligence who orders all the things of nature to their ends, and we call this being God.'

Yet, why just one being? And in what sense could it be thought of as having intelligence? And, even if what Aquinas argues in his Five Ways is remotely cogent, is there not more to be said of God than they have to offer? As I have noted, the text of the Five Ways comprises but a fraction of what Aquinas wrote. And he has much more to say of God than is given by their conclusions. In the next few chapters we shall see something of what that amounts to.

7

The Being of God

In a passage immediately following the text of the Five Ways, Aquinas writes: 'Having recognized that a certain thing exists, we have still to investigate the way in which it exists, that we may come to understand what it is that exists.' Significantly, however, his next words are: 'But we cannot know what God is, but only what he is not.' Yet, can Aquinas really mean what he says here? Is he seriously asserting that we can only know what God is not? Many of his readers have thought that he cannot be doing so since that would leave him concluding that we have no idea as to what God is, which seems a curious line for a Christian theologian to take.

Nonetheless, this is actually Aquinas's position. 'The divine substance', he says, 'surpasses every form that our intellect reaches. Thus we are unable to apprehend it by knowing what it is' (SG I, 14). God, he maintains, 'is greater than all we can say, greater than all we can know; and not merely does he transcend our language and our knowledge, but he is beyond the comprehension of every mind whatsoever, even of angelic minds, and beyond the being of every substance' (DN I, iii,77). According to Aquinas:

> The most perfect [state] to which we can attain in this life in our knowledge of God is that he transcends all that can be conceived by us, and that the naming of God through remotion (*per remotionem*) is most proper . . . The primary mode of naming God is through the negation of all things, since he is beyond all, and whatever is signified by any name whatsoever is less than that which God is. (DN I, iii,83–4)

Comments like these can be found throughout Aquinas's writings. Their content is a central aspect of his thinking. But what, precisely, are they trying to express?

KNOWING WHAT GOD IS

In fairness to those who cannot bring themselves to believe that Aquinas really holds that we do not know what we are talking about when we speak about God, perhaps the first thing to say is that passages such as those just quoted are not suggesting that we cannot make any *true statements* when it comes to divinity. In fact, Aquinas argues, there are things to be said of God which are both *true* and such that we can *know* them to be true. Examples include 'God is living', 'God is good', 'God is perfect', 'God is eternal', and 'God is omnipresent'. Aquinas also thinks that there are things to be said of God which are true even though we cannot *know* them to be true. Examples include 'God is three persons in one nature' and 'God became a human being so that people might share in the life of God'.

And yet, of course, one can speak truly of things without understanding what they are. I do so all the time, and I would be surprised if you do not also. If someone were to ask me why televisions work, I should quickly tell them that one reason is electricity. But what is electricity? There are people who can answer this question in a learned and technical manner (people who know what electricity is). But I, maybe like you, am not one of them. Nor do I belong to the happy few who really know what they are talking about when they say, for instance, that physical things are composed of atoms, or that there is a high front around when the weather is dry, or that the AIDS virus attacks the human immune system. I certainly assert that these are all truths, and I offer some kind of justification for doing so. But, if pressed, I have to admit that I really do not understand what I am saying, not only with respect to these examples, but also with respect to much else that I talk about. And, Aquinas thinks, this is the way all of us stand when it comes to talk and truths about God.

To understand him, it helps to note the difference between knowing (or having good reason to think) *that what one says is true*, and knowing *what it is that makes one's statements true*. Suppose that a doctor tells me that I have a brain tumour. In that case I have grounds for claiming that this is what I have. And, in saying that I have a brain tumour, I clearly understand to some degree what I am saying. But what makes it true that someone has a brain tumour? The obvious answer is: 'The existence of the tumour in the person's brain.' If I have a tumour, that is because there is a tumour in me. Yet, must I understand what, precisely, a tumour is in order rightly and intelligibly (and with some understanding on my part) to claim that I am the victim of a brain tumour? Obviously not. It is one thing to know or to have reason for claiming that a proposition is true; it is another to know what it is that makes the proposition true. And the difference here is what Aquinas has in mind when saying that there are truths to be proclaimed about God even though we do not (and cannot) know what God is.

For Aquinas, knowing what something is involves more than being able to talk about it, or even to talk about it truly. It means having what we have in mind when we say that doctors understand what is going on when patients have brain tumours. Aquinas thinks that we know what a thing is insofar as we possess a scientific understanding of it, insofar as we are able to single it out and to locate it precisely in terms of genus and species, insofar as we know what it is essentially. And this, he holds, is what we cannot do when it comes to God. Why not? Because God is not part of the world but the reason why there is any world at all. For Aquinas, God is not something with respect to which we can develop a scientific understanding.

But why not? Why should we be doomed to lack a science of God? Though frequently ignored in accounts of his thinking (and frequently ridiculed by those aware of it), Aquinas's chief answer to this question comes in his defence of the claim that God is 'entirely simple' (*totaliter simplex*), to which we now need to turn.

DIVINE SIMPLICITY

The teaching that God is simple is an ancient one. Some have argued that it is implied by certain biblical texts. It is decisively endorsed by several of the early Christian Fathers. It is firmly defended by various medieval thinkers (Jewish, Christian, and Islamic) and by many contemporary philosophers and theologians as well. It is also asserted by Christian ecumenical councils. For example: according to the Fourth Lateran Council (1215), God is 'one absolutely simple essence'; and according to Vatican I (1869–70), God is 'completely simple' (*simplex omnino*).

But what might it mean to say that God is simple? A famous account of divine simplicity comes in St Augustine's *The City of God*, where we read:

> The reason why a nature is called simple is that it cannot lose any attribute it possesses, that there is no difference between what it *is* and what it *has*, as there is, for example, between a vessel and the liquid it contains, a body and its colour, the atmosphere and its light or heat, the soul and its wisdom. None of these *is* what it contains; the vessel is not the liquid, nor the body the colour, nor the atmosphere the light or heat;

nor is the soul the same as its wisdom . . . Further, the soul itself, even though it may be always wise – as it will be, when it is set free for all eternity – will be wise through participation in the changeless Wisdom, which is other than itself. For even if the atmosphere were never bereft of the light which is shed on it, there would still be the difference between its being and the light by which it is illuminated . . . Accordingly, the epithet 'simple' applies to things which are in the fullest and truest sense divine, because in them there is no difference between substance and quality. (*The City of God*, XI, 10)

For Augustine, God is simple because he is immutable. But Augustine also thinks that God is simple as not possessing different properties or attributes. According to Augustine, expressions like 'the knowledge of God' or 'the goodness of God' do not name realities which are truly distinct. Or, as he sometimes observes: 'All that is *in* God *is* God.'

And this is what other defenders of divine simplicity have also wished to assert. Hence, for example, according to Anselm of Canterbury: 'The supreme nature is simple: thus all the things which can be said of its essence are simply one and the same thing in it' (*Monologion* 17). Anselm acknowledges that those who believe in God use many different statements when speaking of God's nature. They say, for example, 'God is good', 'God is just', and 'God is wise'. But, Anselm argues, we should not think of God as having really distinct attributes. Fred might be tall, dark, and handsome. Yet what if he shrinks, turns grey, and loses all his looks? Would he still be Fred? Most people would say that Fred can exist over a long period of time even though he undergoes many changes (thereby losing and acquiring many attributes). Why would they say this? Presumably because they would want to distinguish between Fred and the attributes he possesses at any given time. They would want to say that being Fred can be distinguished from (and is distinct from) being tall, dark, and handsome (or whatever else one takes Fred to be). They would want to say that Fred and his attributes are not one and the same thing. According to Anselm, however, one cannot say this of God. For him there is no difference between God and anything we might want to call 'the attributes of God'. For Anselm (and also for Augustine), the various attributes we ascribe to God in sentences of the form 'God is X', 'God is Y', and so on, are not distinct realities in God. They *are* God.

And this is what Aquinas thinks. Unlike Augustine and Anselm, however, he develops a detailed defence of the position (arguably, the first in Western religious history). For he suggests that 'God is simple' can be defended on three counts. God's simplicity, he says, follows from the fact that God is (a) not changing, (b) not an individual, and (c) not dependent.

(a) Not changing

As we have seen, one reason why Aquinas holds that 'God exists' is true lies in his conviction that something causes change without undergoing change. So he takes it as fairly obvious that God cannot have the complexity which something has just by being a bodily individual, that he cannot have a variety of different physical bits. Why? Because, thinks Aquinas, bodies are always potentially divisible, while God is the source of there being something rather than nothing and must, therefore, be the source of *any* coming to be that occurs. 'For what is able to exist', says Aquinas, 'is brought into existence only by what already exists . . . The first existent is God. In God then there can be no potentiality' (ST Ia, 3,1; cf. ST Ia, 2,3, SG I, 16, and DP VII, 1).

But Aquinas also wants to deny that God changes for another (albeit related) reason. For, what does it mean to say that something is changing or has undergone change? As I noted in Chapter 3, Aquinas recognizes two kinds of change: substantial (as when a cat becomes a corpse) and accidental (as when a cat puts on weight). As I also noted in Chapter 3, Aquinas holds that we can make sense of individuals changing both substantially and accidentally only insofar as they are material (insofar as they are instances of informed matter). In other words, intelligible individuals undergoing substantial and accidental change are, for Aquinas, always a mixture (*compositio*) of form and matter, from which he concludes that God cannot have the complexity of being both form and matter. Instead, so he reasons, God is 'essentially form' (ST Ia, 3,2; cf. ST Ia, 3,1, SG I, 17, and CT I, 16).

(b) Not an individual

Yet how are we to describe such a thing? Normally, we encounter and talk about individual things which are individuals in the sense that they are discrete or particular examples of a kind, so that there can always be more than one of them. But what allows us to single out such things? As we have seen, Aquinas's answer is 'matter'. And, if he is right, it would seem to follow immediately that something which is nothing but form is just not something we can think of as an individual in the usual sense. For such a thing could not be distinguished from its nature.

I am a human being, not human nature. And, Aquinas thinks, I am *this* human being and not *that* human being because of my matter. But what if my existing did not consist in my being a thing of some kind numerically distinguishable from others of the same kind? Granted the notion of matter as making things to be distinct instances of their kind, we might say that I and my nature would be indistinguishable. And, with an eye on divine simplicity, this is precisely what Aquinas wants to say with respect to God. On his account, God must be (substantial) form without matter. And in that case, he thinks, God cannot be thought of as a numerically distinct instance of a kind (or type, or group, or class). 'The individuality of things not composed of matter and [substantial] form', he argues, 'cannot derive from this or that individual matter, and the forms of such things must therefore be intrinsically individual and themselves subsist as things. Such things are thus identical with their own natures' (ST Ia, 3,3).

Aquinas thinks that there are many things the individuality of which is constituted purely by their substantial form. In his view, for instance, angels are form without matter. For the moment, however, the point to stress is that this is also how he thinks of God. On his account, we cannot sensibly distinguish between the individual that God is and the divine nature itself. I am not humanity. But God, Aquinas holds, is rightly described as *being* divinity. Indeed, so Aquinas thinks, God is rightly described as being *whatever* divinity is essentially. Or, as he puts it, God 'is identical with his own godhead, with his own life and with whatever else is similarly said of him' (ST Ia, 3,3). In God, says Aquinas, there is no mixture (*compositio*) of individual (*suppositum*) and nature.

(c) Not dependent

Yet might there be a mixture of another sort? Specifically, could it be the case that in God there is a mixture of nature (or essence) and existence? For Aquinas, the question is worth asking since, he says, there are things with respect to which we can distinguish between nature (or essence) and existence. He thinks that we can do this when it comes, for example, to angels. Why? Because, though he takes them to be immaterial and, therefore, not to be things which come about by physical generation, he also takes them to be derivative when it comes to the fact of their existing. Angels, in his view, owe their existence to something other than themselves. And he thinks that such is the case with everything other than God.

Aquinas's view is that existence in all things except God is what they *have* rather than what they *are*. It is received and not something which belongs to them by nature. And how shall we express this fact (if it is, indeed, a fact)? Aquinas does so by saying that, in everything other than

God, there is a mixture (*compositio*) of essence and existence, while in God there is none. For him, it is God's nature or essence to exist. Or, as he also likes to say, God is 'subsistent existence itself' (*ipsum esse subsistens*).

Aquinas has to take this kind of line because of what we have seen him maintaining about God as the reason why there is anything at all. In his view, whatever accounts for the *esse* of things cannot be something the *esse* of which comes to it from outside, from another, from an antecedent source. It cannot be that the existence of God is dependent on what is not God. So Aquinas concludes that 'God is his own existence' (*suum esse*). For him, so we may say, to be God is to be 'to be' (*esse*).

But notice that, contrary to what some writers have suggested, Aquinas does not take 'God is his own existence' to mean that God is to be identified with existence considered as a property or quality of some kind. As we have seen, Aquinas does not view *esse* as a property or quality. Nor does he believe that God's being his own existence entails that one obviously contradicts oneself in denying that God exists. For, as we have also seen, Aquinas thinks that we cannot know what God is so as to be able to demonstrate that 'God does not exist' is clearly contradictory. Aquinas holds that God cannot but exist. But he does not claim that this can be shown by appealing to anything demonstrably contradictory in 'God does not exist'.

In fact, Aquinas's teaching that essence and existence are identical in God is nothing but what is sometimes called 'negative theology'. Its purpose is not to *describe* God but to indicate what *cannot* be true of him. For Aquinas, if we use the word 'God' to refer to whatever accounts for things having *esse*, if we use it to signify whatever accounts for there being anything at all, then we cannot think of God as owing his existence to another. Aquinas thinks that, if there is a God, he must be 'outside the realm of existents, as a cause which pours forth everything that exists in all its variant forms' (*extra ordinem entium existens, velut causa quaedam profundens totum ens et omnes eius differentias*) (PH I, 14). Aquinas's readers have sometimes described him as professing an understanding of God's nature when asserting that in God there is no distinction between essence (nature) and existence. For Aquinas, however, this assertion, even though we can know it to be true, gives us no understanding of what God is. It gives us no comprehension of the divine essence. For him, all it amounts to is a true expression of what *cannot* be the case with God.

And that is how Aquinas thinks of all that he says on the topic of God's simplicity. None of it purports to tell us what God is or what God is positively like. Indeed, it can be summed up in the claim that God is no 'what' of a kind, that he is nothing we can get our minds around, that we cannot, to use my earlier phrase, have a 'scientific understanding' of God. When Aquinas turns to divine simplicity in the *Summa theologiae*, he prefaces his discussion by saying that what he is about to offer is an account of 'ways in which God does not exist'. And that is precisely what Aquinas's 'doctrine of divine simplicity', as it is sometimes called, amounts to, both in the *Summa theologiae* and in his other writings.

But is there not more to be said of God than that he is *not* this, that, or the other? Can Christian theologians settle only for noting what God *cannot* be? Can they not defend speaking of God in a positive manner? In the next chapter we shall see some ways in which Aquinas seeks to answer these difficult questions.

8

God-Talk

In ST Ia, 13,2 Aquinas refers to the view that sentences of the form 'God is F' (e.g. 'God is living'), 'although they sound like affirmations, are in fact used to deny something of God rather than to assert anything'. Given what we saw of his teaching in the last chapter, one might expect him to agree with this position: but he does not. In ST Ia, 13,2 he says that if, for example, 'God is living' simply means that God 'is not like an inanimate thing', then there is no reason 'why we should use some words about God rather than others', and nothing we say of God would capture what he primarily is. Also, he maintains, when people speak of God, they do not only want to say what God is not. 'When people speak of the "living God",' he observes, 'they do not simply want to say that God . . . differs from a lifeless body.'

These arguments of Aquinas are good ones for exactly the reasons he gives. They also clearly indicate that he believes it to be possible to speak truly and positively of God. Yet how does he think that they square with his view that we cannot know what God is but only what he is not? How can he regard them as compatible with the claim that God transcends all that can be conceived by us?

The short answer is that, though Aquinas accepts that we can speak positively and truly of God and know that we are doing so, he also thinks that the words we thereby use fail to measure up to the reality they are trying to latch on to. In using them, he holds, we are trying to mean more than what we usually do. But that short answer needs some unpacking.

FIGURATIVE DISCOURSE

In one sense, Aquinas sees no problem with the idea that there is talk of God which is positive, true, and fully intelligible to us. That is because he recognizes that much talk of God is manifestly figurative. Suppose I assert that God is a rock, or a mighty fortress, or a father. Aquinas would agree that I am not denying anything of God. And he would accept that I might know what rocks, mighty fortresses, and fathers are. He would also concede that what I say is true since God is solid, firm, unchanging, dependable, protective, caring, a source of my existence, a refuge, and so on. Aquinas thinks that figurative God-talk is true and important. In fact, so he notes, the Bible is full of it.

But what if you ask me: 'Is it *really true* that God is a rock or a mighty fortress or a father?' Even though I might hold that God is all these things, might I not also rightly agree that God is somehow none of them? Aquinas thinks that I might. He believes, for instance, that I might truly deny that God is a rock or a mighty fortress since God is not a physical object. He also believes that I might truly deny that God is a father since God is not a man with sperm who has procreated with a woman. In his view, therefore, positive and figurative talk about God, intelligible as it is because of what we primarily mean or signify by the words we employ when engaging in it, cannot convey what God really is. Why? Because he thinks that what it says can also be denied and that this is not the case with what, as we may put it, is true of God 'absolutely'. For Aquinas believes that there are things which can be said of God which are both true and undeniable. Examples would be 'God is good' and 'God is living'. These, for Aquinas, are propositions which cannot be truly denied. They are true without qualification. They are absolutely true. So he also thinks that not all discourse concerning God is figurative: some of it is literally true.

CAUSES AND EFFECTS

Could it be true in the light of what God has brought about? We sometimes describe things with an eye on their effects, as, for example, when we call people good because of the benefits they shower on others. So, might we not turn to what God has originated as a guide to what can literally be asserted of him? Might we, for instance, say that God is unqualifiedly good because he is somehow the cause of there being many good things?

The suggestion may seem an attractive one. And people often say that the reason they think of God as good lies precisely in the goodness of what he has produced. According to Aquinas, however, such reasoning is confused. For one thing, he observes, if 'God is X' only means that God produces what is X, then God can be described as being like anything we care to mention. As we have seen, Aquinas takes God to be the reason why there is any world at all. But what follows from this conviction with respect to the thesis now in question? For Aquinas, it follows that accepting it would commit us to saying that God is not only good but also, for instance, wooden, feline, and gaseous. For things so describable are as much a part of what God has produced as things which we take to be good. 'God', Aquinas observes, 'is just as much the cause of bodies as he is of goodness in things; so, if "God is good" means no more than that God is the cause of goodness in things, why not say "God is a body" on the grounds that he is the cause of bodies?' (ST Ia, 13,2).

At one level, Aquinas has no problem with saying that God is wooden, feline, gaseous, and so on. For, as we have seen, he allows that we might speak truly of God in a figurative way. Indeed, he says, figurative God-talk might positively save us from a mistaken understanding of divinity since its manifest falsehood (i.e. the fact that it could not be *literally* true even if it is *somehow* true) is unlikely to lead us to take it too seriously (cf. ST Ia, 1,9). Yet Aquinas also wants to insist that talk like this cannot tell us what God in and of himself is without qualification. You may rightly think of me as a lion because I am aggressive and predatory. But you will not know what I am if you do not know that I am human. By the same token, so Aquinas suggests, to assert that God is describable as being like what he produces is not a sufficient answer to the question 'How can God be spoken of truly and literally?'

In particular, he thinks, the answer is insufficient if we are concerned with what God is essentially and unchangingly. As you know by now, I am the proud owner of a cat called Smokey. But would you know what I essentially am if this were all you knew about me? Obviously not. I might never have come across Smokey. My relation to him does not constitute what I am in myself, what I am by nature (or essence). And, Aquinas thinks, a similar line of reasoning is relevant when it comes to God. For, he argues, God's relation to what he produces cannot be what makes him what he is essentially and unchangingly. Aquinas's view is that what God produces must depend on what God essentially and unchangingly is.

UNIVOCALLY, EQUIVOCALLY, AND ANALOGICALLY

Those who believe in God have never laid claim to what we might call a 'private language'. I mean that they have always spoken of God using words which belong to a language which already has a life of its own apart from theology. They sometimes assert that God is what nothing else is; that he is, for example, infinite or omnipotent. But even words like 'infinite' and 'omnipotent' are not uniquely theological. To call something infinite is to say that it is not finite, and both 'not' and 'finite' have meaning apart from any reference to God. The same goes for the elements of which 'omnipotent' is composed. Anything omnipotent is all-powerful, and neither 'all' nor 'powerful' are uniquely theological terms.

Or, as we might put it, when people speak of God, they dress him in borrowed clothes. They characterize or describe him using words which they also (and primarily or normally) use when talking of what is not God. Philosophers and theologians sometimes refer to 'religious language'; but there is really no such thing, and there is certainly no such thing as 'theistic language' (God language). There is obscure language. And there is obscene language. But there is no language which is unique to religious people or, in particular, to those who speak of God. Their language is that of us all.

Aquinas is acutely aware of this fact. So, when turning to the question 'Can we truly say what God essentially is?', he typically begins by distinguishing between three different ways of using (three different ways of meaning) one and the same word on different occasions or with an eye on different things.

Consider the sentences 'Mars is a planet' and 'Venus is a planet'. Does the word 'planet' mean something different in each sentence? The answer, of course, is 'No'. The word means exactly the same thing in both of its occurrences. To call Mars and Venus planets is to assert precisely the same thing of each of them. Or, as Aquinas would say, to call Mars and Venus planets is to use or mean 'planet' *univocally*. According to him, in 'Mars is a planet' and 'Venus is a planet', the word 'planet' signifies exactly the same thing.

But what about 'Cricket players use bats' and 'Bats are winged mammals'? Cricket bats and the bats which fly around in attics are not remotely alike: they are as unalike as could be. So, in 'Cricket players use bats' and 'Bats are winged mammals', the word 'bat' means or signifies something completely different. Or, as Aquinas would say, to speak of cricket bats and winged bats is to use or mean 'bat' *equivocally*. He would say the same of, for example, 'bank' in 'I rowed the boat to the bank' and

'I have money in the bank', or of 'committed' as in 'The judge committed the prisoner to jail' and 'The judge committed a crime'.

So a word used on different occasions can mean or signify something exactly the same or something completely different. Yet, what shall we say of, for instance, the word 'love' in 'I love my wife', 'I love my job' and 'I love chicken soup'? Is a husband's love for his wife the same as his love for his job or his love for chicken soup? Is one's love of one's job normally equivalent to one's love of one's spouse or one's love of certain foods?

With respect to questions like these, the univocal/equivocal distinction seems to break down. To speak of loving one's wife, one's job, and some food seems not to be using or meaning 'love' in exactly the same way. But neither does it seem to involve pure equivocation. One is hardly punning if one employs the word 'love' with respect to even such different objects as a person, an occupation, or a means of nourishment. The same might be said of 'musical' as in 'I have a musical clock' and 'Mozart was musical', though one would hardly be saying exactly the same thing when attributing musicality to Mozart and a clock.

Aquinas expresses this thought by suggesting that the same word may, on different occasions, signify *analogically* (i.e. without meaning exactly the same on each occasion but also without meaning something entirely different). And, he argues, all words employed with respect to God and to what is not God (apart from ones used to speak of him figuratively) must signify or be meant analogically. For he believes that they cannot be construed univocally or equivocally.

Why not univocally? Aquinas thinks that, for example, 'God is good' is literally and not figuratively true. So, why should he be unhappy with the suggestion that 'good' means exactly the same thing in, say, 'John is a good chef' and 'God is good'? Aquinas also thinks that God is literally wise. In that case, however, why should he not accept that in 'God is wise' and in, for example, 'Solomon is wise', the word 'wise' means or signifies exactly the same thing?

His answer to these questions lies in his teaching that God is simple. If John is a good chef, that is because he is good as a substance distinguishable from his nature and from what he is accidentally. For Aquinas, however, God has no accidents and is not distinct from his nature. If Solomon is wise, he is so because he exemplifies what many others do (or might do). For Aquinas, however, God exemplifies nothing. He is not of a kind with attributes shared by others of the same kind. Or, as Aquinas explains:

When we say that a man is wise, we signify his wisdom as distinct from the other things about him – his essence, for example, his powers or his existence. But when we use this word about God we do not intend to signify something distinct from his essence, power or existence. When 'wise' is used of man, it so to speak contains and delimits the aspect of the man that it signifies, but this is not so when it is used of God; what it signifies is not confined by the meaning of our word but goes beyond it. Hence it is clear that the word 'wise' is not used in the same sense of God and man, and the same is true of all other words, so they cannot be used univocally of God and creatures. (ST Ia, 13,5)

Yet what about suggesting that terms used of God and creatures are purely equivocal? Why not say that, for example, 'wise' in 'God is wise' and 'Solomon is wise' mean or signify something entirely different? Here Aquinas's answer is that, if such were the case, then there would be no point in using of God any particular word which we also use of other things.

We might say, for example, 'God is wise.' But if 'wise' here has nothing of the significance which it has in other contexts, and if the same goes for any word as employed with respect to God and to what is not God, we might just as well say that God is rectangular or dusty, which, according to Aquinas, we do not want to say and would be plainly wrong if we did so. 'Where there is pure equivocation,' he writes, 'there is no likeness in things themselves, there is only the unity of a name' (SG I, 33). And this, he thinks, cannot be the case when it comes to what we truly and literally say both of God and of what is not God. Also, he holds, if terms used when talking of God and of other things have a purely equivocal meaning or significance, then there could be no good argument from what is not God to the truth that God exists or to any other truths concerning God.

As we have seen, Aquinas denies that we can know that God exists on the basis of a knowledge of what God is or on the basis of some explicit knowledge of God which we possess innately. The proposition 'God exists' is not, he thinks, self-evidently true so far as we are able to see. And, so he also thinks, if we are cogently to argue for its truth, we need to reason from things which we do know (i.e. from the world which we experience). But what if 'God is X' and 'Something other than God is X' use whatever word we substitute for X in a purely equivocal way? Then, according to Aquinas, cogent arguments from what is not God to the conclusion 'God exists' would be impossible. But this, he thinks, is not the case since there actually are some cogent arguments from what we know of what is not God to the conclusion that God exists. If 'nothing was said of God and creatures except in a purely equivocal way,' says Aquinas, 'no reasoning proceeding from creatures to God could take place' (SG I, 33). He means that, if, for example, to say that God is a cause is to use the word 'cause' in a sense which means something totally different from what it means in any other context, then there could be nothing we could recognize as a cogent causal argument for the conclusion that there is a cause rightly referred to as God.

ANALOGICAL PREDICATION

So Aquinas is of the view that, in talking about God, and forgetting about talk of God which is purely figurative (and, therefore, arguably false), we must be employing words which signify with respect to God and to what is not God in an analogous sense. But can we seriously hold that we do so while also speaking truly? One might concede that, for example, 'good' can signify differently, though not equivocally, as predicated of (as used when affirming something about) different things. But can we know that it is significantly and truly predicated of, say, both God and a good chef? We might agree that acid causes certain things to corrode. But can we know that 'causes' is significantly and truly predicated of both God and acid?

Aquinas would say that the examples I have in mind here are significantly different. As we have seen, he thinks of God as a cause since, among other things, he thinks it to be the case that something must account for, or bring it about, that there is anything at all, and he is happy to use the word 'God' to refer to whatever that is. As we shall see later, however, Aquinas does not think that God *has* to do any causing. In his view, we cannot think of God as having to bring anything about simply in order to be God. So he would say that 'God is a cause' does not latch on to, or truly report, what God essentially is. On the other hand, however, he would certainly say that, for example, 'God is good' does exactly that. Why? Because he takes goodness to belong to God essentially. But why goodness rather than, say, materiality?

Aquinas would reply that materiality cannot belong to God by nature. Why not? Because of what cannot be true of God on the supposition that God is the reason why there is anything at all, or on the supposition that God is what we can think of as that to which the Five Ways reason. Aquinas thinks that there are propositions of the form 'God is an X' (where 'X' is a noun), 'God is Y' (where 'Y' is an adjective), and 'God Fs' (where 'F' is a verb) which simply cannot be true. For example (and in the light of what we have already seen him saying), he would deny that God is an antelope, that God is pink, and that God brushes his teeth.

And yet, Aquinas reasons, there is nothing to stop us from literally affirming that God is truly an X, or that God is Y, or that God Fs, where the X,Y, and F signify what could be truly affirmed of, or predicated of, whatever accounts for there being something rather than nothing, or of whatever accounts for there being what each of the Five Ways take as their starting points. He thinks, for instance, that, if it is reasonable to suppose that something accounts for there being any world at all, then that something, whatever it is, can truly be said to be a cause (a cause of there being anything at all) since it accounts for or brings something about. He also thinks that, of any such thing, we can say that it is a causal agent (that it is Y) and that it causes (that it Fs).

Aquinas is not, of course, suggesting that whatever accounts for there being something rather than nothing is exactly like the causes which we encounter in day-to-day life. Nor is he asking us to believe that making the difference between something and nothing is like bringing it about that a room has a rug in it rather than no rug. But he is suggesting that, when we speak of 'accountability' or of 'causing' with an eye on God, we are not using terms either univocally or equivocally. And he is arguing that we can come to see this by reflecting on what God cannot be if, indeed, he makes for the difference between there being something and nothing, or if he is what the Five Ways take him to be.

Yet, what might we take God to be when thinking of what he is essentially? If God does not have to make anything at all, then he is not essentially a reason for there being something rather than nothing. And he is not essentially the explanation or cause of anything with which the Five Ways are concerned. In that case, however, can we truly and literally say that God is like anything other than God? Aquinas thinks that we can, and that we can do so with an eye on the topic of efficient causation.

CAUSES AND EFFECTS AGAIN

What is going on when efficient causation takes place? A popular view with some thinkers is that efficient causation occurs as one state of affairs is temporally followed by another one. The idea here is that, if, for example, my drinking sulphuric acid is followed by my death, then there is a distinct cause (the sulphuric acid) which exists in its own right (as a cause) apart from and before from my death. And, according to this account, what we call my dying *by* sulphuric acid (my dying *because of* sulphuric acid) is just the fact that there is sulphuric acid there at one time and my dying at another. Causation (efficient causation) is, on this account, simply a matter of what comes after what. It consists of one describable entity followed in time by another.

Yet to know what follows what is not to know what explains that which comes to be. To know that B comes temporally after A is not to know that A explains B. Suppose that I am hale and hearty at time one. I drink sulphuric acid and die at time two. We cannot explain what is going on here by simply reporting the sequence of events. Nor can we do so by reporting the fact that many people have, in the past, drunk sulphuric acid and died. We need to know why the drinking of sulphuric acid is more than coincidentally connected with death in people who drink it. And, as we saw in Chapter 6, Aquinas is well aware of this fact. For him, properly to understand what is going on as efficient causes account for their effects, one needs to see how effects are accounted for by the natures of their causes. As we also saw in Chapter 6, Aquinas is of the view that, in accounting for their effects, efficient causes show forth their nature in them: 'What an agent does reflects what it is' (*omne agens agit sibi simile*) (cf. SG I, 29; I, 73; II, 20). In his view, when I, for example, am the victim of sulphuric acid, I constitute a place where the acid is at work, a place where it is expressing its nature, a place where its likeness can be seen. And, since Aquinas takes God to be the primary efficient cause of what exists apart from God, he concludes that God can be named or described on the basis of all of this. An effect, for Aquinas, is somehow like its cause. So he thinks that from God's effects we can say what God is since God is their cause. God, he says 'is known from the perfections that flow from him and are to be found in creatures yet which exist in him in a transcendent way'. So Aquinas's view is that from God's effects we can know what God is since God is their cause. And that gives us what looks like a rule of thumb offered by Aquinas for speaking truly of God. First take your creature. Then assume that it is like God since God is its Creator. Then speak accordingly of God.

A KNOWLEDGE OF WHAT GOD IS?

But does Aquinas think of this rule of thumb as a tool for achieving a serious knowledge of what God is? The answer is 'No'. For one thing, and as we saw earlier, Aquinas does not think that God can be truly and unqualifiedly described as being like his effects just by noting what these are like. He does not, for instance, think that God can be truly and unqualifiedly described as being wooden, feline, or gaseous, even though he takes God to be the ultimate cause of there being things like this. In fact, Aquinas thinks, from the knowledge that God is the ultimate efficient cause of everything other than himself, we can only conclude that God is truly and without qualification to be described using terms which imply no way of being that is finite or limited. And, he adds, even when we have done this, we have to recognize that we do not really understand what God is. There are effects of God which are good, and Aquinas sees no reason why goodness should not be strictly and literally ascribed to God, since he sees nothing in the meaning of 'good' (or of words such as 'living', 'knowing', or 'wise') which implies finitude or limit. But he also thinks that the goodness of God (like the life, knowledge, or wisdom of God) cannot be what it is in non-simple or complex things.

For Aquinas, as we have seen, God is nothing material. God is also no instance of a kind and cannot be thought of as distinct from his 'attributes' and his existence. So, though Aquinas believes that there are reasons for saying that God is positively and essentially thus and so, he also maintains that there is a serious sense in which we cannot understand what we are saying when we say what God positively and essentially is. We can, he thinks, speak truly and literally of God because God is the efficient cause of perfections which can be appropriately ascribed to him. But he also wants to say that things caused by God which display such perfections fail to represent him adequately, so that words like 'good', 'living', or 'wise', when based on the goodness, life, or wisdom found in what God has brought about and when then applied to him, 'fail to represent adequately what he is' (ST Ia, 13,2). 'Words like "good" and "wise"', Aquinas concludes, 'when used of God do signify something that God really is, but they signify it imperfectly because creatures represent God imperfectly' (ST Ia, 13,2; cf. ST Ia, 4,3 and SG I, 33).

At bottom then, Aquinas is optimistic when it comes to our ability to speak truly and literally of God. But he is also decidedly reserved. What I earlier called his 'rule of thumb' is not something he thinks of as a periscope which allows us to peer at and grasp what divinity is. Why not? As he indicates in the quotation at the end of the last paragraph, because of what he takes to be the difference between creatures and God, their Creator.

But what does Aquinas mean by calling God 'Creator'? And what does he take to be involved in being creaturely? In the next chapter we shall turn to some of his answers to these questions, and to topics related to them.

9

Creature and Creator

Is it only God who creates? Aquinas raises this question at *Summa theologiae* Ia, 45,5. His answer is 'Yes' since only God can bring it about that anything has *esse*. And from this answer alone we can clearly see that he effectively takes the question 'How come anything at all?' to be one of theological significance. In his view, it is a question which anybody ought to be struck by, so he does not see it as a *uniquely* Christian one (like, for example, 'Does the Holy Spirit proceed from the Father alone or from the Father and the Son?' – a question which has led to divisions among Christians, and only among Christians). According to Aquinas, 'How come anything at all?' is a question to which one can correctly and reasonably reply without previously embracing any explicitly religious position. For him, we may say, it is a philosophical question to which a philosophical answer can be given. Yet, as he goes on to explore what the answer might amount to, Aquinas uses language which looks more theological than philosophical. Jews, Muslims, and Christians are not noted for expressing what they believe by saying things like 'We believe that something accounts for there being anything at all.' They more usually say that they believe in God the Creator. And this is what Aquinas wants to say. For him, the cause of there being things having *esse* is rightly described as the Creator, the Maker of heaven and earth. For him, the cause of there being anything at all is what Jews, Muslims, and Christians ultimately believe in and, indeed, worship. But what does he take to be included in and implied by the truth that God is the Creator?

'GOD' AND GOD'S NAME

An important point to note is that Aquinas does not take the word 'God' to be what we would call a proper name. Some people take a different view. They say that 'God' is the name of the Creator just as 'Smokey' is the name of my cat. One might ask them 'Of what is "God" the proper name?' since bearers of proper names are always individuals with identities pre-existing their being named (one can, after all, rename any individual one cares to mention). Yet those who take 'God' to be a proper name normally agree when it comes to the answer to this question. For, so they commonly say, 'God' is the name of the *person* who is the Creator. The idea here is that there are many persons, and one of them is the Creator. And his, her, or its name is 'God'.

From what we have so far seen of Aquinas's thinking, however, it should be obvious how he would respond to this suggestion. For him, God is not *an* anything of any kind. Smokey is a cat. But what is God? Aquinas's answer is: 'something the nature and existence of which cannot be distinguished from itself'. There are people who claim that 'God is a person' is the most fundamental claim of Judaism, Islam, and Christianity. Yet, Aquinas observes, the proposition 'God is a person' is not to be found in the Bible and can be thought of as literally true only in the context of the doctrine of the Trinity, according to which God is three persons, not one person (cf. ST Ia, 29,3, SG IV, 26, and DP IX, 1–8). On Aquinas's account, 'God is a person' (if taken as literally true) is incompatible with what has to be said when expressing what God, as Creator, cannot be (a conclusion which he is justified in holding if he is right in what he says about knowing that 'God exists' is true, and if he is right in what he goes on to say about divine simplicity and the way in which we can truly assert what God literally is). He also (surely rightly) assumes that 'God is a person' conflicts with what Christian orthodoxy seems to require of those who subscribe to it. If we take 'God' to be the name of an individual person, then the assertion that 'God is a person' is clearly incompatible with the doctrine of the Trinity, according to which the three persons of the Trinity are distinct, though equally divine, and there is not more than one God.

We shall return to Aquinas's trinitarian thinking later. The point to grasp now is that Aquinas understands 'God' to be not a proper name but the *name of a nature* (*nomen naturae*) (cf. ST Ia, 13,8). He takes it to signify 'being divine'. We would normally say that all cats are feline. And, in the sense that 'feline' is not a proper name, Aquinas thinks that 'God' is not a proper name. For him, it signifies whatever it takes to be divine. It signifies a nature. Cats exemplify felinity by being individual cats, for they are all felines. But there is no such thing as 'Felinity', considered as something existing apart from the individual feline things we call cats. What if there were, however? What if there were such a thing as Pure Felinity existing in its own right? Then Aquinas would say that there would be something a bit like God. For God is not an instance of a kind. He exists as the individual that he is, indistinguishable from his nature. Cats are not Felinity. But God, Aquinas holds, is *divinity itself*. For him, God is what we name, not when we confer a proper name on an object we might encounter (like a cat), but when we try to use a word (i.e. the word 'God') to refer to what accounts for there being individuals to which we can give proper names. He thinks that our use of such a word is a somewhat feeble attempt to reach out so as to latch onto a way of existing which we cannot understand.

CREATION AND BEGINNINGS

For Aquinas, then, to call God the Creator is not to say that anything classifiable made the heavens and the earth (and whatever else there is apart from God). It is not to say that a 'such and such' named 'God' did so. It is to say that everything other than God comes from what is divine. But when did it do so? When did everything other than God come to be by virtue of the divine nature (which is not different, so Aquinas thinks, from God)?

One might raise these questions since one might think of creation as a feat which God accomplished at some time. The Bible says that God created the heavens and the earth *in the beginning* (Genesis 1:1). And one might naturally take this to mean that there must have been a time at which God's creative activity was focused. In other words, one might take the statement 'God is the Creator' simply to mean that God got things going *at some time in the past*. But Aquinas does not. He agrees that God brought it about that the world or universe (or whatever you want to call what we live in) began to exist (perhaps we might call it 'that whole of things which is not itself a part of some greater whole', which is about the best I can come up with when asked for a definition of 'world' or 'universe'). Yet he does not think that we can philosophically prove that the world (or universe, or whatever you want to call it) must have had a beginning. Nor does he think that a date can be assigned to God's act of creation.

But we can, he thinks, date God's creative acts. Remember that Aquinas takes God to be the reason why there is anything at all. But what might we include under the heading 'What there is'? One might offer different answers, but it seems obvious that 'what there is' at least includes your reading this sentence at the time at which you are doing so. And Aquinas would say that you are reading it by virtue of God your Creator. So your reading of the sentence is, for Aquinas, what God is producing creatively. Yet it occurs at a time. And Aquinas thinks that we can therefore date God's creative activity. We can do so, he reasons, since created events can be dated and since they are there as what God is bringing about.

The tense of 'is bringing about' here is important. As we have seen, Aquinas thinks that the action of a cause lies in the effect as brought about. 'Action and passion', he explains, 'are not two changes but one and the same change, called action in so far as it is caused by an agent, and passion in so far as it takes place in a patient' (IP, 3,3). For him, therefore, to say that God is making things to exist is not to locate what God is doing at a time prior to what is existing because of him. To call God 'Creator' is, for Aquinas, to draw attention to what God is bringing about at any time. For him, creation is not an event in time: it is the making to be of things in time for all the time that they exist. Most typically, Aquinas uses the verb 'to create' when thinking of God as getting the universe started. But he thinks of this divine activity as almost exactly on a level with God's bringing it about that anything, at any time, has *esse*. Hence, for example, under the heading 'On the coming forth of creatures from God' (*de processione creaturum a Deo*), he argues that everything which is, must be caused to be by God (ST Ia, 44,1; cf. ST Ia, 45,1, SL II, 1,1,2–4, and SG II, 6). And he does so by means of an argument now familiar to us. 'We are bound', he says, 'to conclude that everything that exists in any way is from God.' Why? Aquinas answers:

> Whatever perfection we find to exist in things by sharing, needs to be caused in them by something to which the perfection belongs essentially; for example, iron is heated by fire. Moreover . . . God is intrinsically subsisting existence itself . . . Everything other than God is not its existence but shares in existing. (ST Ia, 44,1; cf. ST Ia, 7,1, DP VII, 2, and SG I, 21)

This is essentially the argument of the Fourth Way, which, in turn, is essentially an argument from the *esse* of things to a cause of there being things having *esse*. And what Aquinas is alluding to in it captures the core of his view of God as Creator. For him, God creates by making things to exist, *period*. And God, so he thinks, is doing this for as long as things exist, which is why he maintains that it is God alone who creates. For only God, that which is pure existence itself, can make the difference between there being nothing at all and there being something.

CREATION, CHANGE, AND CREATED CAUSES

But is there really a difference taking place as nothing gives way to something? Obviously not. Smokey is something (a cat), but nothing is just nothing (not anything). We might ask 'What is in the drawer?', and the right answer might be 'Nothing'. Yet the inside of a drawer is not absolute nothingness. For a start, there is air framed by whatever the drawer is made of. And to say that there is nothing in the drawer is not to say that 'Nothing', considered as the name of something, is in the drawer. Rather, it is to say that there is, for example, no pen in the drawer, or no paper clip, knife, fork, or whatever. 'Nothing' in 'There is nothing in the drawer' is (roughly speaking) shorthand for 'No X', where X is the name of something which could be in the drawer.

Aquinas, though, is sensitive to such facts. So he must not be supposed to mean that God makes the difference between nothing and something by acting on or by tinkering with nothing (considered as a thing of some kind). In fact, he says, God's creative activity literally makes no difference to anything. Why? Because Aquinas thinks that it is not the bringing about of change in anything. Rather, it is the making to be of things together with the changes they undergo. How come Smokey? One (true) answer would be 'Smokey's parents'; they brought him about by acting on bits of the world so as to induce change in them. But 'How come anything at all?' According to Aquinas, this question cannot be answered with reference to what (in the world) modified what (also in the world). The answer must lie in something which causes to be, *but not from anything.*

In other words, Aquinas endorses, while giving reason for doing so, the classical claim that God creates *ex nihilo* (from nothing, i.e. not *out of* anything). 'In the case of begetting human beings', he says, 'the latter did not exist beforehand, but they are produced out of something nonhuman, as something now white is made out of something not white.' And yet, he adds,

> if we should consider the emanation of the whole of being in general from the first source, such emanation cannot presuppose any being. But 'nothing' is the same as nonbeing. Thus, as human beings are begotten out of the nonbeing that is nonhuman, so creation, that is, the

emanation of the totality of being, is out of the nonbeing that is nothing. (ST Ia, 45,1)

An objection to this line of reasoning would be to say that, if, as Aquinas thinks, creatures are made to be by God for as long as they exist, a distinction needs to be drawn between, say, 'creating' (on God's part) and 'sustaining' (on God's part). One might suggest that it would be best to say that, while God's making things to begin to exist can rightly be called 'creation from nothing', his keeping things going can hardly be so called since the things God sustains are already there to start with. And this point is not a silly one since the notion of 'sustaining from nothing' sounds slightly odd. Yet Aquinas finds nothing wrong in maintaining that what we might call the 'sustaining' of creatures by God is, in principle, nothing different from God's making them to begin to exist in the first place. For Aquinas, both involve God bringing it about that something has *esse* (being or existing, as opposed to not being or not existing). And, for him, the time at which the thing in question exists is irrelevant. So, on Aquinas's account, I am as much being created by God now as was the universe when it came into being (on the supposition that the universe actually did begin to exist).

Yet, if my being, not to mention that of everything else, is, at bottom, God's creative doing, must it not follow that the only doer (so to speak) is God? My being and my doing are only conceptually distinct, in that one can think of me without, say, thinking of me as feeding my cat. In reality, my being includes all that I am about. If I am a feeder of cats, then my being when I feed my cat is the being of a cat feeder. As I feed my cat, I am hardly doing two things: existing, and feeding my cat. Try feeding a cat while not existing. So, might it not be best to say that it is God, not I, who feeds my cat? Might it not be best to say that, in the end, there is really only one cause which accomplishes anything? Might it not be best to say that only God gets anything done?

To some extent, Aquinas shows sympathy with such questions. For him, every action of a creature is God's action. 'The divine power', he says, 'must needs be present to every acting thing . . . God is the cause of everything's action inasmuch as he gives everything the power to act, and preserves it in being, and applies it to action, and inasmuch as by his power every other power acts' (DP 3,7). According to Aquinas, God operates in every operation since God is the reason why there are any creaturely operations. On the other hand, however, Aquinas also finds it ludicrous to suggest that, for example, people do not feed cats, and he sees no good reason for denying that they actually do so.

To grasp his thinking on this topic, we need to note two things. First, he believes that secondary causes can be genuine causes. Second, as I said above, he thinks that it is literally true that God makes no difference to creatures.

Consider the case of my typing a word by striking the keys on my computer keyboard. The appearance of the word on my computer screen has a causal story behind it, starting with me. I type a key, this connects with something else (maybe with many things). Then we get a letter on the screen. And so on, until a word is formed. But what caused the word to be formed? Since I am the typist, it seems natural to say that I am the cause of it appearing on the screen. Yet other causes were involved. Are they any less causes of the appearance of the word because I initiated the process which brought them in? Surely not. I typed the word. But I did so by means of other things which were also, and in their own right, causally efficacious. Or, so we may say, I am the primary cause of the word appearing on the screen; but there are also secondary causes to be reckoned with (i.e. causes which cause because I cause).

Well, Aquinas would say the same thing when it comes, for example, to my feeding my cat. My cat gets to be a full cat because I have fed it. And Aquinas thinks that my feeding my cat and its becoming full are truly God's doing. But God is not squatting down and spooning meat into a bowl: I am doing that. Or, as Aquinas would say, I am a secondary cause in the cat's becoming a full cat (i.e. God gets the cat fed by means of me). Just as keys, and the insides of computers, can be thought of as genuinely causal when it comes to words appearing on a computer screen (even though their primary cause is the typist), so I, as I feed my cat, can be thought of, according to Aquinas, as genuinely causing (even though my actions, like those of everything else, come from God, the cause of there being any acting creatures).

But can I really be a genuine cause of my cat's getting fed if God is bringing it about that my cat is getting fed by me? If we think that the answer to this question is 'No', we are probably assuming that my being really me, considered as a causal agent, is somehow threatened by the fact that God makes me to be me (where my 'being me' includes my acting as I do). Yet, why should we assume this? It might sensibly be thought somehow threatening if God's making me to exist as a cat feeder involved him modifying me from outside, as, say, a bus would if it knocked me down. In that case, we might think that God's feeding a cat by means of me is a bit like someone forcing a person's finger around the trigger of a gun so as to shoot someone else. As we have seen, however, Aquinas does not think that God's creative act is a case of modifying or changing. In creating, he holds, God is not modifying or changing anything: he is simply making things to be themselves. In this sense, so Aquinas thinks, God makes no difference to anything. Rather, God accounts for a world in which things can make a difference to other things.

10

The Doing of God

Hitler invaded Poland in 1939. But what date or dates can be assigned to God's creative activity? As we have seen, Aquinas thinks that, strictly speaking, this activity is dateable only because events which happen in time can be dated. Yet, does he take this to mean that God's life is simply a matter of what takes place in time? Does he think that there is no life for God apart from changes which occur in the universe? And is there, for him, no divine *when* apart from dates we might assign to historical occurrences?

THE LIFE OF GOD

Aquinas intimately connects God and creatures since, for him, their being and their doing are what God is as an active efficient cause. If you want to know what God is doing (i.e. 'bringing about'), thinks Aquinas, there is a simple answer: look around you. God's doing, in the sense of creating, is not, for Aquinas, one activity going on in God and another activity going on in creatures. For him, the being of creatures is the doing of God (which is why he thinks that God can be 'described' with respect to what he brings about). Yet Aquinas does not want to say that God's life depends on his effects. For him, we can conclude that God is alive because of the fact that God is *able* to create.

More precisely, so Aquinas argues, life can be ascribed to God because he acts of himself. In Chapter 3 we saw Aquinas maintaining that living things are 'automobiles' (i.e. self-moving things), and this idea is what he has in mind when he speaks of God being alive. Only, he stresses, God must be said to have life in the fullest sense. For he argues that there are degrees of self-movement. A plant, he thinks, can truly be said to be self-moving (as a stone, for instance, cannot). Yet he also thinks that the self-movement of plants is fairly limited. In his view, plants in motion simply do what their nature determines them to do. Animals and people have a greater degree of self-movement, he reasons, for they can move towards goals or ends which satisfy them in some way (sensually, in the case of animals; both sensually and intellectually, in the case of people). Yet he also thinks that even animals and people are less self-moving than God must be.

Why? Because, Aquinas argues, God's doing (God's movement or action) is not a response to what impinges on him as part of a world which he occupies. Rather, it springs wholly from himself. When a cat chases a mouse, it does so because the mouse has impinged on the cat. When people strive for what they desire, that is because they are drawn to some good which they do not yet possess. According to Aquinas, however, God's actions can never be a response to any kind of external stimuli. And there is no good for God to desire apart from what he already is. Why? Because, says Aquinas, God is the source of all creaturely good (cf. SG I, 98 and ST Ia, 18,3).

TIME AND ETERNITY

For Aquinas, then, God's life is not to be confused with any created thing or process. Yet he does think that there is, indeed, no divine *when* apart from them. Why? Because he believes that God is not measured by time. For Aquinas, the life of God (which is nothing other than God) is eternal. And, he holds, eternity and time are radically dissimilar.

Considered in its historical context, Aquinas's view of eternity is a fairly conventional one, for it basically reiterates what was commonly said on the subject by Christian authors from the time of St Augustine. According to them, eternity is what you have if you transcend time, if your life is not captured by an account of what comes after what from a temporal perspective. In Book V of his *Consolation of Philosophy*, Boethius (c. 480–c. 524) declares that 'Eternity is the complete and total possession of unending life all at once' (*Aeternitas est interminabilis vitae tota simul et perfecta possessio*). He means that the life of something eternal is not spread out so as to be reportable in terms of earlier than or later than. It lacks successiveness. It is not lived in time. And this is how Aquinas thinks of eternity. God, he declares, is certainly eternal; in God there is no before and after, no past, present, or future, and, therefore, no 'now'. In Chapter 19 of his *Proslogion*, St Anselm, addressing God, writes: 'You were not, therefore, yesterday, nor will you be tomorrow, but yesterday and today and tomorrow you *are*. Indeed, you exist neither yesterday, nor today nor tomorrow but are absolutely outside all time.' And Aquinas could have said just the same. 'Time and eternity clearly differ', he observes (ST Ia, 10,4). For him, eternity is distinct from time. No temporal processes occur in eternity.

According to Aquinas, only God is eternal. So his teaching on eternity is part and parcel of what he has to say about God. And one could summarize it by saying that God, for Aquinas, is timeless. He thinks that we can date God's acts. But he also thinks that this is not to date any stage of God's life or anything in God himself. Why not? Aquinas's answer is: dateable events and things with a temporal location are all parts of a world of change, while God is the reason why there is any such world and cannot, therefore, be part of it.

Aristotle maintains that there is no time without change (*Physics* 218b21 f.), and Aquinas accepts this conclusion. For him, individuals and processes can be dated (are temporal) only because we can identify them in relation to changes which take place in the world. But how can the source of there being any world be identified in this way? Aquinas holds that it cannot be so identified. 'The notion of eternity', he says, 'derives from unchangeableness in the same way that the notion of time derives from change. Eternity therefore principally belongs to God, who is utterly unchangeable' (ST Ia, 10,2).

One might ask why God should be thought to be unchangeable, especially since many contemporary theologians (and philosophers) take it as obvious that God cannot be any such thing. From what we have seen of his thinking so far, however, what Aquinas would say in response to this question should be evident. For him, God is unchangeable since he is the unchanged cause of things which undergo change and also since he is identical with what he is. Twentieth-century authors frequently assert that nothing unchangeable could really be thought of as divine. Aquinas's view is that nothing changeable could be. For him, any changeable individual would merely be part of a world which needs God to make it to be.

DOES GOD HAVE TO CREATE?

If God is unchangeable, however, and if God is, indeed, the maker of creatures, must it not follow that God cannot but create? Aquinas thinks that it follows only on the supposition that God has eternally chosen to create (cf. ST Ia, 19,3; cf. SG II, 23). But can he be thought of as able to do this? In the last chapter we found Aquinas speaking about the 'emanation of the whole of being in general from the first source'. And such language might suggest that he thinks of 'the whole of being in general' as something which just *has* to flow from God. Neoplatonic philosophers such as Plotinus (204/5–270) used the term 'emanation' to refer to the process by which, so they thought, what we take to be things of our acquaintance come from what is above them. Their idea was that what we ordinarily take ourselves to encounter is, to put it crudely, something like vomit: something which gushes from higher realities. Yet Aquinas is at pains to deny that God cannot help but spew out the created order. For one thing, he reasons, nothing created is such that we would formally contradict ourselves by saying that it does not exist (even if it does exist). Smokey is real enough. For Aquinas, however, it would not be contradictory to say 'There is no such cat as "Smokey".' In this sense, Aquinas holds that there is nothing necessary when it comes to the existence of creatures.

Might it not be, however, that God just cannot help creating given what he is by nature? I cannot help but breathe, for I am a human being. Ceasing to breathe is just not something I can do for any length of time (not voluntarily, anyway, though I shall involuntarily do so at some point). So, might creating be to God as breathing is to me? According to Aquinas, the answer is 'No'. Why so? Because God could be forced to create by nature only if there were something other than God which inevitably acted on God so as to force him to create given the nature he has, or if God needed creatures simply in order to exist. And yet, Aquinas suggests, anything other than God must be such that its nature and actions are God's doing, from which it would seem to follow that no such thing can stand to God as forcing him to act in one way rather than another. Furthermore, God can be said to need creatures in order to exist only if the non-existence of creatures would mean that God could not really be God (that nothing could be divine unless something existed as a creature). But how come the existence of creatures? Aquinas's answer is 'God'. So, he (surely rightly) concludes that, if there being the divine nature depended on the existence of creatures, there would be no divine nature. I cannot help breathing, but that, Aquinas thinks, is so because I am a physical organism with needs that flow from what I am considered as such. I might, for example, feel (as many people do) that I cannot be whole until I produce a child. But, Aquinas thinks, God cannot produce anything unless God is essentially what he is quite apart from what he produces (as, in fact, is the case with human parents).

THE POWER OF GOD

But what, exactly, can God produce? Are there limits which constrain him? Or, as some would ask, what is the extent of God's power? Is it limited? Is it unlimited? Classical Jewish, Muslim, and Christian thinkers have repeatedly asserted that God is constrained by nothing and that his power is unlimited. God, so they have said, is omnipotent. And that (unsurprisingly, perhaps) is Aquinas's view as well. But why does he hold it? Why does he think that God must be omnipotent?

The topic of God's omnipotence is a tricky one. And it is especially tricky if we take 'omnipotent' to mean 'able to do anything', and if we then raise questions of the form 'Can God ——?' If 'God is omnipotent' means 'God can do anything', then can God, for example, sing well? Lots of people manage to do this. But God, surely, cannot sing well. For (assuming that God is incorporeal) he lacks vocal organs and a mouth. So God, perhaps, is not omnipotent. Yet those who have believed in divine omnipotence would surely not feel unduly undermined by the fact that God cannot sing well. So perhaps what they want to say is not best captured by an understanding of 'omnipotent' which takes it to mean 'able to do anything'. Aquinas, at any rate, never takes 'omnipotent' to mean 'able to do anything'. On the other hand, however, he is happy to say that God is, indeed, omnipotent. But why?

Because he thinks that God can make to be the case whatever, simply speaking, can possibly be the case. 'There are buildings in Paris' expresses a possible (not to say an actual) truth. So, according to Aquinas, God can make it to be that there are buildings in Paris. 'Smokey is sleeping' also expresses a possible truth. So, according to Aquinas, God can make it to be that Smokey is sleeping. And so on for other examples. 'Something is judged to be possible or impossible', Aquinas argues, 'from the implication of the terms: possible when the predicate is compatible with the subject, for instance, that Socrates is seated; impossible when it is not compatible, for instance, that a human being is a donkey' (ST Ia, 25,3). And, he concludes, to call God omnipotent is just to say that God can bring about what is possible. To focus on omnipotence by concentrating on sentences of the form 'God can . . .' is, in his view, a mistake (for there are obviously lots of things which God cannot do). But Aquinas sees nothing to stop us defining omnipotence in terms of what, absolutely speaking, is able to be.

This, of course, is hardly surprising given his views on what it means to say that God is the Creator. For Aquinas, God is the Creator since he accounts for there being any world at all. And it is a natural development of this view to say that God is omnipotent in that he can make whatever can coherently be thought of as being part of such a world. 'Since every agent enacts its like,' he reasons, 'every active power has a possible objective corresponding to the nature of that activity which the active power is for . . . The divine being, on which the notion of divine power is founded, is infinite existence, not limited to any kind of being, but holding within itself and anticipating the perfection of the whole of existence. Whatever can have the nature of being falls within the range of things that are absolutely possible, and it is with respect to these that God is called all-powerful' (ST Ia, 25,3).

For Aquinas, it is equally natural to add that God can bring about that which things in the world cannot bring about given what they are by nature. Or, as he puts it, God can work miracles. I can bake a cake, but I cannot restore a dead person to life. Can God do this, however? If there is no contradiction involved in the notion of someone dying at time one and coming to life at time two, then Aquinas's answer is 'Yes'. In Aquinas's view, God has made a world consisting of things with distinct natures and distinct ways of working. So he thinks that there are things which they cannot naturally cause to come to pass. But he also thinks that there is nothing to stop God bringing it about that events in the world come to pass which cannot be produced by what is already in the world. 'The divine will', he argues, 'is not limited to this particular order of causes and effects [sc. those which obtain in the world] in such a manner that it is unable to will to produce immediately an effect in things here below without using any other cause' (SG III, 99,6). One may, of course, think that miracles are not to be expected or that they are impossible from a scientific perspective. And Aquinas would agree. For him, a miracle is not just an extraordinary event. It cannot be predicted on the basis of what things in the world are by nature. Or, as he puts it: 'Since their abilities and activities are limited, all creatures are bound by laws of nature, and a work exceeding the world in which they live cannot be produced by any power there. And if it comes about, then it is done immediately by God, such as raising the dead to life, giving sight to the blind, and the like' (ST Ia2ae, 5,6; cf. ST Ia, 105,6–8, and DP VI, 1–2).

THE PRESENCE OF GOD

Aquinas's teaching that God is simple is often said to make God distant or remote. His teaching that God is eternal is often said to make God aloof or static or uninvolved in the things of this world. His teaching that God is omnipotent is often said to depict God as unable to let things be themselves, as something domineering or coercive. Such readings of Aquinas do him a terrible injustice, however. For his view is that God is as involved as it is possible to be in the things of this world. It is also his view that God, far from cramping the style of his creatures, is their ultimate facilitator, the one who, more than anything else, helps them as they strive to be themselves. Why this is so ought to be clear from what we have already seen of his thinking. But the point might be emphasized by casting an eye on what Aquinas thinks of God's presence to his creatures.

We might approach this by considering the topic of intimacy between human beings. Let us, for instance, suppose that I am in love with you. How can I display or express my love? Well, I can try to acquire things for you. Or I can seek to ensure that you remain well and active. Then again, I can be with you. I can meet you, live with you, and even go to bed with you. And very nice, too. Yet in all these scenarios I am still somewhat limited when it comes to being intimate with you. I can buy you a bunch of roses or an oil well, but my presence to you would then consist of nothing but my putting you in contact with objects in the world. I can try to keep you healthy, but, yet again, I can do so only by connecting you to what is distinct from you (such as food or medicine). In the best possible world, I can be physically with you, and I can express my affection towards you in bodily terms. But I can do so only as something outside you, as an object in the world which is proximate to you.

Well, according to Aquinas, God scores better than I when it comes to my intimacy with you. For, to his way of thinking, God is never present to creatures as something outside them which can merely put them in contact with other things outside them. On the contrary. For Aquinas, God is *wholly* in *every* part of what he creates. And he is there as making it to be itself. He is wholly in all that he creates since, Aquinas thinks, he is simple and therefore not divisible (i.e. the notion of there being a part of God here and a part of him there makes no sense). And God is in all that he creates since nothing created would be there if he were not at work in it.

According to Aquinas, God is *nowhere*, if being somewhere means being in a place dimensively. On the other hand, he argues, God is *everywhere* since there being anywhere is a matter of there being God at work. God, says Aquinas, 'is in every place giving it existence and the power to be a place, just as he is in all things giving them existence, power and activity'. He adds: 'Just as anything occupying a place fills that place, so God fills all places. But not as bodies do (for bodies fill places by not suffering other bodies to be there with them, whilst God's presence in a place does not exclude the presence there of other things); rather, God fills all places by giving existence to everything occupying those places' (ST Ia, 8,2).

For Aquinas, God is more intimately present to creatures than any creature can be to any of its fellows. And, though he conceives of God as timelessly eternal, Aquinas certainly does not take the eternity of God to render him static or uninvolved. On his account, the eternity which is God is the source of all creaturely life and activity. Indeed, for Aquinas, this life and activity is the living God at work.

But at work in what? If God is the source of the *esse* of things, an obvious answer is 'Everything'. And Aquinas would (obviously, as we can now see) be happy with this answer. For him, God is at work in rivers, in conifers, in mountains, in buildings, in planets, and even in vacuum cleaners (not to mention cats). And Aquinas is interested in all such things (vacuum cleaners would obviously have delighted him had he known about them). Yet some of God's creatures interest Aquinas more than others. He has a treatise devoted to astronomy, but he has a lot more to say about people. Why? Because he believes that people have a special place in God's created order, one which makes them of interest to theologians as well as to philosophers. But what does Aquinas take people to be? As we shall see in the next chapter, he takes them to be remarkably interesting animals.

11

Lower than the Angels

Aquinas is not inclined to speculate on what God is or is not likely to do. His general view is that we are in no position to predict the behaviour of the Almighty. But he seems to take a different line when he turns to what he calls 'purely spiritual creatures', or 'angels', as the Bible calls them. For, on the supposition that God has created our world, he argues that God must also have created angels since the created universe would be incomplete without them (cf. ST Ia, 50,1 and SG II, 46). This argument is rather feeble as a proof for the existence of angels. And maybe Aquinas never thought otherwise, for he sometimes speaks, not of it being provable that angels exist, but of it being not unreasonable to suppose that they do. As a commentator on Scripture, he can hardly ignore them, for they are very much in evidence in the Bible. And he certainly believes in their existence (he is sometimes referred to as 'the Angelic Doctor'). Whether or not he takes the existence of angels to be demonstrable apart from biblical testimony is, perhaps, open to question.

What is not open to question, however, is that Aquinas thinks that angels are to people as people, on the whole, think that they are to cockroaches. As we survey the living world, we tend to suppose that we are pretty much the greatest things in it. And we take some living things (e.g. cockroaches) to be so vastly inferior or below us that we have no qualms when it comes to stepping on them or otherwise doing our best to eradicate them. For Aquinas, however, people are vastly inferior to angels. Why? Because he thinks of people as essentially material and, therefore, constrained and limited in all sorts of ways. On his account, an angel, not being material, is like God in the sense that there is nothing to distinguish between it and its nature. And angels, he reasons, are nothing so low as to need physical organs as ways by which to acquire knowledge. They are also incorruptible and vastly knowledgeable.

So people, for Aquinas, are lower than the angels: very much lower. On the other hand, Aquinas also thinks that people are greater than angels. For it was, he says, the nature of a human being, not the nature of an angel, that the second person of the Trinity assumed. We shall be turning to Aquinas on the Incarnation of God in a later chapter. For the moment, let it suffice to say that, though Aquinas may be called 'the Angelic Doctor', people interest him more than angels. They are limited, he thinks: but they are also very important. And, unlike angels, they are there for us to examine and to reflect on philosophically. They are potential objects of scientific inquiry. Or so Aquinas thinks, though others have disagreed with him on this (taking people to be something like what Aquinas means by 'angels').

SOUL AND BODY

My aunt Margaret was someone who disagreed with Aquinas at this point, though she did not realize it. At her husband's funeral she said that he must be happy to see all the friends who turned up for it. She was clearly thinking that my uncle Bill was still around as hale and hearty as he ever was. How could she have thought so? She must have been supposing that Bill, both before and after his death, was a kind of angel. She must have been supposing that Bill was always an immaterial individual, in spite of the evidence to the contrary. And, had she but known it, she could have impressed the mourners at Bill's funeral by citing some very well-known philosophers. She could, for example, have mentioned the name of Descartes.

In the course of his *Meditations on First Philosophy* (1641), Descartes seeks to establish a foundation on which to build an account of what he can know. Having decided that he cannot doubt that he exists as long as he is thinking, he then goes on to ask what he is. His conclusion is that he is essentially a non-material thinking thing. He admits that he has a body and that this is something which affects him in many ways, just as he makes a difference to it. But he is not, he says, his body. He can exist without it. He is what he is quite apart from it. A somewhat similar view seems to be offered by Plato (c. 428–c. 348 BC) in his *Phaedo* and other works. Plato takes the view that people must be essentially other than their bodies since they can live lives attached to different bodies, for he believes in reincarnation. He thinks that I am not to be identified with the body I have. Rather, the body I have is something I have acquired. And I can carry on, regardless of what people tend to call my 'death'.

Yet this is not Aquinas's view at all. For him, if my body is not there, then neither am I. As a Christian, he believes that people are not entirely extinguished when they die. But, even from his Christian perspective, he is also happy to say that what of me survives my death is not me. Or, as he says in his commentary on St Paul's first letter to the Corinthians (15:17–19): 'My soul is not me' (*anima mea non est ego*). Aquinas thinks that I can be there as myself after my death. How? Because God can raise my body from the grave. But if there is only my soul, he argues, then I do not exist.

So what does Aquinas take my soul to be? To understand his position, we need to note that people are not the only things to which Aquinas ascribes a soul. On his account, anything living has one. For him, to say that something has a soul is just to say that it lives (is animate as opposed to inanimate). 'Inquiry into the nature of the soul', he explains, 'presupposes an understanding of the soul as the root principle of life in living things within our experience' (ST I, 75,1; cf. ST Ia, 18,1 and SG I, 98). So Aquinas takes plants and non-human animals to have souls. Yet he also thinks that there is a radical difference between these and human beings. To be sure, he agrees, they resemble each other in certain ways. All of them grow and move, for instance. And though plants lack sensation, people and non-human animals do not. Unlike my roses and my cats, however, people can understand and reflect or think accordingly – a fact which leads Aquinas to hold that people are more than the sum of their bodily functions. Why? Because he holds that thought and understanding cannot be identified with any particular physical object.

Why not? Aquinas's answer is that particular physical objects are not intrinsically intelligible and can be raised to the level of intelligibility only by what is not a particular physical object. In his view, you do not understand what a thing is just by coming across instances of it which impinge on your senses. If you could understand what a thing is simply by being in physical contact with it, then, for example, babies would understand what is around them as soon as they are born, which, of course, they do not. And Aquinas is acutely conscious of this fact. For him, there is a huge difference between sensation and understanding.

In particular, he thinks of sensations as being private, while understanding is public. You and I can have the same sensations in that, for example, both of us can feel heat. But I cannot have your feelings of heat any more than I can have your toothache. I can feel hot and you can feel hot, and both of us can have toothache. But our sensations exist as, so to speak, trapped within each of us. Their occurrence is the occurrence of changes in different bodies, and, in this sense, they are private. On the other hand, however, you and I can have exactly the same thoughts. When I recognize that whales are mammals, what is ascribable to me (the recognition that whales are mammals) is not just *like* what is ascribable to you if you recognize that whales are mammals: it is one and the same thing. I, of course, can understand what whales are even if you do not. But, if we both understand what they are, if we can both recognize that whales are mammals, then we have transcended our physical limitations so as to share something: we share the same thought. And, Aquinas thinks that this fact is of major significance. For, in his view, it means that people have to be more than material individuals. Why? Because he believes that if people were simply that, then they could not know or understand. At best, they could simply feel.

Aquinas, of course, thinks that people do, indeed, feel. He is very much aware of the fact that people have senses. And, as we have seen, he thinks that we are able to distinguish between material things of the same kind precisely because of this fact. For Aquinas, however, no material thing is actually understandable considered on its own. Rather, the world is potentially intelligible, and it becomes intelligible as we 'abstract' from sense data and thus come to understand things apart from their individuality. A thing is knowable, says Aquinas, insofar as it is separated from matter. And he therefore concludes that the subject in which anything exists as known must be immaterial.

For Aquinas, the model for knowing is not so much seeing as talking. Rather as Wittgenstein came to do, he denies that an object could ever be the meaning of a word. On his account, meaning (and, therefore, understanding) emerges as those able to know escape from or transcend the particularity of the way of existing had by what is physical. Or, as Aquinas commonly puts it, understanding is of *forms*, and it occurs as these come to be in what is not material. According to him, when I understand what, for example, a lemur is, I have in me the nature of a lemur (its 'form', as Aquinas would say). But I do not have it as the lemur does. For Aquinas, lemurs (and other material things) have their forms (their natures) just by being material things of the kind they are (they have them materially (*materialiter*)). He thinks, however, that I can have forms in a different way (intentionally (*intentionaliter*)): as one who understands what lemurs (and other things) are (cf. ST Ia, 75,2; cf. ST Ia, 84,7 and SG II, 49).

Yet Aquinas does not therefore conclude that I am non-material. He says that the human soul, considered as 'the principle of the act of understanding', is not a material object. He even says that it 'subsists in its own right' since it is a knowing or understanding thing (ST Ia, 75,2). But he also says that the soul is but a part of the whole human being. For people, on Aquinas's reckoning, are not just knowers: they are also things with bodies, things which can move (like plants) and feel (like non-human animals). And they are so essentially.

Speaking in an Aristotelian vein, Aquinas observes that 'the nature of a specific type includes whatever its strict definition includes'. And, he continues: 'In things of the physical world, this means not only form, but form and matter' – from which he concludes that 'it belongs to the very conception of "man" that he have soul, flesh, and bone' (ST Ia, 75,4). Aquinas frequently refers to the view that human beings are essentially substances different from bodies. But he firmly rejects it. For him, people are naturally a composite of the immaterial and the material. Or, as he usually puts it, the human soul is 'the form of the human body' (cf. ST Ia, 76,1 and SG II, 69–71). By that he means that our existence as knowers is what makes our bodies to be the special things which they are, *viz.* bodies of intellectual animals (bodies of people as opposed to bodies of plants or non-human animals).

In terms of this picture, I am not soul plus body: I am an *ensouled body*. There is, Aquinas argues, 'no more reason to ask whether [the human] soul and body make one thing than to ask the same about the wax and the impression sealed on it . . . Just as the body gets its being from the soul, as from its form, so too it makes a unity with this soul' (DA II, 1). For this reason Aquinas argues that, if people are to live after their death, the soul must be reunited to the body. Since he holds that the human soul is subsistent, and since he thinks that (being immaterial and being the principle of life in people) it cannot be destroyed in the ways that bodies can, he agrees that it might survive the corruption of the body. But, he adds, the soul of a human being is not the whole human being. For Aquinas, the union of soul and body 'is a natural one, and any separation of soul from body goes against its nature . . . so, if soul is deprived of body, it will exist imperfectly as long as that situation lasts' (EP 15). In fact, and as I noted above, Aquinas's view is that my soul separated from my body is just not me. Nor is it an angel. According to Aquinas, angels are wholly immaterial, not immaterial parts of what is essentially a whole which includes matter (cf. ST Ia, 75,7 and ST Ia, 76,1; cf. SG II, 50).

THE LIFE TO COME

We might put all this by saying that, when it comes to our life after death, Aquinas does not believe in the immortality of the soul. He does not think that human souls can perish, as bodies do. For him, our souls are incorruptible since they are not material (cf. ST Ia, 75,6, ST Ia, 89,1–2, and SG II, 79) and cannot, therefore, be extinguished by any physical process which occurs, including our bodily death. But even an everlasting soul would not, for him, be a living human being. 'Even if soul achieves well-being in another life,' he observes, 'that does not mean that I do, or that another human being does' (EC 15). Aquinas does not even think that I survive if my soul carries on to enjoy some kind of union with God. I can only survive my death, he thinks, if my soul is reunited with my body, which is to say that, when it comes to our life after death, Aquinas's emphasis is firmly on the notion of bodily resurrection, which he takes to be the emphasis of Scripture as well (cf. SG IV, 79).

But what does Aquinas mean when he speaks of the resurrection of people? Primarily, he means that, when I am raised from the dead, my soul is reunited with the same body as that which I have now. He means that human souls which survive death are reunited with numerically the same bodies as those of the people of which they were formerly parts. The key word here, of course, is 'numerically'. Aquinas does not think that our resurrected bodies need to look like what they do at some particular stage in our lives. Nor does he think that they need to be composed of exactly what they were at some specifiable time before our death. Our bodies, after all, are in a constant process of change, as Aquinas is well aware (cf. SG IV, 81). The bodies of people aged 90 look vastly different from those of babies. They are also physically different because of what happens as aging occurs. But 90-year-old Fred has a body which is *numerically* identical with that which he had at birth. An ideal observer tracking it through the years would be tracking one and the same thing, albeit one and the same *changing* thing. That is why we can point to someone decades after they performed an action and say 'You did it.' And it is with this point in mind that Aquinas thinks of human resurrection. For him, we can be raised from the dead if God brings it about that our souls are reunited with what is materially continuous with what came from our mother's womb and subsequently acquired a name. God, as he puts it, 'can restore the corrupted to integrity' even though created things in nature can do no such thing (cf. SG IV, 81), even though 'the human body substantially dissolves at death . . . [and] . . . cannot be restored to numerical identity by the action of nature' (CT, 154).

This line of thinking raises all sorts of questions, of course. What if my body is eaten by lions after my death? And what if these lions are subsequently eaten by other ones? Would there be anything left of me to which my soul could be reunited? What if I perish by being burned to a crisp? Could anything of my body survive? Aquinas is aware of the need to ask such questions, and he raises them as he defends the view that people can rise again (cf. SG IV, 80 and CT I, 161). On reflection, however, he does not think that they ought to lead one to declare that human resurrection is impossible. In his view, my remains might undergo any number of changes. Yet, so long as the world continues to exist, there must still be something materially continuous with them as they go through these changes. And, for Aquinas, it is material continuity which is needed for resurrection. If my physical remains can be thought to be trackable (at least in principle) as time goes on, then, Aquinas thinks, it can be thought that, as time goes on, there is something which is numerically identical with them. And this can be raised and reunited with my soul. It may not look much like what I ever looked like. But, says Aquinas, God can restore it to do just that. If my hands are amputated, I am still there. Can God give me hands again without turning me into a numerically different physical thing? Aquinas sees no reason for saying that he cannot. And he argues that there is nothing to stop God from making what is left of my body into something rather more recognizable as me. Or, as he writes in Chapter 154 of the *Compendium of Theology*:

> The matter composing this human body of ours, whatever form it may take after a person's death, evidently does not elude the power or the knowledge of God. Such matter remains numerically the same, in the sense that it exists under quantitative dimensions, by reason of which it can be said to be this particular matter, and is the principle of individuation. If, then, this matter remains the same, and if the human body is again fashioned from it by divine power, and if, also, the rational soul which remains the same in its incorruptibility is united to the same body, the result is that identically the same man is restored to life.

As we have seen, Aquinas thinks that it is not form which makes a physical thing to be the individual that it is. In his view, material things are the individuals which they are since they are materially distinct. And matter, for Aquinas, is always able to take on different forms. He is not, therefore, worried about the prospect of my remains taking on different forms. When it comes to the thought of my resurrection, all he is worried about is the possibility of there being a world in which there is nothing which was once materially part of me. If there were such a world, then, he thinks, there would be nothing once physically me to be raised from the dead. Yet he sees no reason to think that there is such a world. In his opinion, our world retains that which is numerically continuous with all who have died in it. He thinks that it is pregnant with resurrected bodies.

Yet Aquinas does not for a moment suppose that human resurrection is subject to philosophical proof or demonstration. For him, we can only expect it on the basis of faith. In later chapters we shall be turning to what Aquinas means by 'faith'. We shall also be seeing more of what he takes to be true on the basis of faith. At this point, however, we need to follow him further in his account of what people are. In particular, we need to note how he thinks of them as subjects who act.

12

The Acting Person

If you think that cats are living animals, then you can make sense of saying that they have experiences and sensations. You can also make sense of supposing that they have memory, that they can learn, that they can behave willingly or unwillingly, that they can suffer, and search, and try to get things done. In short, you can make sense of supposing that cats have a perspective on the world and can act in it accordingly. And, if this is your view, then Aquinas would agree with it.

Yet he also wants to say that cats are different from people. In his view, non-linguistic animals interpret their world through what he calls the *species sensibilis*: the sensation (in the nose or the ear or the eye) as relevant to the rest of the animal's body and behaviour. His view is that, when a cat looks at a king, the appearance which is in the king as a set of physical properties is (given suitable illumination) in the cat's eye as part of the cat's life, as making a difference to what it will do next. But he does not think that cats can act as people do. Why not? Because, he thinks, people have ways of interpreting the world which involve more than sensation and reaction which spring from it.

ACTING FOR ENDS

As we have seen, Aquinas believes that human understanding should never be confused with encountering a thing at the sensory level and should never be identified with any particular physical process. He holds that we cannot understand material individuals. We can meet them at a bodily level. But to do this, he argues, is different from understanding them. For Aquinas, understanding is expressible in judgements or statements, and it can be shared by human beings (though not with other animals) in a way that sensations cannot. Since statements can be either true or false, he also argues that knowledge or understanding can lead us to recognize alternatives.

Aquinas thinks that to understand a statement is also to understand its negation. And he is obviously right to think so. When you understand that the cat is on the mat, and when you understand that it is not the case that the cat is on the mat, there is no expressible difference when it comes to what you understand. The difference has to do with what 'it is not the case that' expresses, which is not itself a thought. It is, so to speak, an attempt to erase a thought, a device to encourage us not to accept it. And, with this point in mind, Aquinas holds that to understand a statement is to be able to view the world as containing possibilities, as possibly being other than it is in fact now. For this reason, he also holds that with the ability to understand comes the ability to *act* and not simply to *react*. Why? Because he thinks that action (as ascribable to people and not to animals) involves more than being affected by external stimuli and responding accordingly: it depends on understanding how things are and how they could be. And it consists in seeking that they should be one way as opposed to some other way.

According to Aquinas, non-human animals can also be said to seek. For he thinks that they have tendencies to behave in accordance with their natures, that they have 'appetites'. We speak of water naturally 'seeking' its own level, and Aquinas, in a similar way, speaks of animals 'seeking' to be what they naturally are and to have what they naturally need. Left to themselves, he thinks, they just are what they are by nature. They may be interfered with and may, therefore, become thwarted or defective. And how they behave in particular circumstances may be impossible for us to predict with a high degree of accuracy. According to Aquinas, however, in the absence of interference, animals simply realize their natures: they 'seek' to be themselves.

But not, Aquinas holds, in a conscious sense. Their seeking is not based on knowing how things might be and moving accordingly. It is not a matter of planning that a possibly attainable end should come to pass. Rather, it is a combination of instinct affected by circumstances. It is a product of complex and given structures. It is lived out rather than chosen. And Aquinas thinks that it therefore falls short of action – or, at any rate, of what he takes to be involved in genuine human action. For, in his view, this is irreducibly and consciously end-directed, and it depends on under-standing since it is only by understanding the world that we can consciously seek to affect it.

Aquinas does not want to say that we cannot act unless we have a complete understanding of the world and of how things are within it. Indeed, he thinks, we often act in ignorance. But he also holds that we cannot truly act without some conception of how things are and of how they might be. So he views human action as end or goal directed (i.e. intentional). For Aquinas, human action differs from the behaviour of non-human animals since it is done with reasons. It always invites the question 'With a view to what are you doing that?' And, so he also thinks, acting for reasons is always a matter of seeking what one takes to be good.

GOODNESS, ACTION, AND WILL

But how are we to understood the word 'good' in this context? In general, Aquinas associates goodness with success or achievement. He thinks that when we seek what we take to be good we are trying to succeed or achieve in some way. When he explains what goodness is, however, he more typically suggests that to be good is to be *desirable*. 'The goodness of a thing', he says, 'consists in its being desirable . . . Now clearly desirability is consequent upon perfection, for things always desire their perfection' (ST Ia, 5,1; cf. DV I, 21,1 and SG I, 37). Aquinas frequently observes that anything can be called good (though not, perhaps, as good as it might be) insofar as its natural tendencies or appetites remain in operation. His view is that something is good if it has features which are desirable for it, features to which it is naturally attracted. So he thinks of goodness as that to which everything naturally tends, as that which everything seeks. And it is with this thought in mind that he argues that, when people act with reasons, they always aim at what they take to be good. In his view, all things always tend to what is good for them. But he does not think that people always do simply what their nature dictates (as is the case with non-human animals). They can understand what they are able to do, and they can perceive alternatives. Their tending can be governed by understanding, in which case, says Aquinas, it will always be influenced not just by the draw of goodness in general but also by what is *thought* to be good. In his view, we do not just seek what is naturally good for us: we also seek what we believe to be so. In this sense, he thinks, acting people can never consciously fail to aim at what attracts them. Their actions will always reflect their desires.

Another way of making the point is to say that Aquinas sees human actions as always expressing the *will* of those who perform them. But it is important to recognize that 'will', for him, does not signify some kind of entity which is radically to be distinguished from anything we might think of as knowledge or understanding. He believes that human action involves will inasmuch as acting people do what they find it desirable to do. But he also thinks that what we find desirable depends on how we view things, that willing and understanding are inseparable.

According to Aquinas, there is no operation of the will which is not also an operation of the reason, and *vice versa*. There is an interweaving of being attracted and understanding that cannot be unravelled in practice. We think of what we are *attracted* to thinking of, and we are attracted to what we *think* of. Insofar as we consciously aim at what we are attracted to, we act voluntarily, or with will. This, of course, means that, for Aquinas, there is no place for the notion of willing as something we have to do *after* we have cleared our minds and decided what it is good for us to do. On some accounts of human agency, people first decide what is good and then (maybe with difficulty) will it. Hence we have the notion that people need 'willpower' – the idea being that one can have a clear view of what needs to be done, or of what ought to be done, without the will to do it. But this is not how it is on Aquinas's account. For him, our perception and wanting of what is good are of a piece. We naturally want what we take to be good. And what we take to be good depends on what we want. Aquinas does not doubt that we might often be mistaken about what is good for us. For him, however, our actions (as opposed to our mechanical reactions, or to bits of behaviour in which we engage unthinkingly) are always directed to what we take to be good for us. They always express our desires (our will) and, in this sense, are voluntary. 'A good understood', says Aquinas, 'is will's object and moves it by being something to aim for' (ST Ia, 82,4).

Does this, however, mean that we can only act in one way at any given time? Is Aquinas saying that people inevitably follow their desires? At one level he is, for he is committed to the view that there is a sense in which people can only aim for what they desire. For he thinks that, whether they realize it or not, what people ultimately desire (their ultimate and true good) is God, to whom they cannot but be attracted (cf. ST Ia2ae, 2,8, ST Ia, 82,1, SG I, 37, and SG III, 24). At the same time, however, he is equally clear that God is not an immediate object of knowledge for people in this life. If we enjoyed a clear understanding of God, then, he thinks, we would simply aim at God. Instead, however, we find ourselves presented by a variety of competing goods. And for this reason Aquinas holds that we do not of necessity desire as we do. 'The will of one who sees God's essence', he writes, 'necessarily clings to God, because then we cannot help willing to be happy.' Yet he also says that 'there are individual good things that have no necessary connection with happiness because a man can be happy without them, and the will does not have to cling to these' (ST Ia, 82,2). In general, Aquinas thinks, we cannot but aim at what we desire. But he also believes that our desires depend on what we know in particular and different circumstances. 'The will can tend towards nothing that is not conceived to be good,' he explains, 'but, because there are many kinds of good things, it is not by any necessity determined to any particular one' (ST Ia, 82,2).

ACTING IN PRACTICE

For Aquinas, then, acting persons intend (aim at) what attracts them. But what is going on as they act in specific circumstances? Aquinas's answer is that they live out or engage in examples of what he calls 'practical reasoning'. He thinks that human action is always a reasonable business since it always involves seeking what one takes (even if mistakenly) to be somehow desirable. In this sense, he conceives of it as always conforming to a pattern of reasonableness comparable to what is involved when we reason about what is the case (theoretical reasoning). We may reason to the *truth* of some matter. We might work out how things *are*. But we can also, says Aquinas, reason as to *what is to be done*. We might work out *how to behave*. And he thinks that this is what we are doing as we settle down to action in practice.

On Aquinas's account, essential to human action is what he calls 'choice' or 'decision' (*electio*). Aquinas takes human action as a *doing in the light of alternatives*. In saying so, however, he does not mean that action follows choice or decision – as if acting people first make choices or decisions and then subsequently act on them. For Aquinas, actual human actions are human choices or decisions, and to describe them is to state how we have chosen or decided (what our choices or decisions have amounted to). Yet Aquinas does not think that our actions come out of the blue, as it were. For him, particular choices or decisions reflect the way in which people think. They also reflect the character of the people in question. Or, as Aquinas says, choice (*electio*) springs from *deliberation* (*consilium*), and both choice and deliberation arise from *dispositions* of various kinds.

When he refers to deliberation (*consilium*), Aquinas has in mind a reasoning process having to do with how to obtain what we want. Action, he thinks, starts with desire for what one finds attractive or takes to be good. But how is one's goal to be reached? Here, he says, reason comes in as suggesting the recipe for success. Before choosing what to do (before actually acting), we may have to consider how best to get what we are looking for at the outset. We may be clear as to what we want to achieve, but we might have to think about how to do so. Or, as Aquinas puts it:

> The field of practice is attended with much uncertainty, for our acts are engaged with contingent individual cases, which offer no fixed and certain points because they are so variable. The reason does not pronounce a verdict in matters doubtful and open to question without having conducted an investigation. Such an inquiry is necessary before coming to a decision on what is to be chosen; it is called deliberation. (ST Ia2ae, 14,1)

The end to be achieved is not, one should notice, the business of what Aquinas means by deliberation. He does not conceive of this as helping us to determine what we want or should want. In his view, we deliberate in the light of desire. We do not desire in the light of deliberation. For Aquinas, deliberation presupposes goals, ends, or intentions (cf. ST Ia2ae, 14,2, DV I, 5; DV III, 24, and DM, II, 5). But not all courses of action lead to the same goal. And some courses of action can be better at getting us what we want than others. For Aquinas, therefore, deliberation has to do with means. It is a way of helping our will to have its full rein. It is rational reflection on how to obtain what we want.

But what about our wants? How does Aquinas see these as entering into the occurrence of genuine human actions? This is where the notion of dispositions comes in. For, to put it as simply as possible, Aquinas views the wants reflected in particular human actions as deriving from what we are (or, rather, from what we have become), considered not just as doing this or that but as people *of a certain kind* – people who find it desirable to act in certain kinds of ways, people with certain tastes, likes, and dislikes. For Aquinas, concrete actions reflect our characters or settled personalities. He thinks that there are patterns of action to which we tend as individuals, and that our tendencies can be affected or influenced by our past and by choices we make. We do not, he holds, act in an historical vacuum: we act on the basis of dispositions.

What I am calling a 'disposition' Aquinas calls a *habitus* (cf. ST Ia2ae, 49–54), and, though *habitus* can be translated 'habit', it is better rendered by 'disposition'. For Aquinas's *habitus* is not a 'habit' in the modern sense. When we speak today of people having a habit, we normally imply that they would find it hard *not* to act in certain ways. Hence, for example, we speak of someone having the habit of smoking. A habit, for us, is a kind of addiction. For Aquinas, however, a *habitus* places one's activity more under one's control than it might otherwise be. In this sense, to have a *habitus* is to be disposed to some activity or other – not because one tends to that activity on every possible occasion, but because one finds it natural, readily coped with, an obvious activity to engage in, and so on.

In Aquinas's thinking, fluency in a foreign language is a *habitus*. Someone who possesses it may refrain from displaying it for one reason or another. But, when speaking the language, such a person will do so easily and with a proficiency which many lack entirely. Or, again, people who are naturally or instinctively generous would, according to Aquinas, have a *habitus*. They would be generous without effort. There would be little or no question of 'going against the grain'. A *habitus*, for Aquinas, is halfway between a capacity and an action. You can be said to speak French even though you are not actually doing so. But to say that you can speak French means more than that it is logically possible for you to do so. It is to say that you have a genuine ability which not everyone has. In this sense, 'You can speak French' ascribes to you an ability or skill which endures over time, one which can really be displayed. In the thinking of Aquinas, it ascribes to you a *habitus* or disposition.

We may put it by saying that, in Aquinas's view, people can acquire settled ways of acting. And, for him, this means that they can acquire a settled range of aims, tastes, or wants which play a vital role when it comes to concrete decisions. For he holds that these express our wants – even insofar as they spring from deliberation. In choosing, he thinks, we aim for what attracts us and we ignore or avoid what does not. And we pay attention to what attracts us even as we consider how to obtain what we want – since how we choose to achieve our purposes depends on what we are prepared to take seriously and on what we are prepared to disregard. Or, as Aquinas frequently explains, human actions reflect the virtues and vices of people. For, on his account, virtues and vices are dispositions to act in certain ways – the difference between them being that virtues help us to act well as human beings, while vices help us to act badly.

SIN

Notice, however, that Aquinas often contrasts virtuous activity not with what is vicious but with what is sinful. Why so? The reason lies in the fact that he thinks of people not just as able to act well or badly in general but also as able to act well or badly when considered as creatures of God.

According to Aquinas, one can explain how people come to act as they do even if one has no particular theological commitment. He also thinks that, even from a non-theological perspective, one can say something about the difference between acting well or badly – the difference between succeeding as a human being (being a good human being) and failing as such (being a bad human being). In other words, Aquinas thinks that it is possible to offer a sound philosophical account of human action. He also thinks it possible to give good philosophical reasons for acting in some ways rather than others. So he says, for example, that, though 'there is a true bliss located after this life', it is also true that 'a certain imitation of bliss is possible in this life if human beings perfect themselves in the goods firstly of contemplative and secondly of practical reason' and that 'this is the happiness Aristotle discusses in his *Ethics* without either advocating or rejecting another bliss after this life' (SL IV, 49,1,1). Yet Aquinas takes God to be the ultimate (even if unrecognized) object of human desire. And his approach to human conduct is infected by this conviction. For it leads him to see human actions as having more than what we might call a merely human significance. It leads him to see them as significant before God and as affecting our standing considered as God's creatures.

More precisely, it leads him to see human actions as being in or out of tune with what he calls 'Eternal Law'. According to Aquinas, 'Law is nothing but a dictate of practical reason issued by a sovereign who governs a complete community' (ST Ia2ae, 91,1). And, he adds, 'The whole community of the universe is governed by God's mind.' 'Through his wisdom', says Aquinas, 'God is the founder of the universe of things, and . . . in relation to them he is like an artist with regard the things he makes . . . And so, as being the principle through which the universe is created, divine wisdom means art, or exemplar, or idea, and likewise it also means law, as moving all things to their due ends. Accordingly, the Eternal Law is nothing other than the exemplar of divine wisdom as directing the motions and actions of everything' (ST Ia2ae, 93,1; cf. ST Ia, 16,1).

Since Aquinas takes God to be simple (non-composite), since he believes that all that is *in* God *is* God, he thinks that God and the Eternal Law are one and the same reality. For him, therefore, human actions must ultimately be viewed as conforming, or as failing to conform, with the goodness that God is essentially. On Aquinas's account, God, who is perfectly good, is the standard by which creatures can be thought of as good or as failing to be good. So, when people succeed or fail in goodness, they succeed or fail with respect to God. Insofar as they succeed, then, so Aquinas thinks, they reflect the goodness that is God. Insofar as they fail, they stray from this goodness. Or, as Aquinas says, they sin. Drawing on St Augustine of Hippo, he defines sin as 'nothing else than to neglect eternal things, and to seek after temporal things'. All human wickedness, he adds, 'consists in making means of ends and ends of means' (ST Ia2ae, 71,6).

In other words, Aquinas takes bad human actions to be actions the nature of which can be properly grasped only if we see them as leaving us short of what God is all about. Or, as he puts it:

> A human act is human because it is voluntary . . . A human act is evil because it does not meet the standard for human behaviour. Standards are nothing other than rules. The human will is subject to a twofold rule: one is proximate and on his own level, i.e. human reason; the other is the first rule beyond man's own level, i.e. the eternal law which is the mind of God. (ST Ia2ae, 71,6; cf. ST Ia2ae, 1,1)

On this account, there is no conflict between rational human action and action which conforms to the goodness that is God. But the former is seen as an instance of the latter – the idea being that sound moral philosophy is, in the end, also sound from the viewpoint of theology. This is not to say that Aquinas thinks of moral philosophers (even the best of them) as our most trustworthy advisers when it comes to matters theological (when it comes to conforming to the mind of God). Nor is it to say that he thinks of rational reflection as able, by itself, to lead us to ultimate happiness. It is, however, to say that Aquinas finds no difficulty with the suggestion that genuine moral failure (which he thinks can be understood at a philosophical level) can also be viewed as failure with respect to God – as a matter of people failing to rise to the goodness which God is.

And it is on this basis that Aquinas reasons throughout his writings. Much that he calls 'sin' is something which he thinks can be analyzed and reflected on in the light of what he thinks about goodness and badness in general, and with no explicit reliance on the teachings of theology. And much that Aquinas calls 'sin' is something which he believes to be understandable in terms of his approach to human action as I have described it above – an approach which is, therefore, of philosophical and not just theological relevance. For, though it is mainly presented by Aquinas in writings which are primarily intended by him to be contributions to Christian theology (notably the *Summa theologiae*), it is also presented by him as teaching which ought to seem acceptable to any clear-thinking person.

Presumably, however, one cannot sin if one is unable to help doing what one does. And thinking persons from time immemorial have tended to insist that there can be no full account of what human action amounts to that pays no attention to the notion of human freedom. So, what does Aquinas have to say on this topic? That is our next question.

13

The Free Human Creature

People can believe the wildest things. But it would surely seem odd, and plainly false, to say that, when you blow your nose in a handkerchief, the handkerchief can help getting wet. It would seem equally odd, and false, to claim that trees can help growing. So there are things which go through processes not of their own devising, things whose careers are entirely determined by their nature and their environment. What about people, however? Sometimes these seem to be in much the same boat as handkerchiefs and trees. Push me from the top of a ten-storey building, and I shall surely fall to the ground. Fill me with alcohol, and I shall inevitably sway and stagger. But are people always, in this way, nothing but the victims of nature and circumstances? Aquinas's answer is 'No', for he firmly believes in the reality of human freedom. But what does he take this to be? And why does he believe in it?

HUMAN FREEDOM

It is sometimes said that to hold that people are (at least sometimes) free is to hold that people have free will. But such is not Aquinas's view. He believes, not that people have free will, but that they have freedom of choice. When Aquinas attributes freedom to people, he frequently says that they have *liberum arbitrium*. And, though translators of Aquinas often render this phrase by the English expression 'free will', its significance is different. For the thesis that people have free will is commonly taken to mean that freedom belongs only to the will, that it is, if you like, the prerogative of will or a peculiar property of it. And Aquinas does not share this assumption. For, as we saw in the last chapter, he believes that will and understanding are intimately co-mingled when it comes to human action. On his account, intellect and will are at no point separated in the exercise of practical reason. There is no act of practical intelligence which is not also one of will, and vice versa.

Yet Aquinas is prepared to ask whether or not the choices people make on the basis of what they think and are attracted to can be genuinely attributed to *them* and are not, in fact, the action of something else working in them in a way which always renders them non-responsible for what they do. And this is the question he has in mind when, for example, he asks in the *De malo*, 'Do human beings have free choice in their acts or do they choose necessarily?', and when he asks, in other works, 'Do people have *liberum arbitrium*?'

The operative word in the question 'Do human beings have free choice in their acts or do they choose necessarily?' is 'necessarily'. And, in this context, it means 'inevitably' or 'unavoidably'. If you pour acid on a human hand, the skin will immediately corrode. And it does so inevitably, unavoidably, or, as we might say, necessarily. If you drop a ton weight on a mouse, the mouse will become an ex-mouse. And it will do so inevitably, unavoidably, or, as we might say, necessarily. But what about the actions of people? Are these what they are inevitably, unavoidably, or necessarily? Is everything we do to be thought of as coming to pass as skin reacts to acid and as mice get squashed by weights? Aquinas's answer is 'No'. And he takes this to be the correct answer for a number of different reasons.

To begin with, he has theological ones. For he believes that Scripture teaches that people have freedom. In the book of Ecclesiastes, we read: 'God from the beginning constituted and left human beings in the hands of their own deliberation.' Aquinas takes this passage as ascribing to people the freedom to decide (cf. DM VI and ST Ia, 83,1). And, in general, he reads Scripture as teaching, or implying, that people can act with freedom.

He also thinks that, if people lacked freedom, there would be nothing we could recognize as moral philosophy, or that there would be no point in trying to engage in it. Just as various natural sciences rest on the assumption that things undergo change, so, in Aquinas's view, thinking about morality rests on the assumption that people act with freedom. If you believe there is no change, then you cannot consistently be a research chemist. By the same token, Aquinas suggests, you cannot seriously engage in ethical thinking if you deny human freedom. 'People', he says, 'are free to make decisions. Otherwise counsels, precepts, prohibitions, rewards, and punishment would all be pointless' (ST Ia, 83,1).

But Aquinas's most developed defence of human freedom springs from his conviction that human actions are done for reasons and cannot, therefore, be assimilated to processes which come about inevitably, unavoidably, or necessarily. Why does he think this? Because he holds that it belongs to the very nature of reason to deliberate with an eye on alternatives. Some of the changes which things undergo happen, he believes, because things are doing what they cannot, in the circumstances, avoid doing. But, he insists, this is not the case when people act for reasons. Why not? Basically, he argues, because acting for reasons means thinking and because reasons for action can never compel assent.

Here, once again, it is important to note how, in Aquinas's view, human animals differ from non-human ones. He thinks that they have a great deal in common. For, as we have seen, he takes both to be living things with the ability to undergo sensations. He also takes both to have various inbuilt desires, tendencies, or instincts which greatly affect the ways in which they behave. For Aquinas, however, people can understand how things are and respond (rather than merely react) to them on this basis. They do not just behave. They can describe what is around them. And they can do what they do for reasons which are different from what might be mentioned when accounting for the behaviour of non-human animals.

One might well speak of the reason why the cat chased the mouse. But 'reason' here has nothing to do with framed intentions. There may be reasons why the cat chased the mouse, but they are not the cat's reasons. In Aquinas's opinion, however, human action is precisely a matter of things acting with reasons of their own. And, he thinks, with the ability to act from reasons of one's own comes an understanding of the world under many different descriptions. Or, rather, as Aquinas sees it, the ability to understand the world under many different descriptions is why people have the ability to act from reasons of their own. For him, it is the root of our capacity to make actions really our own, and also, of course, the root of our capacity to deceive ourselves and to behave irrationally and badly.

It might help here if we focus on the notion of interpreting the world. For Aquinas, this is something which both human and non-human animals do. For both of them have senses in terms of which the world becomes significant for them. According to Aquinas, however, people can interpret the world, not just as sensed, but also as understood. So they can speak about it. They can, for example, not just feel wetness: they can talk about it raining. And they can ask what rain is and why it is raining now though it was not raining yesterday. For Aquinas, people can interpret the world by describing it. And, he thinks, this opens out for them possibilities of interpretation which are just not available to non-human animals.

For, as he sees it, to be aware of things, not just in terms of their sensible appearance, but under a description as well, is also to be aware of things under an indefinite number of descriptions.

Suppose that I and a mouse smell a piece of cheese. On Aquinas's account, the cheese is significant for the mouse. And, all things being equal, the mouse will be drawn to the cheese. According to Aquinas, however, I can perceive the cheese as more than something to eat without thinking. I can see it, for example, as somebody else's cheese, or as bad for me if I want to lose weight, or as what I promised to give up for Lent, or as more expensive than I can decently afford, and so on. And Aquinas views my ability to think of the cheese in these ways as the root of my human freedom. For, he argues, there is a big difference between how we might think of something like a piece of cheese and how we inevitably think about certain other matters.

Take, for example, the way in which we think when reasoning as follows:

If all human beings are mortal
and all Australians are human beings
then all Australians are mortal.

Here we cannot but accept the conclusion given the premises supplied. And no additional information can leave us with any alternative but to accept it. We accept the conclusion of necessity. But now consider this argument:

I want to get to Paris.
If I catch this flight it will get me to Paris.
So I should catch this flight.

Might additional information force me to change my conclusion that I should catch the flight? Well hardly. What about 'If I catch this flight, I shall be boarding an aeroplane with terrorists on it'? If I consider the flight under that description, then I will conclude that I should not catch it. And yet, Aquinas thinks, when reflecting on the world, we can always view it under different descriptions. So he also thinks that we can engage with it not because we are forced to think about it only in one way. We can engage with it as able to think about it in different ways. For Aquinas, people have freedom of choice since, unlike non-human animals, they can interpret the world in different ways (under different descriptions) and act in the light of the ways in which they interpret it. In this sense, he thinks, their actions are governed by reasons which are fully their own.

One might, of course, suggest, as some philosophers have done, that our thinking is identical with processes in our brains over which we have no control. And one might therefore suggest that our actions have irreducibly physical causes which determine them to be as they are. For Aquinas, however (and, again, as we have seen), thinking cannot be identified with any physical process. On his account, we depend on our bodies in order to interpret the world. Indeed, he says, all our knowledge depends on the ways in which we function as bodily things. But he also suggests that our interpreting the world cannot be identified with a particular physical process. If it were, he reasons, then meanings would be the same as physical objects, which, in his view, they are not. For Aquinas, no configuration or activity of my brain cells could be an idea or concept or meaning. Any such configuration would be my private property distinct from yours, just as my toenails are distinct from yours. To the argument that you can interfere with people's ability to entertain meanings by damaging their bodies, especially their brains, Aquinas replies that this is so because we depend on bodies (and not just our own) for thinking and understanding. But our thinking and understanding, he holds, are not to be identified with them.

In short, Aquinas thinks that we are drawn to what we take to be good. But he also thinks that we are not compelled to act in any particular way simply because of our tastes. On his account, we aim for what we want in a world in which we (as thinkers) can recognize different things as likely to satisfy us in different ways. And on this basis we deliberate with an eye on means and ends. He therefore concludes that the choices we make are not necessary as, for example, the scorching of skin is a necessary consequence of acid being poured on it or as the eating of a piece of cheese might be inevitable for a mouse. Our choices, he reasons, are actions which flow from what we, as individuals, are. They reflect our desires and our view of things. And they might have been otherwise. Aquinas thinks that, in place of a particular repertoire of particular instincts, people have a general capacity to reason. Since he holds that particular matters, like what to do in this or that situation, are not subject to conclusive argument, he suggests that people are not determined to any one course.

FREEDOM AND GOD

Yet Aquinas does not think that our actions come about as wholly uncaused. Some philosophers have argued that people can be free only if their actions have absolutely no cause outside themselves. But this is not

Aquinas's view. He argues that, even when people act freely, their actions must be caused by God. Aquinas finds it unthinkable that any created event, including whatever we take to be there when human choosing occurs, should come to pass without God making it to be.

Why? Because of what we have already seen him teaching about God as Creator. For Aquinas, God is the cause of the existence of everything, the reason why there is something rather than nothing, the source of *esse*. And since he takes human free actions to be perfectly real, he concludes that they must, like anything else, be caused to exist by God. 'We must', he says, 'unequivocally concede that God is at work in all activity, whether of nature or of will.' For Aquinas, God 'causes everything's activity inasmuch as he gives it the power to act, maintains it in existence, applies it to its activity, and inasmuch as it is by his power that every other power acts' (DP III, 7; cf. SG II, 89 and 90).

One may, of course, say that, if my actions are caused by God, then I do not act freely at all. And this is what many philosophers and theologians have said. On their account, God cannot cause my free actions. He must wait to find out what I shall freely do, or he must give me space freely to act independently of him. Aquinas, however, would reply that my actions are free if nothing *in the world* is acting on me so as to make me perform them, not if God is not acting in me. According to him, what is incompatible with freedom is 'necessity of coercion' or the effect of violence, as when something acts on one and 'applies force to the point where one cannot act otherwise' (ST Ia, 82,1).

Aquinas's position is that for people to be free is for them not to be under the influence of some other creature. On his account, freely acting persons act independently of other bits of the universe, not independently of God. For him, God, as Creator *ex nihilo*, cannot interfere with created free agents so as to push them into action in a way that prevents them acting freely. For God never acts *on* them (as Aquinas thinks created things do when they cause others to act as determined by them). He makes them to be what they are – freely acting agents. And, with these points in mind, Aquinas argues that human freedom is not threatened by God's causality. On the contrary: his position is that we are free, not in spite of God, but because of God. In his words:

> God's will is to be thought of as existing outside the realm of existents, as a cause from which pours forth everything that exists in all its variant forms. Now what can be and what must be are variants of being, so that it is from God's will itself that things derive whether they must be or may or may not be and the distinction of the two according

to the nature of their immediate causes. For he prepares causes that must cause for those effects that he wills must be, and causes that might cause but might fail to cause for those effects that he wills might or might not be. And it is because of the nature of these causes that these effects are said to be effects that must be and those effects that need not be, although all depend on God's will as primary cause, a cause which transcends this distinction between must and might not. But the same cannot be said of human will or of any other cause, since every other cause exists within the realm of must and might not. So of every other cause it must be said either that it can fail to cause, or that its effect must be and cannot not be; God's will however cannot fail, and yet not all his effects must be, but some can be or not be. (DI I, 14)

In terms of this account, God is not to be thought of as an external agent able to interfere with human freedom by acting on it coercively from outside. Rather, God is the cause of all that is real as both free created agents and non-free created agents exist and operate. Or, as Aquinas says in the *Summa theologiae*:

Free decision spells self-determination because people, by their free decisions, move themselves to action. Freedom does not require that a thing is its own first cause, just as in order to be the cause of something else a thing does not have to be its first cause. God is the first cause on which both natural and free agents depend. And, just as his initiative does not prevent natural causes from being natural, so it does not prevent voluntary action from being voluntary, but, rather, makes it be precisely this. For God works in each according to its nature. (ST Ia, 83,1)

What Aquinas is arguing here is simply what seems entailed by his view that, as I put it in Chapter 9, God makes no difference to anything. I can make a difference to something by acting on it from outside and by causing it to be how I want it to be. For Aquinas, however, God is never outside creatures, as creatures are to each other. He is creatively making all of them just what they are for as long as they exist. So his causality can never be thought of as coercive. For Aquinas, the action of God is, indeed, in everything created. So it can be said, therefore, that the being of the world is the doing of God. But this doing is one which makes things to be exactly as they are. When he asks whether God is everywhere, Aquinas replies that God is, indeed, everywhere but that God is not in any place as a body is (i.e. dimensionally). God, he says, is everywhere since God makes (is creatively present to) all bodies which constitute places by their relation to each other. He does not think that God's creative presence to bodies inhibits them from being the bodies that they are. And, by the same token, he does not think that God's creative presence in the choices of creatures renders them less than the choices they are.

You might, however, think that it shows God to be somewhat distasteful, if not wholly obnoxious. For consider what people might be thought of as choosing to do. Some choose to torture people. Some choose to cheat. Some choose to lie, to rape, and to murder. If Aquinas is right, does it not follow that what such people do is also what God is doing? And if God is doing that, how can we possibly regard him as anything but a monster? These questions bring us to the topic of God's goodness and to what is commonly called 'the problem of evil'.

14

God and Goodness

Those who believe that God exists find it natural to say that God is good. But what might it mean to call God good? And is there any reason for believing in God's goodness? For that matter, is there any reason to suppose that God is bad? These questions are perennial ones, and Aquinas is aware of them. His basic position with respect to them is that God is indeed good and that this conclusion can be argued for. But, in saying so, he does not mean what people often do when professing belief in God's goodness. It is commonly said that God is good since God is morally good (that he is, if you like, well behaved). Yet this is not at all what Aquinas thinks.

WHAT GOD'S GOODNESS CANNOT BE

When we think of moral goodness, we are, of course, thinking primarily of people, for it is these whom we chiefly take to be morally good (or morally bad). Can we say what it is that makes people morally good? Two main answers have been given to this question. According to the first, morally good people are people who do what they ought to do. They do their duty. They obey 'the moral law'. According to the second, morally good people are virtuous people. They are prudent, just, temperate, and courageous.

For Aquinas, however, neither line of thinking is applicable when it comes to sound reflection on the goodness of God. For him, there is no duty, or law regarding conduct, which stands over and against God as something to which his conformity (or non-conformity) provides grounds for us morally to evaluate him (whether positively or negatively). Aquinas is happy to speak of what people are bound to do, or of what they owe. But he never supposes that God is bound to do what people are bound to do. And he consistently teaches that God owes nothing to anyone or anything since he is the source of everything other than himself, and of all that it has. As we have seen, Aquinas has time for the notion of law. But he never conceives of there being a law which is binding on God. For him, law either derives from God, or is God himself (cf. Chapter 12). As for virtues, Aquinas takes these to be dispositions which people need in order to be happy. And he thinks that they can no more be ascribed to God than they can to a stone since he does not think that God is a human being needing certain dispositions in order to be happy.

One might suppose that moral laws are something like logical laws. And one might therefore suggest that they are binding even on God. But this is not Aquinas's view. He would agree that there is a sense in which logical laws are binding on God. As we saw in Chapter 10, his account of divine omnipotence holds that God can make to be whatever can be thought to be without contradiction. According to Aquinas, God cannot bring about anything which is logically impossible, from which one might deduce that he takes God to be bound by logical laws. Yet Aquinas does not take these to be a set of commands which God must obey. For him, God is 'bound' by logical laws only in the sense that to speak of God doing what is logically impossible would be to fail to describe anything which could be consistently said to be done. There could not be a genuine description of a logically impossible state of affairs, and Aquinas thinks that there could not be a true proposition reporting that God has brought about such a thing.

But moral laws are not like logical laws. If there are such things as moral laws, then they, presumably, take the form of imperatives stating what ought or ought not to be done. Aquinas agrees that they have a kind of necessity since he thinks that, if someone ought or ought not to do something, then anyone in exactly equivalent circumstances is constrained in the same way. But he does not think of God as being like people who find themselves in circumstances. For him, God is not a person, and he is certainly not a human being. And there is no context when it comes to his action. For God, Aquinas holds, is the maker of contexts.

Let us say that those who do not murder innocent people conform to a law (a moral law) which prohibits the murder of innocent people. Aquinas would be happy to say that this law (which he thinks to be one of the Ten Commandments issued by God to the Israelites) is binding on everybody. What he would not be happy to say, however, is that this is a law which could sensibly be thought of as binding on God. For he does not take God to be capable of murder (since God is not a human being and can no more commit murder than he can pick his nose). Perhaps we should say that God should refrain from bringing it about that innocent people die. Yet Aquinas sees no reason to suppose that there is a law which obliges God to do this. Lots of innocent people die. Lots of good and saintly people die. Is there a law to which God stands accountable in not preventing their death? Aquinas does not think so.

In general, and unsurprisingly from what we have seen in previous chapters, Aquinas does not think that God's goodness can consist in being what a good human being is. He thinks that people have duties and obligations. He also thinks that they can be evaluated with an eye on the notion of virtues and vices. For him, however, God is not a human being, and it would be folly to try to comment on his goodness or badness without paying attention to that fact. On Aquinas's account, God is not a good *anything*, for he is not an individual sharing a nature with other things.

If God is not morally good, however, can he be good at all? To understand Aquinas's response to this question, we need to consider what he has to say on the topic of goodness in general. In particular, we need to note that 'good', for him, is not a word which by itself tells us what something in particular is actually like.

THE MEANING OF 'GOOD'

Does the word 'good' always signify the same thing? The correct answer is evidently 'No'. We speak of there being good meals, good singers, good surgeons, good holidays, good television programmes, good athletes, and so on. But is what makes for goodness in, for example, a singer the same as what makes for goodness in, for example, a surgeon? Hardly. Good singers are people who can read a musical score and transfer it into sound. They can hit the high notes without cracking. They are musically adept, both intellectually and in terms of performance. But one would not go to them for surgery. Good surgeons might, of course, be great singers, but we do not place ourselves in their hands for that reason. We want them to be medically competent. We want them to have a steady hand. We want to know that they have performed a lot of successful operations.

One might make the point by saying that 'good', unlike 'green', is not an adjective which signifies a single property had by everything which can be described by means of it. You can understand 'X is green' without knowing what X is (to say that grass is green and that my carpet is green is to ascribe exactly the same property to each of them). But you cannot in the same way understand 'X is good' if you do not know what X is. X might be a singer. X might also be a surgeon. Do all good singers possess a property had by all good surgeons, this being what makes them all good? If they did, then from 'Fred is a good singer' we could infer that, if he is also a surgeon, he is a good surgeon, which we obviously cannot. Fred might be an excellent singer but an awful surgeon. 'Good' resembles adjectives such as 'big' and 'small'. 'X is a big elephant' does not mean (a) 'X is big' and (b) 'X is an elephant' (these being understandable apart from each other). And 'X is a small cat' does not mean (a) 'X is small' and (b) 'X is a cat' (these also being understandable apart from each other). To suppose otherwise, and on the assumption that elephants and cats are both animals, would license us to conclude that a big cat is a big animal and that a small elephant is a small animal, which we obviously should not.

Yet, should we conclude that 'good' means something entirely different when we use it to describe things? Taking his lead from Aristotle (cf. *Ethics* I, 1, 1094a3), Aquinas suggests that to call things good is, indeed, to say the same thing about all of them. He does not think that it is to say that they all have some shared property (as all green things do). But he believes that it is still to say the same thing of them. For he holds that it is to assert that all of them are somehow desirable.

Suppose that you want to hire a good singer. What are you looking for? You are looking for someone who meets your requirements when it comes to singing. You are looking for what you find to be desirable in singers (what you want a singer to be). And this is what Aquinas thinks.

Suppose that you want to put yourself in the hands of a good surgeon. What are you looking for? You are looking for someone who meets your requirements when it comes to surgery. You are looking for what you find to be desirable in surgeons (what you want a surgeon to be). And this is what Aquinas thinks.

For Aquinas, we can make no sense of the word 'good' if we do not take it to mean 'desirable'. We would, of course, normally say that people can desire what is not good. Suppose that my tastes run to disembowelling babies. Does that mean that what I desire to do is good? Surely not. And Aquinas does not suggest otherwise. But why not? Because he thinks that a disembowelled baby is not desirable. He is perfectly aware that people can desire all sorts of things. For him, though, we need to ask: 'What can we mean when calling something "good"?' And, he says, the only general answer available is: 'It is desirable.' His point is that, if Jack the Ripper thinks that the results of his actions are good, that must be because he is drawn to them, because he finds them desirable, just as we are drawn to justice and peace, which, so we say, is good. His point is that we and Jack the Ripper agree when we speak of goodness. We and he mean the same by 'good', even though we are of different minds as to what is actually good.

You might put this by saying that goodness, for Aquinas, is subjective. For he thinks that 'good' means the same even though people dissent when it comes to what is good. But the sameness in question here is, so to speak, very thin. Aquinas wants to say that 'good' signifies 'desirable' regardless of who it is that uses the term and regardless of what turns different people on. Yet he is not prepared to say that goodness is just a matter of taste.

Why not? Well, think about surgeons again. Suppose my desire is that the surgeon who operates on me botches his job and causes my death. Such a surgeon will, *for me*, be good. But does that fact prevent us from asking whether or not the surgeon in question is a good one? Surely not. For it seems reasonable to say that a good surgeon is one who regularly operates successfully on people. And, in general, it seems reasonable to say that, though 'good' means desirable, there are criteria for distinguishing between what is *desired* and what is *desirable* when it comes to concrete cases. I might be looking for (might desire) an incompetent surgeon. But it makes sense to say that I am not thereby looking for a good surgeon. I am looking for (desiring) someone to kill me. I might be looking for (might desire) something to help me scale a wall, and a bicycle to hand might enable me to do so. But I am not thereby looking for a good bicycle. I am looking for (desiring) something to help me get over a wall.

With examples such as these in mind, Aquinas suggests that, though not everything desired by people is good, 'good' must mean 'desirable'. And, in doing so, he means that, though goodness can be thought to be subjective (since people can take different things to be good without using 'good' in different senses), it is not relative. If I applaud Fred for singing badly, if I say that he is good, then, Aquinas thinks, I am saying that Fred's way of singing is desirable to me. But he also thinks that we can speak of Fred being good as a singer whether or not I like the way in which he performs. His view is that 'X is good' means 'X is desirable' without it following that X is really desirable.

On the face of it, this conclusion seems to be self-contradictory. But it is no more so than is the assertion that people can be wrong in their choice of surgeons. Nobody chooses to go under a knife held by someone they take to be incompetent. People entering surgery presume that they are going to be worked on by someone they want (desire) to work on them. They presume that they are about to be in the hands of good surgeons. But the surgeons in question might not be up to the job. So they would be bad surgeons, regardless of what their victims think. They might be desirable (as called good by their patients). But they might be bad as surgeons to those who observe how they work.

GOODNESS AND GOD

For Aquinas, then, 'God is good' can mean nothing more than that God is desirable. God, he says, is good since 'an object is good insofar as it is desirable' and since God is just that (ST Ia, 6,1; cf. ST Ia, 5,1–4 and SG I, 37–38). Yet, what could he have in mind when saying this? And how does he claim to know that what he says is true?

To understand him, it helps to think yet again about surgeons. For Aquinas, a good surgeon is what we look for (desire) in a surgeon if we are, indeed, thinking about surgeons (as opposed, say, to people who can kill us). But how come there are any good surgeons? For that matter, how come there are any individuals which can be thought of as good of their kind? Aquinas, of course, thinks that the answer to these questions is 'God'. In his view, goodness in its many forms is what God has creatively brought about. And, since he also thinks that the effects of efficient causes reflect their causes, since he thinks that their causes express themselves in them (that they are what their causes look like in action), he concludes that God is good, as the source of things which are good in their various ways, and desirable, since 'good' means 'desirable'. 'The perfection and form of an effect', he argues, 'is a certain likeness of the efficient cause, since every efficient cause produces an effect like itself . . . [and] . . . since God is the first efficient cause of everything . . . the aspect of good and desirable manifestly belongs to him' (ST Ia, 6,1). He means that God is good since the goodness of creatures pre-exists in him as their cause. He also means that, insofar as they seek (desire) their own goodness, they are seeking what is first in God and only secondly in them. He does not, of course, mean that we cannot call something good without logically committing ourselves to the claims that God exists and that God is good. His point is that, given that God exists as the maker of a world in which things can be singled out and taken to be good, we should conclude that the goodness of created things reflects what God is. Aquinas thinks that goodness and desirability are equivalent since we cannot make sense of 'X is good' if we do not take it to mean that 'X is desirable'. So his conclusion is that God is desirable. And, he reasons, to think that this is so is to think that God is good.

But not, of course, good of a kind. For him, God is not a good *such and such*. We normally call things good with an eye on what kind of thing they are (as in 'good surgeons', 'good people', and so on). On Aquinas's account, however, God is not an instance of a kind. And he thinks that we are just as entitled to say that God is goodness as we are to say that God is good. In other words, Aquinas's understanding of 'God is good' leaves us with no expectations as to what is to be expected when it comes to God.

If you tell me that you are going to give me a good television for Christmas, I would rightly form views as to what to expect from you. When politicians promise a good economy, we know what to look for. For Aquinas, however, knowing that God is good is not to comprehend what he is essentially. Nor is it to know what to expect from him. For, that God is good, Aquinas thinks, is a truth knowable to us only on the basis of the fact that God is the maker of all that we can single out and speak of as good. The Bible, of course, frequently speaks of God as good. And Aquinas fervently holds that we should believe what the Bible tells us. But, as we shall later be seeing, he also holds that it is one thing to believe and another to know. Why believe that God is good? Aquinas is more than content to reply 'Read the Scriptures.' But can we know that God is good? Aquinas's answer to this question lies in those views of his which I have just tried to summarize. These, we might say, comprise his philosophical answer to the question, though we might not fully grasp what that amounts to if we do not note another point he makes about goodness in general.

BEING AND GOODNESS

A good surgeon is a living person who works wonders in the operating theatre. There are no non-existing good surgeons. So to be a good surgeon is to be an existing (a real) surgeon. And this, in turn, would seem to imply that goodness has to do with existing. If X is good, then, presumably, X *is* in some form. I do not mean that a good X is both good and existing in the sense that a skating person is both skating and a person. I do not mean that good things also have an attribute or property called 'existing'. I simply mean that nothing can be good if it is not there to be singled out and truly described as good. As a way of countering the suggestion that existence is an attribute or property which something might possess (in addition to its other attributes or properties), some contemporary logicians like to say that 'existence is what the existential quantifier expresses'. They mean that to speak of something as existing is to say that one can speak truly about it, that, for example, 'John is an existing man' means that 'John is a man' is a true proposition. And I think that they are right. But John cannot be a good man if 'John is a man' is false. In this sense, so we may say, being and goodness converge. To be good is *to be* in some way.

And this conclusion is one which Aquinas takes with the utmost seriousness (cf. Chapter 6). In his view, anything good *is* in some way. Yet he also wants to say that anything which is in some way is also *good*, which, on the face of it, seems a curious conclusion at which to arrive. Are bad people good? Is a bad surgeon also a good one? Surely not. Something can exist without being good, so one might naturally think. And, at one level, Aquinas would agree. He has no objection to the suggestion that, for example, John might be a bad man. Yet he also thinks that John cannot be a bad man if John is not a man.

What must John be if he is a man? The obvious answer is that he must be a male human being. And he must be this even though he spends his time torturing people. So John needs to be what it takes to be a male human being before he can be judged to be a bad man. In that case, however, John can be deemed to be both good and bad. If he is a human being, then he has managed to make it into a category. He has succeeded in being a human being. Since he tortures people, he has not, alas, placed himself into the class of people we might morally admire. As a fit and living man, he is good in one way. As a torturer, he is bad in another. And this is what Aquinas has in mind when saying that anything which *is* in some way is also good. In his view, a wicked man must at least succeed in being a man, just as a bad pint of beer must be beer. He thinks that a wicked man must have whatever is needed to be a man, just as a bad pint of beer must have whatever it takes to be beer (as opposed, say, to water or milk).

In short, he thinks that everything is good insofar as it exists as what it is. If we want a good pint of beer, we want something which is, at least, beer. And we take this fact for granted as we go on to evaluate the beer before us. Or, as Aquinas puts it, 'to be good is really the same thing as to exist', even though 'good' and 'exists' have different meanings (ST Ia, 5,1). He means that, though things may not be as good as they might be, they have to be good in some way simply in order to be things of the kind to which they belong. For, otherwise, they just would not be there, which is to say that their being and their being good are not optional activities for them. I might choose to be walking but not to be reading. For Aquinas, however, nothing can exist without somehow being good. In this sense, he thinks, everything real is good, even though it might not be as good as it could be.

Yet many things are bad. People dying of cancer might be wonderful, but they are not what we should like them to be as human beings. Unless we think that they are morally wicked, we would not call them bad. But they are surely not thriving. And they can be thought of as bad on this count. It is bad for people to have cancer. Why? Because cancer eats away at people. It stops them from being living human beings. It stops them from being able to make moral choices, in the light of which we might deem them to be good or bad people. So people dying of cancer are losing the goodness which they need in order to be hale and hearty. In this sense, they are bad since there is a good way to be which is falling away from them. And this fact surely raises a question for people who believe that God exists and that God is good.

For why does God countenance a world in which people die of cancer? And why does he preside over a world in which there is more to complain about than physical diseases? What about murder and rape? How do these square with the thesis that God is good? Some have suggested that they prove that there is no God. In the next chapter we shall see what Aquinas has to say with respect to this conclusion.

15

The Problem of Evil

Why is there physical pain? Why do people suffer from anxiety and psychological distress? Why are there people who act badly? These are the questions which have given rise to what contemporary philosophers and theologians call the 'problem of evil'. But what exactly is the problem supposed to be?

If Fred is dying of cancer, I might acknowledge a practical problem. I might ask 'What can I do to make Fred as comfortable as possible?' And I might take myself to have an equally practical problem on my hands should I have to deal with people who are morally wicked. I might wonder 'What can I do to get rid of them?' or (more charitably) 'What can I do to help them to become better human beings?' But the general nastiness of much that occurs has led some to hold that there is what we might deem to be an 'intellectual problem of evil', one which is regularly presented as a problem for those who believe that God exists. The general idea here is that it is hard to see how pain, wickedness, and so on could ever have come to pass in a world created by God.

This 'intellectual problem of evil', however, could amount to different problems depending on who is raising it. For, suppose you believe (or think that you know) that God exists. In that case your problem might be that of fathoming the place of evil in a world made by God. You might be trying to penetrate the mystery of the God in whom you believe. And you might feel that this is a very difficult job, something in which you might never succeed in this life.

You might also take a different line, however. For you might say that there is a problem of evil which positively undermines belief in God's existence. There cannot be a circle which is also square. But can there be a world made by God which contains evil? Taking it as obvious that the world contains evil, you might conclude that God's non-existence is as certain as that of square circles. Alternatively, you might say that, though 'Evil exists' and 'God exists' are logically compatible, the evil that exists is positive or strong evidence that God does not exist. If one's house is dirty, that is evidence that it lacks a cleaner (even though it might have a bad one). By the same token, so you might argue, the evil in the world is evidence that the world is not created by God and that God, therefore, does not exist.

As we have seen, Aquinas thinks that God exists and that we have very good reason for saying so. In his view, we can know that God exists. So he does not think of evil as something which we ought to regard as grounds for thinking that God *cannot* exist. Nor does he take it as a reason for thinking that God's existence is unlikely or improbable. But he acknowledges that people might take a different view, for he offers what might be regarded as a classical formulation of the problem of evil. It comes at the point in the *Summa theologiae* where he turns to the question 'Does God exist?' Here he wants to argue that God, indeed, exists. To begin with, however, he cites reasons why one might say that the answer must be 'No'. One such reason is this: 'If one of two contraries be infinite, the other would be completely destroyed. But we understand by the term "God" something infinite, namely, something good without limit. Therefore, if God were to exist, we would not find anything bad. But we do find bad things in the world. Therefore God does not exist' (ST Ia, 2,3).

So Aquinas is aware of what I have called the 'intellectual problem of evil' considered as giving us grounds for an argument that God cannot, or probably does not, exist. He does not take it to show that God cannot or does not exist, for he thinks that we can know that God does exist. Yet he has things to say to those who think that evil constitutes some kind of case in favour of atheism. In particular, he says that evil cannot be thought of as something which God wills directly and as an end in itself.

'EVIL SUFFERED' AND 'EVIL DONE'

People often distinguish between what they call 'natural evil' (or 'naturally occurring evil') and 'moral evil'. The idea here is that some evil can be explained in terms of inanimate things which have effects which can be thought of as bad, and that some evil consists in what people freely choose to do. And, to some extent, the distinction is a clear one since we can cite obvious examples which seem to support it. It was clearly bad for the dinosaurs when life on earth left them unable to survive. They suffered and perished. And no human beings were around to account for this. We might say that their anguish and their demise is a perfect example of 'natural evil' since it occurred because of what the world apart from us was like as they died. It is to be explained only by science. Yet, what about the fact that John beats his wife? Here we might want to say that John is a bad man whose actions are morally evil. Most of us, however, would presume that, if John's beating his wife makes him a bad man, that can only be because he chose to do so. Nothing was choosing as the dinosaurs suffered. But, if John was responsible for beating his wife, then, so it seems, he was responsible for what he was doing. Hence he counts as a clear example of moral evil.

The distinction between 'natural evil' and 'moral evil' can, of course, become blurred. Suppose I perish in an earthquake. Is that a natural evil? Perhaps it is since people cannot (at present) control the occurrence of earthquakes. But is my perishing in an earthquake a purely natural occurrence? It might be if I were a dinosaur. But what if I die in an earthquake which occurs in a place where I have chosen to live knowing that earthquakes are likely to happen there? Is it only because of nature that I have died? If you think that my choices are on a level with what happened as the dinosaurs died, then your answer will be 'Yes'. But if you think that nothing in the natural world forced me to be where the earthquake occurred, then your answer will be 'No'. You will say that I chose to be where I was. And, if you say that, then it would seem that you agree that my sad demise is not just explicable in terms of how things in nature behave. You will want to say that it is also explicable in terms of what I chose to do, just as the climate which countries experience as a result of climate change is partly explicable in scientific terms and partly explicable in terms of people's choices when it comes to their treatment of their environment.

If this is what you want to say, then Aquinas would agree with you. So, for example, he thinks that we should be very cautious about blaming people for what they do since their behaviour, he suggests, might have been influenced by any number of factors. He also thinks that we should be careful before supposing that what we take to be naturally explicable events are simply that. At the same time, however, he has a place for a distinction between natural evil and moral evil. He says, for example, that, if a lion eats a lamb, something bad is happening to the lamb, something which cannot be captured by talk about what is morally good or morally bad. He also says that, if I choose to murder you, something bad is also there, though something which is not completely captured by the thought that you, like a lamb, are a naturally suffering victim.

Aquinas, of course, thinks that, if I murder you, then you suffer at my hands and are, therefore, a victim of mine. But do we capture what is bad about my murdering you by noting the fact that you are dead at my feet? Obviously not. Your being dead is a tragedy for you and for those who loved you. So we grieve and lament when we learn about it. Yet what we describe as we speak about your corpse and what it was like after I attacked you need not include me. Suppose that I killed you by clubbing you with the branch of a tree. Then I am to blame for your death because I did this. But suppose you were struck by the branch of a tree which fell in a gale. Would you be descriptively any different from what you would be had I clubbed you with a branch? Possibly not. Effects that we aim at intentionally can often come about regardless of our intentions. And for this reason, Aquinas suggests that moral evil does not consist in the fact that people bring about bad effects. For him, it consists in the fact that they are bad people. They are people who choose to do what is bad.

What I am here calling 'natural evil' Aquinas calls *malum poena* (which we might render as 'evil suffered'). And what I am calling 'moral evil' he calls *malum culpae* (which we might render as 'evil done'). Evil, he says, is twofold. First, there is 'evil consisting in the loss of a form or part required for a thing's integrity, as when someone is blind or lacks a limb' (i.e. 'evil suffered'). Second, there is 'evil of withdrawal in activity that is due, either by its omission or by its malfunctioning according to manner and measure' (i.e. 'evil done') (cf. ST Ia, 48,5). And he certainly thinks it worth asking how they are to be thought of with an eye on the proposition 'God exists'. As we have seen, Aquinas holds that creatures are totally dependent on God for being there at all and for being as they are. Ought he not, therefore, to conclude that God is the cause both of evil suffered and evil done? And, if he does so conclude, ought he not to reconsider his claim that God is good? For, how can what is good be responsible for evil suffered and evil done?

WHAT GOD CAN BE SAID TO PRODUCE

Aquinas is sensitive to the need to ask such questions. In responding to them, he chiefly concentrates on the sense in which God can be said to be responsible for evil. Unlike many people, however, he does not take the view that God is responsible for this as merely putting up with it, perhaps for some morally justifiable reason. As we have seen, God's goodness, for Aquinas, is not moral goodness. And he can make no sense of the suggestion that God has to put up with anything created. So he does not try to argue that God regretfully has to tolerate evil suffered as a means to some very good end. Nor does he claim that evil done can be attributed only to the choices of people and is, therefore, not really God's doing, or is something he permits so as to let people be truly free (a move which philosophers discussing the problem of evil commonly call the 'Free Will Defence'). He claims that God is responsible for evil suffered only because he is producing a good. And he argues that God is responsible for evil suffered only because he is not making people to be better than they choose to be.

With respect to evil suffered, Aquinas's position is basically that of St Augustine, who says that evil can be thought of as a 'privation of a good' (*privatio boni*) which ought to be there (cf. *Enchiridion* XI and *Confessions* III, vii,12). What am I doing if I say that it is bad for someone to be blind? I am, presumably, lamenting the fact that the person cannot see. So it seems that I am worried about what the person lacks (the ability to see). What am I saying if I say that it is bad for a lamb to be eaten by a lion? I am, presumably, lamenting the fact that the lamb, which formerly functioned as a happy and flourishing lamb, has lost what made it happy and flourishing (in this case it was literally eaten away). And this is how Aquinas thinks.

For Aquinas, evil suffered is no illusion. It is perfectly real in the sense that we can truly say things like 'This person is blind' and 'That lamb is suffering'. Yet Aquinas also thinks that to say such things is not to refer to something which exists in its own right (cf. Chapter 3). There are, he holds, no such things as blindnesses: there are only people who cannot see. There are, he holds, no such things as sufferings: there are only things which lack what they need to be whole and hearty. One might say that blindness is a real and positive property or attribute since there are things which are actually blind (just as there are things which are carnivorous). And one might say that suffering is a real and positive property or attribute since there are animals and people who are suffering (just as there are animals and people who are singing). For Aquinas, however, the question is 'Why is blindness or suffering bad?' And his answer is that it is bad since what we expect or want to be there, is not there. Just as to say 'There is nothing here' is not to say of *something* that *it* is here, so, in Aquinas's view, to say that there is evil suffered is not to say that there is any real individual or any positive quality. He recognizes that pains, for instance, are felt. He does not want to deny that animals and people can *suffer* pain. Yet he takes it as obvious that things which suffer are always lacking in some respect and that this is what their suffering consists in. 'Evil', Aquinas says, 'cannot signify a certain way of existing or a certain form or a nature. We conclude, therefore, that we signify a certain absence of good by the term "evil"' (ST Ia, 48,1; cf. SG III, 6). And he takes this to imply that evil suffered cannot be created by God, that it cannot be produced by God when he makes it to be that there is something rather than nothing.

At the same time, however, Aquinas is equally clear that no created reality can exist without God making it to be. If I am blind, then I cannot see. But Aquinas holds that God must still be creating what I am, what is actually there in me, even though I am blind. If a lamb is being eaten by a lion, then it is rapidly ceasing to be at various levels. But, Aquinas holds, God must still be creating what it actually is even as it is being eaten. So he concludes that all of that is there, all of that exists or is real, when it comes to evil suffered. As he sees it, there is no evil suffered which is not also a case of God making to be that which is positive, or real, and therefore good. Why 'therefore good'? Because, as we saw in the last chapter, Aquinas thinks that for something to be is for something to be good. A bad pint of beer is perfectly real, and Aquinas does not ask us to suppose that a bad pint of beer is really a good one. He does, however, ask us to accept that a bad pint of beer must at least succeed in being beer, that even a good pint of milk cannot be a bad pint of beer. And he thinks that to be beer at all is to be good in some way, to be what we are looking for when we are looking for beer as opposed, say, to milk.

So Aquinas certainly thinks that God is very much involved in the occurrence of evil suffered. But not as creating it, not as making it to be something real and positive. In that case, however, how does Aquinas account for its occurrence? Does he, for instance, take it to be an anti-miracle worked by a malignant deity? Does he take it to be wholly inexplicable?

Aquinas has no belief in malignant deities. He believes in the existence of devils, but he does not take them to be divine. He does, however, think that evil suffered is explicable. For he argues that there can be no evil suffered which is not the effect of something created which, by being good in its way, causes another thing to be bad in its way. Suppose that my kidneys start to fail. We would naturally wonder what is causing them to do so. We would suppose that there is something, or maybe a number of things (whether still around or not), which are (or were) responsible for the fact that my kidneys are packing up. And Aquinas would agree with us here. In his view, evil suffered always admits of a natural explanation. He thinks that there must be something in nature which accounts for my kidneys breaking down, and for any comparable occurrence.

And yet this, he reasons, cannot be anything bad. Let us suppose that my kidneys fail because a virus is at work on them. In these circumstances I would not be happy, and I would say that something bad is happening to me. Yet a defective virus cannot wreak havoc in people any more than a polio victim can run a mile. You have to be a pretty healthy human being in order to run a mile. And you have to be a pretty flourishing virus to bring about dramatic effects in human beings. To make me bad in *my* way (to make me lack what is good for a human being), a virus, Aquinas would say, has to be good of *its* kind. It has to be good in its way, just as the lion who eats a lamb needs to be good. A sick and maimed lion will get nowhere with a lamb. It takes a healthy (or, as Aquinas would say, a good) lion to inflict damage on a lamb. And, though he knew nothing of viruses, Aquinas would be saying the same thing of them were he alive today.

In other words, his view is that evil suffered is always a case of something lacking what it needs to be good (or, more accurately, better than it is) because something else is good (or, at least, good enough to account for evil suffered). It is always a case of something failing to be there since something good is there. For Aquinas, evil suffered is parasitic on good, and to speak of it existing as created by God is only to speak of what God is making to be good. From one point of view (with an eye on the victims of evil suffered), Aquinas accepts that evil suffered is bad. From another (with an eye on what God can be thought to be producing when evil suffered occurs), he argues that it consists of nothing but what is good. So he concludes that God can only be said *indirectly* to 'produce' evil suffered.

It has been suggested that there is more evil suffered than there need be and that this should lead us to conclude that God is somehow bad. For Aquinas, however, there is absolutely no more evil suffered than there need be. In his view, any evil suffered is neither more nor less than what we can expect in a material world in which scientific explanations can be given for what happens. One might say that God is bad since he produces a world in which scientific explanations can be given for evil suffered. According to Aquinas, however, such a charge could amount to no more than an expression of dislike for the world in which we find ourselves. It would be equivalent to the statement 'I wish that there was no world at all' (an expression of feeling, not an argument). It would not, for Aquinas, amount to a proof for the badness of God.

What about evil done, however? Unlike evil suffered, this can hardly be thought of as *benefitting* anyone or anything. People who wrong others harm their victims. And, in doing so, they are bad in themselves (so most of us would say, and so Aquinas would certainly say). With evil done, unlike evil suffered, there seems to be no concomitant good. There is nothing but failure. Evil done often involves success, of course. The perpetrator of genocide may be succeeding in all sorts of ways – as a killer, a strategist, and so on. But agents of evil done, regardless of how they succeed when viewed under certain descriptions, are fundamentally failing to be good, and nothing is benefitting from this (except accidentally). The evil in their actions is nothing but failure.

If that is true, however, then evil done can hardly be thought to be made to be by God. Or so Aquinas thinks. The evil in a morally evil act is not, for him, something which God can make to be since it is not an existing thing. It is no kind of individual or positive quality. It can no more be made to be by God than can square circles. Aquinas therefore concludes that evil done represents no action of God. He thinks that evil suffered does, and that the same goes for the positive realities which are there in those who are morally wicked. But the evil in evil done is, for him, nothing but failure. Considered as such, it is not, he thinks, something produced by those who are morally evil. Nor can it be thought of as something produced by God. The evil in evil done is, for Aquinas, a failure on the part of a human being to be in some way or other. If I shoot you, then I succeed as a shooter, but I fail when it comes to being just or charitable. According to Aquinas, such failure cannot be thought of as anything which God creatively makes to be.

But does not Aquinas hold that God causes all our free actions? We have seen that he does. So, ought he not to admit that God is the cause of evil done? Ought he not to admit that it was God who put people into the Nazi concentration camps, assuming that the people who did this acted freely and were not victims of evil suffered? And ought he not to admit that it was God who destroyed the New York World Trade Center on 11 September 2001, assuming that those who did so acted freely?

In one sense, Aquinas agrees that the answer to these questions is 'Yes'. For he holds that our free choices are God's work in us and that this is the case even when we are choosing to behave badly. He asks 'Is God the cause of sinful acts?' And his answer is 'Yes'. Acts of sin, he says, come from God since they are as real as anything else created (cf. DM III, 2 and ST Ia2ae, 79,2). I may amputate your infected leg to save your life, and this would be a good thing for me to do, assuming that I know of no other way to save your life. But what if I cut off your leg so as to satisfy my sadistic desires? In both cases I remove your leg. And Aquinas would say that I could not do so unless God not only permitted what I do (as a patient might permit a surgeon to operate), but also made to be all that is real as I act.

In another sense, however, Aquinas denies that God causes evil done.

For one thing, he thinks, God cannot be said to do what people do when they fail from the moral point of view. I can make a bed. Can God make a bed? Not if he is not a human being who can be in a room so as to make a bed, as I do (cf. Chapters 10 and 15). And, with this point in mind, Aquinas presumes that God cannot be thought of as sinning, as I might by shooting you. He also thinks that God is unable to sin since God, as the source of all creaturely goodness, can be sensibly said to be 'Goodness Itself' (i.e., not a good *such and such*, but the reason why there are any things to be singled out as good).

More importantly for our present concerns, however, Aquinas also maintains that God cannot be thought of as creatively causing me to be bad when I indulge in my sinful actions. Why not? Because he thinks that my sin consists in my failing when it comes to action, albeit that this might take the form of my choosing to do something. Maybe I ought to look after you. Instead, I murder you. Aquinas would say that I am sinning here since I am choosing to do what I ought not to do. But what does it mean to say so? Aquinas thinks that it means to say that I *am doing something* which amounts to a failure to do something *else*. My sin is not entirely nothing: it lies in what I do. But, Aquinas reasons, if I am acting freely, then I am aiming at what I take to be good, and, regardless of my aims, something good is there. For my action is there. And this, he holds, could only be there as made to exist by God. In this sense, he thinks that God causes sinful actions.

But the evil involved in sin is not, he maintains, creatable, for it consists in the gap between what I am doing and what I ought to be doing but am not doing. Sin, for Aquinas, is essentially a failure in being, though the forms it takes might be regarded as examples of marvellous success (as when assassins expertly manage to polish off their targets). On this understanding, Aquinas concludes that sin is not God's doing. It is not, he thinks, created by God, which he takes to mean that God does not cause sin. People, he holds, can be said to cause sin since they commit sinful acts. But God, he thinks, is not the cause of sin, even though the actions of people can be thought of as the doing of God. For Aquinas, a sinner chooses what is bad as opposed to what is good. The exercise of this choice, which one might reasonably take to be nothing different from the choice, must, Aquinas thinks, be created and, therefore, brought about by God. But the badness of the act and the culpability for it are not, for Aquinas, to be attributed to God. For him, God is responsible for all that is positive and real in it, not for the gap between what it is and what it ought to be. And it is sinners who are culpable for what they do. For they choose to do what they do while refraining from what they should do.

WHAT GOD MIGHT HAVE MADE

If that is Aquinas's view, however, ought he not to agree that God could have made a world in which people never do anything morally wrong? Ought he not to agree that God could have made a world consisting of nothing but saints? And ought he not to agree that God could have made a world in which there was nothing that we could describe as 'evil suffered'? And, if his answer to these questions is 'Yes', ought he not to agree that God is bad?

His answer to these questions is, indeed, 'Yes'. In his view, God could have made me to be a saint, someone who always did nothing but good, someone who did good to an extraordinary degree (which a writer of my obituary shall not, alas, be able to say of me). He also thinks that God could have made a world in which there occurred no evil suffered. Why? Because of his view of divine omnipotence, as sketched in Chapter 10. There seems to be no intrinsic impossibility in there being someone who always acts well. So Aquinas thinks that God could bring it about that there is such a person (he thought that God did so in the case of Jesus Christ). And, as for evil suffered, Aquinas holds that this need not be part of a world created by God since one might coherently suppose that creatures might only have comprised a realm of beings who are not affected by it (as he took angels to do).

Yet Aquinas does not therefore conclude that God is bad. If you suggested to him that he should do so, his immediate reply would be (I presume) 'Bad as what?' For, as we have seen, he takes 'bad' to be understandable only if we know what kind of thing we are talking about. On Aquinas's account, God is not a good *such and such*. Nor can he be a bad *such and such*. So you might suggest to him that God is bad since there are things which he could have created which he has not. But then, as what he writes suggests, he would ask why we should therefore think that God is bad. Could it be that God has an obligation to create a world of a certain kind? Aquinas can make no sense of the notion that God has obligations when it comes to creation. So he does not think that God is bad because he has not produced more goodness than he has.

16

Father, Son, and Spirit

Aquinas holds that we cannot comprehend what God is and that the little we do understand of him derives from what he has produced. According to Aquinas, we come to a knowledge of God only by means of creatures. Yet, is God nothing but the maker of creatures? Aquinas thinks not. In his view, it is absurd to suggest that God has to create in order to be God. I have to breathe in order to be human. Yet God, Aquinas maintains, needs nothing in order to be what he essentially is. He is utterly independent. Some have suggested that God would be somehow unhappy or unfulfilled if he did not create. For Aquinas, however, God could not create if his essence depended for its well-being on anything other than itself (cf. ST Ia, 19,3). His view is that God is God regardless of creation, that God has a life of his own, one lived in the changeless eternity which is nothing other than God himself. Why? Because, says Aquinas, God is Father, Son, and Spirit. His view is that the fundamental truth about God has nothing to do with creation at all. For him, it is captured in the doctrine of the Trinity, a teaching which he thinks of as telling us much more of God than we could ever glean from our study of and reflection on creatures.

PHILOSOPHY AND THE TRINITY

It has been suggested that any right thinking person ought to accept the doctrine of the Trinity since it can be shown to be true (or since it can be shown to be probably true) by means of purely philosophical arguments. Yet Aquinas judges differently. 'The truth that God is three and one', he says, 'is altogether a matter of faith; and in no way can it be demonstratively proved' (DT 3,4). 'No one', he asserts, 'can know the trinity of persons by natural powers of reason' (ST Ia, 32,1; cf. CT 36 and DT 1,4).

Why does Aquinas take this view? Because he thinks that philosophical argument can lead us to see only the need to speak of there being divinity, not distinction within divinity. 'By natural knowledge', he says, 'we can know of God only what characterizes him necessarily as the source of all beings.' Yet 'the creative power of God is shared by the whole Trinity and, therefore, goes with the unity of nature, not the distinction of persons' (ST Ia, 32,1; cf. ST Ia, 45,6). In other words, we can know that there is a Creator but not that God is somehow essentially three. Or, as Aquinas puts it, 'through natural reason we can know what has to do with the unity of nature but not with the distinction of persons' (ST Ia, 32,1). To try to prove the doctrine of the Trinity, says Aquinas, detracts from faith in two ways.

> First on the point of its dignity, for the object of faith is those invisible realities which are beyond the reach of human reason . . . Secondly, on the point of advantage in bringing others to faith. For, when someone wants to support faith by unconvincing arguments, he becomes a laughing stock for the unbelievers, who think that we rely on such arguments and believe because of them. (ST Ia, 32,1)

In that case, however, just what can mere philosophers say when it comes to the doctrine of the Trinity? Aquinas's answer is a fairly simple one. He thinks that they should content themselves with seeking to show that there must be a mistake in attempts to prove that the doctrine is somehow impossible or disprovable. His view is that truth cannot contradict truth. So, since he believes that the doctrine of the Trinity is true, he is convinced that attempts to show that it is false must somehow be mistaken (cf. ST Ia, 1,8 and SG I, 6 f.). And, he suggests, to deal successfully with such attempts is all that a philosopher can hope to manage when it comes to the doctrine. In his view, the doctrine of the Trinity is a truth of faith, not one which can be demonstrated philosophically. And he thinks that 'one should try to prove the truths of faith only by authoritative texts to those who are ready to accept them' (ST Ia, 32,1). He means that if, for example, someone asks you for a proof of the doctrine of the Trinity, you should rest content with appeals to Scripture or to the Councils of the Church; you should not suggest that the doctrine can be proved philosophically. At the philosophical level, Aquinas says, 'it is enough to defend the position that what faith upholds is not impossible' (ST Ia, 32,1).

It should be obvious that Aquinas is not maintaining that there is no reason to believe in the doctrine of the Trinity. In fact, he thinks that there are a number of reasons for doing so. For one thing, he holds that the doctrine was taught by God since it was taught by Christ. He also thinks that the doctrine as formulated by the Christian Church conforms to the meaning of Scripture. But he does not think that we therefore have reasons which force us to agree that God is three in one – not, at any rate, if we do not begin by accepting the authority of Christ and the Church.

If I believe that someone is out to kill me because my friends tell me so, and if I have no other grounds for believing as I do, then I might be well advised not to make a fool of myself by trying to claim otherwise to people who take no account of anything that my friends have to say. If it comes to an argument, I should content myself with trying to show that reasons which might be given for supposing that I am safe do not, in fact, show that I am. By the same token, Aquinas thinks, when it comes to the doctrine of the Trinity, believers must satisfy themselves with seeking to rebut arguments purporting to show that the doctrine is false. One such argument might be: nothing in the teaching of Jesus or in his life as recorded in the New Testament goes anywhere near to justifying the doctrine of the Trinity as it later came to be formulated. And Aquinas evidently takes this argument seriously since he makes a point of citing New Testament texts as sources for, or as reasons to believe in, the doctrine of the Trinity. For him, the doctrine is a thoroughly biblical one, and he defends it by appeal to the Bible (cf. ST 2a2ae, 174,6). Yet to those who place no credence in what the Bible teaches, his response is: 'State your case against the doctrine of the Trinity, and let us take things from there.'

But what kind of case might someone make against the doctrine and with no reference to sources which Christians take to be authoritative? Presumably, it would need to be a conceptual one to the effect that the doctrine is somehow logically confused. But is it? In various places, Aquinas takes note of reasons for suggesting that it is, reasons which he deals with individually. In general, however, his basic position is that the doctrine is thinkable since one can say enough to show that what it asserts is not obviously nonsense. We cannot, he thinks, understand what God is. But he thinks that we can say something of what might be involved in God being three persons, something which is not obviously incoherent.

THREE PERSONS AND ONE GOD

When Aquinas says that God is three persons, he does not, of course, mean that God is three distinct things, even three distinct things of the same kind. Since he believes that God is entirely simple, he thinks that it would be silly to suppose that God is, for example, like three human beings. If all that is in God is God, then no divine person can be anything other than the one simple God. Yet might one make sense of there being distinction in God which is not a distinction between members of a kind (or, between members of different kinds)? Aquinas thinks that one might.

To begin with, he suggests that we need to take seriously what St John's gospel has to say when it speaks of there being a Word which was in the beginning with God and which was God (John 1:1). The Latin for 'word' is *verbum*, and Aquinas maintains that it is possible to think of (though not to understand) a word which is God's word without it being other than God. Or, to put it another way, he thinks that it is possible to think of (though not to understand) the idea that God might bring forth one distinct from himself without bringing forth something which is not God.

For, what if I form a true conception of myself? Is what is in me distinct from me or not? Aquinas thinks that it is wholly in me since he takes forming a concept to be an *intransitive*, as opposed to a *transitive*, activity. When I kick my cat (which, of course, I never do), my action is transitive because it takes place not only in me as one who behaves in a certain way but also in my cat (which is why cats do not like being kicked). Is it like this, however, when I form a concept of something? Aquinas thinks that it is not. I can come to understand, though everything around remains unchanged, and Aquinas thinks that my forming a true conception of myself is nothing other than something in me.

When Aquinas speaks of our forming a conception of something (which, for him, is the same as understanding what something is), he says that there comes to be in us a *verbum cordis* (a 'word of the heart'). Does he mean that we can understand, or form concepts, without recourse to language? St Augustine seems to have held that we can (cf. *Confessions* I, vi,8), but Aquinas does not. He never denies that we understand because we are able to employ the symbols we call words. Indeed, he thinks that we are maimed as human beings (and, therefore, as human thinkers) if we lack the ability to use language or to engage with others who do so (a view which influences his teaching on human souls after death described in Chapter 11). Yet Aquinas does hold that our actually understanding what something is cannot be identified with anything that a dictionary might have written in its pages. In his view, words in dictionaries are there only because people can understand. And different words in different languages can mean the same (from which it would seem to follow that the meaning of a word is not just the word itself). Can one be said to understand what words mean if one does not exhibit certain ways of behaving? Can one be said to understand what, for example, a dog is if one does not respond in certain ways to questions about dogs? Aquinas's view is that one's knowledge of what a word means is certainly shown in one's ability to use it intelligibly in different contexts. But he does not think that understanding what something is can, therefore, be reduced to behaving or talking in certain ways. For him, our talk and our behaviour indicate that we understand what something is, and there is a distinction to be drawn between them and the fact that we actually understand.

In short, Aquinas holds that, when I come to understand what something is, something comes to be in me which is not literally a word, even though it might amount to what a word means since I am understanding what something is. And he thinks that this is so even if what happens in me is that I form a conception of myself. Yet, what if we substitute 'God' for 'me' in that last sentence? Aquinas would say that my understanding what I am is an accident in me. It is not me since I could exist without it. But what if God understands what God is? Is his understanding an accident in him?

If God is wholly simple, then it is obviously not. So God's conception of himself (should there be such a thing, and insofar as we can make sense of it) must be nothing other than God. Or so Aquinas suggests. Yet he also believes that it can be thought of as making for a distinction in God. Why? Because he thinks that God's conception of himself comes to be in God, albeit from eternity, and because he thinks it reasonable to speak of something coming to be in God as being distinct from that from which it comes to be (cf. CJ I, 25–29).

Aquinas, of course, does not mean that there could be anything which comes to be in God which is not God. His point is that, if something comes to be in God from eternity, then something comes to be which is both wholly divine and yet more than can be captured by an account of what 'God' means. In Aquinas's view, God's concept of himself, should God have one, must come from God and must therefore 'proceed' from him. So it is *in* God as proceeding *from* God. And, Aquinas suggests, we can therefore think of there being distinction in God by virtue of relation. God's concept of himself can be nothing other than God. And it is, after all, God's concept of himself. So it comes from God without being distinct from God. Hence, Aquinas suggests, it is not absurd to say that the Triune God consists of a Father who begets a Son, who is not the

136

Father but who is also God (cf. ST Ia, 27,2; cf. ST Ia, 14,4 and SG IV, 10–14).

In writing along these lines, Aquinas is trying only to indicate ways in which one might make some sense of the notion that God is a Father with a Son. He holds that God is an impenetrable mystery, and he does not regard the doctrine of the Trinity as teaching us that God is even more mysterious to us than he would be if we did not believe it. Yet he also thinks that there can be distinction established only by relation. So he thinks that one can reasonably countenance the suggestion that, in God, the Father has no features or properties which the Son lacks, and that the only thing that distinguishes them is that they are at opposite ends of a relationship. As Aquinas puts it, using traditional language, the Father *generates* the Son, and the Son *is generated by* the Father. For Aquinas, being God the Father is standing in a relationship to God the Son. It is nothing else. And being God the Son is standing in a relationship to God the Father, and nothing else. The Father *is* a relation. And so is the Son. It is not that they *have* a relation. A subsisting relation (which is how Aquinas categorizes both the Father and the Son) is not something that Aquinas takes us to be familiar with, any more than he takes us to be familiar with subsisting Being Itself, or subsisting Goodness, or subsisting Power (all of which he regards as good phrases to use as we feebly try to say what God is). Yet he thinks that to speak of the Father and the Son as subsisting relations is helpful. And he does so since he believes that the notion of there being such relations is not incoherent and since it allows us to say that the Son proceeds from the Father, though both Father and Son are equally divine.

And it is somewhat along these lines that Aquinas is thinking when it comes to the third person of the Trinity. For the Holy Spirit, he says, can also be thought of as nothing but a subsisting relation.

If the Father knows the Son for what he is (i.e. God) and if the Son knows the Father in exactly the same way, then, Aquinas suggests, each must love each other equally since each is divine and since divinity cannot but love divinity (for an omniscient being must know and will what is absolutely good, which is what God is). With an eye on people, Aquinas maintains that knowledge and will are inseparable. To will, he thinks, is to be attracted. But to what? To what we take to be good. We cannot make sense of human willing, says Aquinas, if we do not take it to be what is there as we strive for what we take to be good. We cannot, he holds, aim at anything else (cf. Chapter 12). And so, he is happy to say, an omniscient and willing God must will nothing but that which is perfectly good.

But what is perfectly good? Aquinas thinks that only God is. So he holds that God must inevitably will, or love, God. In his view, the Father must love the Son, and the Son must love the Father. But what is love as it comes to be in divinity?

It cannot, Aquinas thinks, be an accident. It cannot be other than God. So it must be God. Yet Aquinas also thinks that it comes forth from God and can, therefore, be said to be a relation within the Godhead. The Father and the Son, Aquinas suggests, can be thought to love each other and, therefore, to bring forth the love between them considered as a subsisting relation. This love, he says, is the Holy Spirit.

One might ask how anything is *produced* when love is there since love seems to be a matter of attraction and not of production. For Aquinas, however, there being love can be thought of as there being joy, which can be thought of as what comes to be when will meets what delights it. So he thinks it not silly to suggest that the Holy Spirit is what God is as the Father and the Son know and love each other. In the traditional language, he thinks it acceptable to say that the Spirit is one person and that the Father and the Son are two persons distinct from it. It should be obvious, however, that 'person', in this context, means, for Aquinas, 'subsisting relation', not what we might have in mind in calling each other persons.

Boethius says that a person is an individual substance of rational nature (*Contra Eutychen* 3). And, with this definition in mind, one which Aquinas is happy to accept (cf. ST Ia, 29,1 and DP IX, 2), we might well agree that all of our friends are persons. Yet, with this definition in mind, Aquinas would also deny that God is a person. For, he reasons, God is *not* an individual substance, and he does not *have* a nature. Aquinas agrees that there is knowledge in God, and he does not want baldly to deny that God is rational. But he certainly does not want to say that God is rational in that, for instance, he can do a crossword in under five minutes or work through a mathematical proof to decide on its validity. So, in one sense, Aquinas denies that God is a 'person' even though he is prepared to use the word when it comes to the Father, the Son, and the Spirit. His position with respect to these, however, is that they are persons only in the sense that they are subsisting relations. For him, the Father is not a kindly individual who spends a lot of fun time with his Son. And the Spirit is not someone who is always there to observe or to participate in what they get up to. For Aquinas, the persons of the Trinity, as unknowable and incomprehensible as God is, can be thought of only in terms of relation, and that, only insofar as they can be thought of at all. Or, as he puts it:

When something springs from a principle which has the same nature, then necessarily both that which issues and that from which it issues belong to the same order; and so must have real relationships with each other. Since processions in God are in the identical nature . . . the relations rising from the divine processions must be real relations . . . While relation in created things exists as an accident in a subject, in God a really existing relation has the existence of the divine nature and is completely identical with it . . . [so] . . . a real relation in God is in reality identical with his nature and differs only in our mind's understanding, inasmuch as relation implies a reference to the correlative term, which is not implied by the term 'nature'. Therefore it is clear that in God relation and nature are existentially not two things but one and the same . . . By definition relation implies reference to another, according to which the two things stand in relative opposition to each other. Therefore, since in God there is a real relation . . . relative opposition must also really be there. Now by its very meaning such opposition implies distinction. Therefore there must be real distinction in God, not indeed when we consider the absolute reality of his nature, where there is sheer unity and simplicity, but when we think of him in terms of relation. (ST Ia, 28,1 ff.; cf. ST Ia, 27,3 and SG IV, 14)

In terms of this account, the persons of the Trinity are nothing but what Father, Son, and Spirit are to each other. And since Aquinas takes this to be nothing less than God, his conclusion is that each of the persons of the Trinity is everything that God is. Each, for example, is whatever accounts for there being something rather than nothing (which, as we have seen, is why Aquinas thinks it impossible to prove that God is three persons).

Yet Aquinas also believes that God, the eternal Trinity, has, so to speak, gone out of itself so as to make more than the difference between something and nothing. Theologians sometimes distinguish between what they (perhaps infelicitously) call 'the immanent Trinity' and the 'economic Trinity'. By the first phrase, they mean the Trinity as it eternally is. By the second, they are trying to signify what the New Testament calls the sending of the Son and the Holy Spirit: the Trinity in history, as it were. And this is a distinction which Aquinas also acknowledges, though without using the terms 'immanent' and 'economic'. For him, the Trinity is all that it is essentially quite on its own. It has no need of creatures. Yet it is also, he holds, at work in the world, and in a sense which goes beyond what is meant by saying that God has created. Why? Because of the Incarnation and because of the work of grace, topics which Aquinas takes to bring us to the heart of the Christian Gospel. In the next chapter we shall see how he deals with the first of them. His approach to the second will be the focus of Chapter 18.

17

God Incarnate

In the *Summa theologiae*, Aquinas waits until 3a,1 before turning formally to belief in the Incarnation. In the *Summa contra Gentiles*, he waits until Chapter 27 of Book IV. In the *Compendium of Theology*, he embarks on a discussion of the Incarnation only at Chapter 185 of Part I. Some have accounted for this apparent delay by suggesting that Aquinas is not really interested in Christology and prefers to spend his time dealing with 'philosophical' matters. Yet nothing could be further from the truth.

For Aquinas, the Incarnation is at the heart of the Christian religion. And all that he writes in texts like the *Summa theologiae* and the *Summa contra Gentiles* is penned with an eye on it. These works certainly contain much that can be viewed as pure philosophy. But the philosophy is there so as to straighten the way to a solid and intelligent grasp of what revelation teaches. And, for Aquinas, central to revelation is the claim that God became human. 'Not only must Christians believe that there is one God, who is creator of heaven and earth and all things', he insists, 'but they must also believe that God is the Father, and Christ is the very Son of God' (AC IV).

That God is the Father is, for Aquinas, part of the doctrine of the Trinity, and that Christ is the Son of God is what the doctrine of the Incarnation teaches. For him, the two doctrines are bound up with each other. And, to some extent, what he has to say about them is the same. It is, for example, the same when it comes to what philosophy can establish concerning them. As we have seen, Aquinas takes philosophy to be unable to show that God is three in one. Yet he also claims that philosophy cannot show that Christ was divine. To believe that Christ is divine, he thinks, is to believe that God is at least somehow two. And he takes it as evident that, if duality in God cannot be established philosophically, then neither can the doctrine of the Trinity. He also thinks that God does not have to become incarnate (cf. ST 3a, 1,2). And, so he concludes, there is no proof of the Incarnation to be derived from reflection on what God is essentially.

One might suppose that the divinity of Christ is manifest because of some empirically observable phenomenon: the resurrected Jesus, for instance. But Aquinas thinks otherwise. Referring, for instance, to the story of doubting Thomas as recorded in John's gospel, he envisages someone suggesting that Christ can be known to be God since Thomas saw him as risen and was led to call him 'My Lord and my God' (John 20:28). Yet, Aquinas argues, 'Thomas saw one thing, and believed another. He saw a man; he believed him to be God' (ST 2a2ae, 1,4). Aquinas means that nothing Thomas could ever have observed could have led him to know that Christ was God. In ST 3a, 43,4 Aquinas accepts that Christ's miracles suffice to show his divinity. But he clearly takes this to mean that they were miracles and, therefore, like any miracle, were wrought by God, not that they prove the doctrine of the Incarnation. He thinks that Christ claimed divine status and that his miracles confirm this claim. They mark him, so to speak, with the seal of God (especially since, as recorded in the gospels, they come to pass at his word and not just as miracles happening in his presence). But Aquinas does not take miracles to demonstrate the doctrine of the Incarnation in any formal sense. He thinks that they give reasons for believing that Christ was God, but he does not take them to give us knowledge that this must have been so.

THE LOGIC OF GOD INCARNATE

Yet the doctrine of the Incarnation, like the doctrine of the Trinity, is not, for Aquinas, unthinkable. We can, he thinks, state it, and we can do so in a way which indicates that we are not talking nonsense. It has, of course, been said that nonsense is just what the doctrine of the Incarnation is. It has been said, for example, that a man can no more be literally God than a circle can be literally square. And some theologians have tried to accommodate this suggestion by proposing that Christ, though not God, was divinely inspired or that he was not really human but God in a human disguise. Yet Aquinas believes that Christ was literally God and that it is not absurd to say so. For he thinks that the doctrine of the Incarnation can be coherently asserted as long as we keep our logical wits about us. He does not, of course, mean that the Word made flesh is nothing but an opportunity for people to engage in logical gymnastics. Yet he does hold that some logical distinctions can help us to see why speaking of God incarnate is not to speak of what is provably impossible.

For example, he thinks that making sense of the Incarnation will be easier if we get it right when it comes to the question 'What is a proposition?' One answer to this question, sometimes referred to as the 'Two Name Theory', says that a proposition is a linking of names to assert identity by means of the verb 'to be'. Suppose I assert that Smokey is a cat. According to the Two Name Theory, I use 'Smokey' and 'cat' as names, and I claim that they stand for the same thing. Yet, though he sometimes writes so as to suggest that this is how he thinks of propositions, Aquinas is resolutely opposed to anything like the Two Name Theory. In common with most contemporary logicians, he holds that propositions single out subjects and then tell us something about them. On this account, 'Smokey is a cat' is best construed as a name ('Smokey') and a predicate ('—— is a cat'). So, for Aquinas, there is a fundamental distinction to be made between subjects which can be named and predicates which are truly ascribable to them. Such predicates, he thinks, tell us what something is. In no sense are they names.

In that case, however, what are we doing when we say what something is? For Aquinas, we are describing it. But we are also locating it within a context of possibly true description. If I say that Smokey is a cat, I am, in a sense, describing him. But I am not doing so half as well as I would if I said that he is grey or that he is lively. To call Smokey a cat is not to say what he, a particular cat, is like. Rather, it is to give notice that a certain range of things might sensibly be said of him: that he is living, mammalian, carnivorous, and so on. And this is what Aquinas thinks. As we have seen, he holds that there is a big difference between what a thing is essentially and what it is accidentally. And he holds that to say what something is essentially is to single it out and to indicate what might sensibly be said of it regardless of what might be true of it simply because of what it happens to be but might not be. For him, 'Smokey is a cat' ascribes a *nature* to Smokey. And he thinks that the same goes for 'Christ is a man' and 'Christ is God'. In his opinion, each of these propositions should be taken as singling out a subject (Christ) and asserting of him that two distinct predicates are applicable to him ('—— is a man' and '—— is God'). And these predicates, he thinks, signify, not an accident of any kind, but a nature. They give notice that certain ways of talking are appropriate when it comes to Christ.

Take, to begin with, 'Christ is a man'. For Aquinas, this means that Christ is whatever it takes to be human. Wisely, perhaps, he does not want to say that we can be clear, in some definitive sense, as to what is and is not possible for human beings. So he does not want to suggest that to assert that Christ is a man commits us irrevocably to any account we might presently give as to what Christ, for example, is and is not capable of. Yet he thinks that we can have some idea as to what is needed for it to be true that Christ is a man. Nothing is a man if it is made of plastic. Nothing is a man if it grows in the earth and sprouts leaves. So Aquinas takes 'Christ is a man' to be incompatible with statements such as 'Christ is made of plastic' or 'Christ grows in the earth and sprouts leaves'. And of men it makes sense to say things like 'They can run', 'They can breathe', and 'They can die'. So Aquinas takes 'Christ is a man' to be compatible with statements such as 'Christ can run', 'Christ can breathe', and 'Christ can die'.

What about 'Christ is God'? Well, we now know what sort of thing Aquinas takes to be true of God essentially. So he takes 'Christ is God' to signify that Christ is just that. He holds that God is incorporeal. So he is happy to say that Christ is incorporeal. He holds that God is omnipotent, omniscient, perfectly good, eternal, and simple. So he is happy to say that Christ is all these things too. He seems to have been worried with respect to the assertion that Christ came to know certain things as people come to know them. For, at one time, he taught that Christ knew everything to be known from the moment of his conception, while, at another time, he taught that Christ's knowledge must somehow have developed by virtue of his human experience, as is the case with all people (cf. ST 3a 12,1; cf. ST 3a, 9,4). In general, however, Aquinas's rule of thumb is a simple one: if it makes sense to predicate **F** of a human being, then it makes sense to predicate **F** of Christ.

In short, therefore, Aquinas maintains that we have two ways of speaking about Christ, only one of which we understand (since we do not know what God is). In virtue of his human nature, we speak of Christ in exactly the same way that we would speak of any other human being. In virtue of his divine nature, we can also say more enigmatic and mysterious things. Yet, how can what it makes sense to say of God make sense to say of what is a man? How can Aquinas cope with the fact that what is human seems not to be divine and that what is divine seems not to be human?

He copes with the fact by accepting it. For he thinks that we must rigidly distinguish between what it takes to be human and what it takes to be God. And he holds that we must never confuse the two. But he does not believe that this entails that we contradict ourselves when saying that Christ is both human and divine. For Aquinas, the name 'Christ' singles out a subject and has no descriptive force. And he suggests that to say that

Christ is human and that Christ is God is simply to say of a single subject that different ways of talking about it can be equally true since the subject in question has, not one, but two distinct natures. For Aquinas, the two natures of Christ are precisely that: two natures, not different aspects of the nature of one thing, or different accidental features of it. So he says that what we can sensibly say of Christ depends on whether we are speaking of what he is as God or of what he is as human. As God, he holds, Christ is omnipotent. But he can hardly be omnipotent as human. As human, he believes, Christ is mutable. But he can hardly be mutable as God.

Yet, if we say that Christ is omnipotent as God, but not as human, or that he is mutable as human, but not as divine, are we not contradicting ourselves? Aquinas thinks that we would be if we were saying that divinity is both omnipotent and not omnipotent, or if we were claiming that humanity is both mutable and immutable. Yet he does not take the doctrine of the Incarnation to imply either of these things, or any suggestions like them. He takes it as obvious that the divine nature cannot be anything but omnipotent and that human nature is essentially mutable. But what if there were a single subject with both a divine and human nature? Then, Aquinas thinks, it would make sense to say of it whatever it makes sense to say of God and whatever it makes sense to say of what is human.

In Aquinas's view, the essential thing to grasp is that the Incarnation is a union between divinity and humanity by virtue of a single subject, not a single nature. For him, God incarnate is the second person of the Trinity, who is essentially divine from eternity and essentially human in history. 'The Word', he observes, 'has a human nature united to himself, even though it does not form part of his divine nature . . . [and] . . . this union was effected in the person of the Word, not in the nature' (ST 3a, 2,2). To say that the divine nature is human or that human nature is divine would, for Aquinas, be to say what is contradictory. Yet it is not, he thinks, contradictory to maintain that one subject is essentially both divine and human. For to do so, he holds, is just to assert that different kinds of predicates can be truly ascribed to one and the same subject, who, if divine and human, can therefore be referred to indifferently either as God or as a human being. Christ drank wine. And, if Christ was divine, he was the eternal Son of the Father. Aquinas therefore thinks that we can consistently say both that the eternal Son of the Father drank wine and that one who drank wine was the eternal Son of the Father. We cannot, he believes, say that the eternal Son of the Father, *as such*, drank wine or that one who drank wine was, *as such*, the eternal Son of the Father. But that is so only because it does not belong to divinity, *as such*, to drink wine and because it does not belong to humanity, *as such*, to be the eternal Son of the Father.

Yet, if Christ drank wine and if Christ is God, does it not follow that God drank wine? And if Christ is God and if God is omnipotent, does it not follow that Christ is omnipotent? Presumably it does. So, how can we fail to contradict ourselves if we accept the implications here? Surely, it is ridiculous to say that God drank wine, just as it is to say that some human being is omnipotent. And what about the notion of identity? If X and Y are identical, then what we can say of X must be what we should also say of Y. Yet if X is Christ and if Y is God, how can we fail to land ourselves in absurdity when claiming that Christ is God?

Well, Aquinas thinks, we must certainly say that God drank wine, just as we must declare that God was born and that he suffered and died. And he reckons that we also need to hold that Christ was omnipotent, not to mention eternal, omniscient, incorporeal, and everything else that God is by nature (cf. ST 3a, 16,4). But it is not, he protests, contradictory to maintain such positions. For, in the case of the Incarnation, we are dealing with one subject having two distinct natures. And we contradict ourselves only if we speak of God incarnate without bearing this point firmly in mind.

Suppose, for example, that we assert 'God is a man'. Then, Aquinas holds, there is no contradiction involved. For 'God' here stands for what 'Christ' stands for (as in sentences like 'Christ taught in Galilee'), and it is not contradictory to say that Christ is a man (cf. ST 3a, 16,1). Then again, what if we claim that 'Christ created the heavens and the earth'? In Aquinas's view, we would be speaking truly and, therefore, consistently since 'Christ' here stands for what 'God' stands for (as in sentences like 'God created the heavens and the earth').

But what about 'Christ is God *insofar as* he is a man' or 'God is a man *insofar as* he is God'? Or what of 'Christ is a creature'? Aquinas does not think that human beings are essentially divine, so he would say that Christ cannot be God insofar as he is a man. And, since he takes divinity to be incorporeal, he would say that God cannot be a man insofar as he is God. And he would add that 'Christ is a creature' is evidently false since it would seem to imply that God is a creature. Aquinas emphatically agrees that Christ is a creature when it comes to his human nature. But he thinks it absurd to hold that, if 'Christ' stands for 'the eternal Word of God', then Christ is a creature. For that would make God the Son a creature insofar as he is God the Son. 'It should not', says Aquinas, 'be stated without quali-fication that Christ is a creature or is subordinate to the Father; such statements should be qualified by the phrase "according to his human nature"' (ST 3a, 16,8).

Yet what is a divine subject with both a Godly and a human nature? At one level, Aquinas does not pretend to have an answer to this question. For, at one level, we may take it to be looking for a description of God, and Aquinas does not think that God can be described. His view is that we can make many true statements about God. But he does not take any of them to be descriptions in the most common sense of the word (as we saw in Chapter 8 and, from time to time, in a number of other preceding chapters). Yet, just as he thinks that we can say things about God which are true, though also beyond our comprehension, he believes that we can speak truly of God incarnate without ascribing to ourselves a knowledge of what is actually there as God becomes incarnate. Aquinas is, for example, clear that, if to say 'God is X' or 'A human being is X' cannot be true, then 'X' cannot be predicated of God incarnate. So he is also convinced that Christ is all that God is, as well as nothing less than what it takes to be human. And, to someone who thinks that this cannot be so, his basic response is: 'You have to be wrong. But explain yourself, and let us discuss the matter further.'

In other words, Aquinas has what we might take to be both a closed and an open mind when it comes to the belief that the Word became flesh (John 1:14). He starts from it and is certain that it cannot be false. But he is prepared to say why he thinks that it is not certainly false. He is even prepared to concede that some traditional ways of talking about the Incarnation might be subject to revision. For example, he suggests we might think twice before agreeing that Christ, as man, is an independent person.

The word 'person' naturally conjures up the notion of a human being, with a human personality. But can God incarnate be such a thing? Aquinas thinks not. If we take 'person' to mean 'human being', then he emphatically agrees that Christ is a person (and that God is, therefore, a person) since Christ is a human being.

But, so he notes, 'Christ, as man, is a subject or person' could be taken to mean that 'the human nature of Christ ought to have its own personality, having its causal origin in the human nature' (ST 3a, 16,12). And, he continues, 'in this sense, Christ, as man, is not a person; for his human nature does not exist by itself apart from the divine nature, as would be required if it were to have its own personality'. He means that we shall be thinking to no good effect if we try to talk of the Incarnation while drawing only on what we know people to be. He means that Christ's human nature does not define his existence in the sense that there is an existence of Christ according to his humanity and another according to his divinity.

For Aquinas, Christ is one existence, divine and human. Some thinkers have tried to defend belief in the Incarnation by suggesting ways in which we can make sense of it by thinking of what might be possible for people. It has been suggested, for example, that God incarnate might have been a human being, part of whose mind worked one way (divinely), while another part worked differently. According to Aquinas, however, to think of God incarnate is, most definitely, not to think simply of what is conceivable for people. With his human nature, says Aquinas, God the Son does not 'acquire a new personal existence, but simply a new relation of his already existing personal existence to the human nature' (ST 3a 17,2). Aquinas is therefore happy to deny that Christ is not a person as a man. He is a person since he is God the Word. And Aquinas is happy to agree that he would have been just as much such had he been God the Father or God the Holy Spirit, each of whom, in his view, could have become incarnate, so far as mere mortals can surmise (cf. ST 3a, 3,1).

AND WHY DOES IT MATTER?

Yet, why should it be thought that the Incarnation is of any special significance to us? What can we draw from the teaching that Christ is God? According to Aquinas, 'if one earnestly and devoutly weighs the mysteries of the Incarnation, one will find so great a depth of wisdom that it exceeds human knowledge' (SC IV, 54). He does, however, think it possible to give some account of the importance of the Incarnation. His basic position is that, by virtue of God incarnate, we are united to God as to a loving friend. One might naturally suppose that the gulf between people and God is too great for them to come together in any way. And one might, therefore, conclude that it could never make sense to speak of God truly loving people since they are in no way equal to him. For Aquinas, however, to believe in God incarnate is to believe that God has, indeed, found something like an equal in people.

Aquinas is confident that we can sensibly ascribe love to God just by reflecting on the created order, for he thinks that love goes with will and that God must be said to will. Why? Because will is nothing but desire for what one takes to be good, because God knows the perfect good, which is himself, and because God is therefore drawn to it. He loves it. He delights in it. Aquinas never supposes that knowledge in God is like knowledge in us. He argues, for example, that God's knowledge cannot depend on what is not God and that it cannot be acquired, lost, or arrived at by sensory awareness or inference (cf. ST Ia, 14,1–7, DV II, 1, 13, and 14). Yet, since knowledge is what we have as we transcend our material limitations,

Aquinas thinks that it cannot be lacking in God. For him, knowledge is nothing but existence not confined to matter (it is nothing but form without matter). And, since he takes God to be wholly non-material, he argues (following his policy of seeking to note what God cannot be) that there must, therefore, be knowledge in God (or, rather, that God must be Knowledge, pure and simple). 'Since God is immaterial in the highest degree', he says, 'it follows that he has knowledge in the highest degree' (ST Ia, 14,1; cf. ST Ia, 7,1 and SG I, 44). And since perfectly to know is perfectly to know what is perfectly good, Aquinas also thinks it follows that God knows what is good and, therefore, is drawn to it. As we have seen, Aquinas takes goodness to be what we aim at insofar as we will. So he finds it natural to conclude that God has will since God knows, and is therefore drawn to, what is perfectly good (i.e. himself). And he takes this to mean that there is love in God. 'Wherever there is appetite or will', he observes, 'there must be love' (ST Ia, 20,1).

In terms of this account, however, God is clearly loving nothing other than himself. He is an eternal and self-contained loving of eternal and perfect goodness. One might say that if God has made creatures, then he must surely love them. And Aquinas agrees that God can be said to do so since creatures are all, somehow, good, and since God is essentially a lover of what is good (or 'Goodness-Loving Itself'). Yet he does not therefore concede that God can intelligibly be thought to be, as one might put it, 'in love with' any creature.

I love Smokey. I also love good literature, good meals, good wine, good holidays, and a good night's sleep. But I would never say that I am *in love* with such things. For I take being in love to imply equality (cf. ST 2a2ae, 25,3). We naturally speak of people as being in love with each other, and of them as giving themselves in love to each other. We do not naturally speak of people as being in love with their cats, or with books, meals, and so on. When we are thinking of mature, adult love (the sort of thing that poets like John Donne write about so effectively), we have in mind a relation between equals. And this, Aquinas believes, is something that could never be thought to obtain between God and creatures simply on the basis of what can be said of God as we reflect on the fact that God is the Creator. We might, he agrees, speak of God as being good to creatures insofar as he gives them what is good for them. And, since he does this, we might even say that God loves creatures, just as we might say that I love Smokey since I feed him so regularly. But we have no warrant for any suggestion to the effect that God might deem creatures to be equal to himself. We have no warrant for suggesting that God might be in love with a creature as people can be in love with each other. We have no warrant for supposing that God might take a creature to be in any way on a level with himself.

But that, Aquinas holds, is precisely what we *can* suppose in the light of the Incarnation. For he takes this to show that God loves people as he loves himself. Aquinas relishes passages in the New Testament such as the one in which Jesus says to his disciples 'As the Father has loved me, so have I loved you' (John 15:9). And, since he believes that Jesus is God the Son, he concludes that people are loved by God, not just as creatures, but as what God loves insofar as he loves himself. Or, to put it another way, Aquinas teaches that people can share in what the Trinity is. 'The human mind and will', he says, 'could never imagine, understand, or ask that God become man, and that man become God and a sharer in the divine nature. But he has done this in us by his power, and it was accomplished in the Incarnation of his Son' (CE 3,5). How so? Through what Aquinas calls grace, our concern in the next two chapters.

18

Nature Enabled

If you want to know what Aquinas takes the significance of the Incarnation to be, you are going to have to spend a lot of time reading through many pages of his writings. For it is not easy to summarize his reflections on God incarnate, which are numerous and which appear in a number of different texts. There is, however, an interesting chapter in the *Summa contra Gentiles* in which Aquinas tries briefly to state why it is good that God became one of us. Here (SG IV, 54), he says that we should rejoice in the Incarnation since it shows:

1. that humanity and divinity are not so distant as one might naturally suppose simply by accepting that God is our creator and that we are his creatures;
2. that people should not downgrade themselves so as to grovel before angels, or demons, or any non-human creature;
3. that God has taught us what our reason cannot discover;
4. that God has shown that he truly loves us as equals, not just as things he has made;
5. that God forgives our faults and wills to draw all of us to himself.

Aquinas does not elaborate on these points in the chapter to which I am now referring. He offers them as a kind of abridgement, as a sketch to be subsequently amplified. Yet they effectively encapsulate the whole range of his thinking when it comes to the significance of the Incarnation.

Do these points have a common theme? They seem to, since all of them imply that, because of the Incarnation, people can take themselves to be other than they might suppose when considering themselves simply as human beings. Aquinas appears to be suggesting that people can be more than merely human. Yet, what could he have in mind in making such a suggestion? To appreciate the nature of his answer to this question, we now need to follow him further when it comes to what he takes people to be.

PEOPLE AS PEOPLE

In one place, Aquinas says that it is dangerous to claim fully to understand the essence of a fly (AC I). Not surprisingly, therefore, he lays no claim to know what, in detail, is and is not possible when it comes to human beings. As we saw in Chapters 11–13, however, he does think that we can know quite a lot about them: that they are, for example, living animals with understanding and the ability to choose, and that they are capable of acquiring virtues and vices. According to Aquinas, virtues are dispositions which enable people to act well, and vices are dispositions which help them to act badly. Yet what does 'well' and 'badly' mean in this context?

Some would say that the words signify nothing but matters of autobiography when it comes to those who use them. On such an account, to say that X acts well or that X acts badly is merely to express how we feel about the actions of X. And Aquinas can make sense of this use of 'acts well' and 'acts badly' when thinking of things such as artefacts. In his view, these can do well or badly, and whether they do so or not depends on nothing but what their makers or users want them to be. He thinks, for example, that, if I produce an object to stop the door from closing, then it does its job well if it does just that. Someone else, liking it as an ornament, might think that it does its job well just because it looks good on a shelf. And Aquinas would have no problem with that position either. He would say: 'If that is what you are looking for in a good ornament, then that is exactly what it is.'

Yet Aquinas is also at pains to distinguish between people and artefacts. He accepts that people can sometimes be compared with artefacts since they are often described with reference to some special function in society which they happen to have, as when we speak of them being television reporters or traffic wardens (cf. Chapter 3). People, says Aquinas, are neither of these things *naturally*. And to speak of them acting well or badly as reporters or wardens is only to speak in terms of human conventions or decisions as to what counts as 'well' and 'bad' with respect to a function determined by us. But Aquinas also thinks that people are *naturally* human beings, and that there are ways in which they can be said to act well or badly that have nothing to do with what we happen to want of them in terms of what might be laid out in, say, a job description. Aquinas maintains that people can act well or badly regardless of how they feel about their own actions and regardless of how others feel about them. He also holds that people can act well or badly regardless of a convention when it comes to deciding between the good and the less good.

Why? Because he thinks, as we saw in Chapters 12 and 14, that goodness is what is desirable, and because he also holds that what is desirable for people is not a matter of our feelings or conventions. You may happen to enjoy having pneumonia, but it still remains the case that pneumonia is bad for you. You may take pleasure in your heart attack, but it still remains the case that it is bad for you to have a damaged heart. And Aquinas holds that there are some fairly straightforward ways of deciding whether or not someone is disposed to act well or badly.

Suppose that I am bad at working out what I and others need in order to flourish as people. And suppose that I regularly disregard reason, or proceed without it, as I go about my business. Then, so Aquinas would say, I would lack prudence or good sense (cf. ST 2a2ae, 47–56).

Or suppose that I incline to act by seeking to undermine others as I live with them in society. Then, so Aquinas would say, I would be lacking in justice (cf. ST 2a2ae, 58).

Or suppose that I am unreasonably frightened by certain things, or unable to face and deal with what is truly threatening. Then, so Aquinas would say, I would lack courage (cf. ST 2a2ae, 123).

Or suppose that I eat and drink, or refrain from eating and drinking, so as to damage my health. Then, so Aquinas would say, I would lack temperateness or moderation (cf. ST 2a2ae, 141).

Aquinas, of course, does not mean that I shall automatically do well if I am prudent, just, temperate, and courageous. He knows well enough that prudent people can be murdered precisely because they are prudent. And he is perfectly aware that the same goes for those who are just, temperate, and courageous. Yet he is also convinced that prudence, justice, temperateness, and courage are dispositions which people can be said to need. I need to be able to see. If I am blind, then I am maimed as a human being. But what if my seeing results in my death because I witness a crime done by someone who kills me just because I am a witness to it? Does that mean that I do not, considered as a human being, need to see? Does it mean that blindness is good for me as a human being? Obviously not. So Aquinas holds that people need to be prudent, just, temperate, and courageous. He agrees that to be so may lead to their destruction. Yet it is also, he thinks, what they need to be considered as people rather than as the victims of circumstances.

Aquinas often makes this point by saying that their human goodness lies in their having 'cardinal virtues' (cf. ST Ia2ae, 61,1 and 2). And he takes these to be what people can come to have as parts of the world in which things with natures act in terms of their natures. In his view, the lucky person is one who has been brought up in an environment which successfully fosters the development of cardinal virtues. The right kind of upbringing, coupled with certain genetic factors, can make a child someone who is naturally disposed to read books. And Aquinas thinks that the right kind of environment, or the right kind of background, might make someone naturally disposed to be prudent, just, temperate, and courageous.

Yet what if the environment is not there, or what if it does not successfully foster the development of the cardinal virtues in some individual? Then, Aquinas holds, it is, in principle, open to the person in question to acquire them by deliberate effort. 'In principle' because, of course, circumstances can vary and because some of them might render people incapable of making anything remotely describable as a human choice (cf. ST Ia2ae, 63,1).

In short, Aquinas holds that possession of the cardinal virtues is not miraculous. His view is that, as human beings, we have it in our power to inculcate them in others or to be somehow effective when it comes to their having them. And he thinks that we might be able to foster them in ourselves. But he also believes that there are virtues which cannot be explained only in terms of what people are or can do simply as human beings, or in terms of anything else in nature. For, as well as believing in cardinal virtues, Aquinas also believes in what he calls 'theological' virtues, which he thinks of in somewhat the same way that he thinks of miracles and human free choices.

THEOLOGICAL VIRTUES

Aquinas does not think of human free choices as strictly miraculous since he takes them to be ascribable to people. In one sense, however, for him they are miraculous since he does not take them to be explicable in terms of the agency of anything in nature other than the person whose actions they are. When it comes to free human choices, he holds, the only cause of them, apart from the person whose choices they are, is God (which is not, of course, to say that people can make free choices without them and their environment being of a certain kind). With human free choices, says Aquinas, we have the direct creative activity of God, not the effect of a creature (cf. Chapter 13). And that is how he thinks when it comes to theological virtues.

For Aquinas, these are dispositions which cannot be accounted for naturalistically. They cannot arise in people by inheritance or education. Nor can they be acquired by personal effort. They direct us, says Aquinas, to a supernatural end, and they are not themselves explicable in naturalistic terms. 'People', he writes, 'are perfected by virtue towards those actions by which they are directed towards happiness.' Yet, he adds, human happiness is twofold: 'One depends on human nature, and this is something that people can achieve through their own resources [while] the other is a happiness surpassing human nature, which people can arrive at only by the power of God, by a kind of participation in divinity.' And this participation, Aquinas argues, can be brought about only by God. 'Because such happiness goes beyond what can be produced by human nature,' he says, 'people cannot arrive at it by virtue of what they naturally are; they have to receive from God that by which they may be led to supernatural happiness' (ST Ia2ae, 62,1). Or, as Aquinas immediately goes on to say, they need theological virtues and not just the cardinal ones.

Why does he say so? Aristotle says nothing comparable, though his teaching is much the same as Aquinas's when it comes to the topic of cardinal virtues, as one can see from the *Nicomachean Ethics*, from which Aquinas often approvingly quotes. So, what leads Aquinas to speak of the need for theological virtues as well as cardinal ones? The answer lies in what I reported of his teaching in the previous two chapters.

Aristotle has no belief in God as a Trinity. And he has no notion of God becoming human so that people may come to share in the divine life. Aquinas, however, does. He also thinks that there can be no sharing in the life of the Trinity unless God brings about in us more than what Aristotle would have taken people to be able to bring about simply considered as human beings. Aquinas introduces the notion of theological virtues since he believes that God is prepared to give us more than we are, or are capable of achieving, simply by being human. And he does so because of the way in which he reads the Bible, especially the New Testament. In particular, he does so because he takes the significance of the Incarnation to lie in what we saw him saying at the beginning of this chapter: that God offers people something they cannot achieve on their own.

Aquinas, of course, thinks that there is a sense in which we can achieve nothing on our own. For him, we cannot exist from moment to moment unless God makes us to be. Yet things can be what they are even though they are helped to become what they cannot be by nature. Smokey (once again) has all sorts of natural abilities. Yet, what if Smokey comes to be flying through the air faster than the speed of sound? Is that explicable in terms of his nature? Hardly. He needs a Concorde to help him to do that. And Aquinas thinks that we need help to become sharers in the divine nature. We are not naturally divine: something has to help us to become so. But what?

According to Aquinas, the answer has to be 'Nothing other than God' or, as he sometimes says, 'Nothing other than grace' since to say that people are graced by God is to say 'that an effect of God's gratuitous will is present' in them (cf. ST Ia2ae, 110,2). And it is with this thought in mind that Aquinas's discussion of theological virtues proceeds. There is, he says, 'a general love, by which God loves all things that are'. Yet, and with an eye on theological virtues, he adds that there is also 'a special love, by which God draws the rational creature above its natural condition to have a part in the divine goodness' (ST Ia2ae, 110,1).

BACK TO CHRIST

Aquinas holds that there are three theological virtues: faith, hope, and charity; and we shall see what he takes them to be in Chapter 19. At this point, however, it is worth noting how he understands them with respect to God incarnate, for he cannot make sense of them apart from what, in his view, Christ is all about. According to Aquinas, we are brought to what our nature cannot achieve (we are graced) by God, who became a man. He takes Christ to have taught that we are able to be more than merely human. And he takes Christ to be a cause of the fact that people become so. But why does he hold these opinions? What, in his view, is the achievement of Christ?

Some of his readers have taken him to have held that it chiefly consists in mollifying an angry God. According to Aquinas, 'the work of the Incarnation was directed chiefly to the restoration of the human race through the removal of sin' (ST 3a, 1,5). He also says that God 'was appeased' by the passion of Christ (ST 3a, 49,5). Putting such statements together, some have read Aquinas as viewing the Incarnation, and, especially, the death of Christ, as a calming-down operation, with Christ as the calmer and God as the calmed.

By now, however, the reader should be able to recognize immediately that this cannot be what Aquinas thinks. For him, talk of God's anger is nothing but metaphor. It is on a level with talk of God being a mighty fortress or having an outstretched arm. And, given his teaching on the Trinity, there is, for Aquinas, *no* God *over and against* Christ. Aquinas certainly believes that the Incarnation is a remedy for sin. Yet he also holds that the consequences of sin could have been dealt with without it (cf. 3a, 1,2). And he speaks of its effects by drawing on a whole range of different images or models rather than by being hypnotized by one.

We are brought to God through Christ, he says, since Christ was a teacher, a priest, head of the Church, a meritorious human being, a remedy for sin, a loving God, a sacrifice, a brother, a victim, a means of redemption, an example, and a means of satisfaction. Some have insisted that God cannot draw us to himself until his Son has been tortured to death for us, but this is not Aquinas's view. 'Simply and absolutely speaking,' he says, 'God could have freed us [from the effects of sin] otherwise than by Christ's passion, for nothing is impossible with God' (ST 3a, 46,2). He also observes that 'the Incarnation was not necessary for the restoration of human nature, since by his infinite power God had many other ways to accomplish this end' (ST 3a, 1,2), and also that God is drawing us to him by the mere fact of the Incarnation, regardless of the details of the biography of Jesus. 'From the moment of his conception', he says, 'Christ merited eternal salvation for us' (3a, 48,1).

When he speaks of eternal salvation, Aquinas is thinking of a union with God which raises people to a share in the life of the Trinity. And, when it comes to the topic of grace and the work of Christ, the key to his thinking lies in his insistence that Christ is truly divine. He speaks of Christ's achievement by drawing on many models (just as he does when trying to say what God is), but his appeal to them is always governed by the conviction that Jesus of Nazareth was what God looks like when projected onto the screen of human history (which is, perhaps, better compared to a rubbish dump than to a screen).

In Christ, Aquinas finds someone who views people as friends rather than as servants. In Christ, he finds someone who offers God's forgiveness to sinners who repent. In Christ, he finds someone who is willing to die for what he stands for, someone who does so patiently and who can, therefore, be thought of as cancelling any debt that might be thought of as owed by humanity to God (even though God can waive debts by fiat since he is Justice Itself and is not bound by a standard of justice over and against him and to which he is bound). In Christ, he finds someone who is perfectly human, someone who is what people are meant to be. In Christ, he finds someone who can say that we come to the Father through him (cf. John 14:6) since he is the way in which the Father comes to us. So in Christ he finds humanity loved and accepted by God. And this is why he thinks that people can be more than merely human.

In Aquinas's view, those who love Christ for what he is are well on the way to being more than can be captured by any scientific account of what human beings are and are capable of. 'The gift of grace', he says, 'surpasses every capacity of created nature, since it is nothing other than a certain participation in the divine nature, which surpasses every other nature' (ST Ia2ae, 112,1). And it is with this conviction in mind that he writes about faith, hope, and charity, as we shall now see.

19

Faith, Hope, and Charity

According to Aquinas, voluntary behaviour is a tending to what one takes to be good. He thinks that, if people are acting voluntarily, it always makes sense to ask them 'Why are you doing that?', meaning 'What good are you aiming at?' Since Aquinas thinks that God is Goodness Itself, one might suppose that he would also hold that all human willing is an aiming at nothing less than God. And he does, in a sense, believe that this is so. For he takes God, as Goodness Itself, to be what everyone ultimately desires, whether they realize so or not. 'The object of the will, that is the human appetite, is', he says, 'the Good without reserve . . . Clearly, then, nothing can satisfy our will except such goodness, which is found, not in anything created, but in God alone' (ST Ia2ae, 2,8).

Yet, reasonably enough, Aquinas also thinks that, in being drawn to what we take to be good, we are not necessarily aiming at God's goodness consciously or explicitly. We could be, he agrees. But he also assumes that we might not, which is why he is prepared to talk about human action, and to evaluate it, with no special reference to God (as he does, for example, in *Summa theologiae* Ia2ae, 16–23 and 36–43). Aquinas is someone who can accurately be described as what some of our contemporaries would naturally call a 'moral philosopher'. His view is that reasonable people, regardless of divine revelation, can arrive at a sensible understanding of what human action amounts to, and of how people ought to behave. That is why he takes Aristotle to be a serious guide when it comes to what is and what is not good for people.

For Aristotle, however, the true good for people is not what Aquinas takes it to be. Aristotle says that sound ethical thinking should be focused on *eudaimonia*, which we might translate as 'flourishing', 'well-being', or 'happiness'. Yet Aristotle's *eudaimonia* signifies something which people can achieve simply by drawing on their natural, human resources. And Aquinas thinks that people are capable of more than this. For him, the true good for people is not *eudaimonia* but *beatitudo*, which he takes to be human flourishing, well-being, or happiness *in union with God* (cf. ST Ia2ae, 3,8).

As a disciple of Aristotle, and yet focusing on what he takes people to be able to achieve on their own, Aquinas has much to say on what they can and ought to do, and on what they should aim at being, even though they might perish in the attempt. But he also believes that there are ways of being for people which derive from, and which lead them to, something other than what people naturally are. And this is what he has in mind when he speaks of faith, hope, and charity. For Aquinas, these virtues are subsequent to any identifiable by philosophy (cf. ST 2a2ae, 4,7).

Why? Because he takes them to be more than what we need to be as good as we can, given only our natural resources, and because he takes them to be what we need in order to share God's life, which is not produced or producible by anything in nature. He sometimes calls them 'supernatural virtues', which sounds somewhat spooky, and which might be taken to suggest that he thinks of them as external to people or as somehow at odds with their humanity. For Aquinas, however, the theological (or supernatural) virtues are nothing more than ways in which people can be helped to be more than a philosopher can expect or prove them to be. I am not capable of flying to the moon; but give me a space craft and I might get there. Would my subsequently being on the moon be external to me? Would it make me less human than I now am? Obviously not. And Aquinas reasons that the same would be true if I came to possess the theological virtues. These, he thinks, are the work of grace. But he takes grace to enhance or to build on nature, not to add something alien to it or to destroy it. 'The full development of the rational creature', says Aquinas, 'consists not only in what is proper to it in keeping with its own nature, but also in what can be ascribed to it by reason of a certain supernatural share in the divine good' (ST 2a2ae, 2,3).

FAITH

One can quickly see how Aquinas develops this conclusion by turning to what he says on the topic of faith, which he takes to be the first of the theological virtues. For he compares it with what is utterly familiar, while adding that it takes people beyond that to which the familiar can lead us. He says that it is like opinion, on the one hand, and like knowledge, on the other, though its object is not knowable. According to Aquinas, people with faith are like those who know. The only difference is that they do *not* know. In his view, they are also like people holding an opinion, though they do *not* hold an opinion.

To appreciate what Aquinas means here, we might start by noting that knowledge, for him, is not just a psychological state. He would say that whether or not I have knowledge is not to be determined by how I happen to think. For this reason, and for others, he sharply distinguishes between knowledge and belief. The fact that I am convinced of something does not, he thinks, mean that I have knowledge. Suppose, for example, that I feel certain that water is a metal. In Aquinas's view, my feelings here do nothing to show that water is truly metallic. For him, knowledge occurs only when a grasp of truth occurs.

And when does he take that to happen? He typically says that we have knowledge only when we see what something is and why it is as it is. On his account, a paradigm example of the knowable is that human beings are rational animals. Yet, what of knowing that Smokey is sitting on my lap? Strictly speaking, Aquinas would deny that this is something that we can know. For Smokey is an individual cat, and Aquinas does not think that individuals, as such, are intelligible to us. 'Smokey is sitting on Brian's lap' seems innocuous enough as a proposition, and one might readily think that it is either true or false, and also that someone can know whether or not it is true or false. According to Aquinas, however, 'Smokey is sitting on Brian's lap' needs a bit of unpacking.

Let us begin with 'Smokey' and 'Brian'. These are names of bodily individuals. So Aquinas, as we saw in Chapter 3, would immediately say that what they signify is not intelligible and, therefore, not knowable.

What about 'is sitting on' and 'lap'? We can understand what these expressions signify without reference to any particular material individual, so we can, Aquinas holds, understand what they signify.

Yet where does this leave us? For Aquinas, it leaves us using names so as to construct a proposition which might be true. But it does not, he thinks, leave us with knowledge since there are too many gaps when it comes to what is intelligible.

Aquinas does not deny that I can know that Smokey is sitting on my lap, for he thinks that I can have physical contact with Smokey, that Smokey can impinge on my senses. But what does 'I know that Smokey is sitting on my lap' mean over and above the fact that I am undergoing sense impressions caused by a cat on my lap? For Aquinas, it means something like 'There is a cat on my lap' and that I cannot know that this is the case unless I know what cats and laps are. In this sense, he holds, knowledge is always of universals, not particulars. And, as a consequence, he takes it to reflect necessity rather than contingency. It is not accidental that cats are what they are essentially, for they would not otherwise be cats. And, Aquinas reasons, that which is knowable is also that which is necessarily what it is given that it is. He is convinced that everything is what it is and not anything else. He believes that things have essences. So his view is that what is knowable about them is never accidental to them. To know what something is, he thinks, is to know what it is essentially. And he says that a similar necessity is involved in knowledge which is not just a matter of knowing what something is.

Suppose I argue that any horse has four legs and that Dobbin has four legs since Dobbin is a horse. Can you doubt that Dobbin has four legs if you agree that he is a horse and that nothing is a horse if it lacks four legs? Obviously not. It is, of course, true that a three-legged horse is just as much a horse as a four-legged one. But that is not what is now in question. The issue is one of valid inference. And, according to Aquinas, this has to do with necessity, as is the case when it comes to things being what they essentially are. In his view, we might have knowledge when we see that a conclusion is entailed by premises on which it is based.

But he also thinks that we might not. For, what if one or more of our premises are false? In that case, he holds, we would lack knowledge when it comes to what is actually the case, even though we would have knowledge when it comes to matters of logic. Wittgenstein said that logical truths are not matters of fact. 'The limits of my language', he observes, 'are the limits of my world', which he goes on to explain by asserting, 'Logic pervades the world: the limits of the world are also its limits. So we cannot say in logic, "The world has this in it, and this, but not that"' (*Tractatus* 5.6 and 5.61). And Aquinas has a similar view. According to him, we can know what follows logically from what without knowing what is actually the case (what is there for logic to get to work on). Yet he also holds that to start from premises which we know to express what is actually the case, or what cannot but be the case, and validly to draw a conclusion from them can, indeed, give us knowledge.

But what knowledge of God can we arrive at on this basis? Not much, Aquinas thinks (and as we have seen him thinking). His line is that we can know that God exists since we need to ask certain questions, like 'How come something rather than nothing?' And we can know what God cannot be: but we cannot know what it is to be God.

In that case, however, what should we say when it comes to Christians? They do not just say that God exists. They speak of God being Father, Son, and Spirit. And they speak of God incarnate. Can they know that what they say is true? We have already seen that Aquinas thinks that they cannot, and why. Now we need to note that according to Aquinas they might proclaim what they believe on the basis of faith, which, for him, is different from knowledge, but intelligible with an eye on it.

For what is going on when we know? Aquinas takes the known and the knower to be like iron filings and a magnet. He thinks that knowers just automatically zoom in on objects of knowledge. In his view, I cannot help conceding the cogency of a formally valid argument, on the supposition that I understand it. He also thinks that I cannot but concede that, for example, all whales are mammals, on the supposition that I understand what whales are. But must I necessarily concede that the Christian Gospel is true? Aquinas's answer is 'No'. And it is for this reason that he takes faith to be a theological virtue. The truths of the Christian faith, as proclaimed in texts like the Apostles' Creed are, he holds, not ones which we can show to be true given some knowledge of what something is or in the light of a valid argument proceeding from what is known.

But should we conclude that those who accept them are being unreasonable? Aquinas thinks not since, as I noted in Chapter 5, he sees nothing intrinsically irrational in believing without knowing. In his last notes *On Certainty* (Oxford, 1974), Wittgenstein writes: 'The child learns by believing the adult. Doubt comes after belief . . . The difficulty is to realize the groundlessness of our believing' (§§160–166). Wittgenstein's point is that, far from being manifestly irrational, believing without knowing is essential when it comes to developing a system of knowledge. And Aquinas is of a similar mind. He is perfectly aware that beliefs can be mistaken. But he does not therefore conclude that it is always intellectually dubious for people to accept that such and such is the case, even though they do not know that it is (cf. Chapter 5). In particular, and anticipating Wittgenstein's teaching example, he thinks that one might be perfectly reasonable in accepting that such and such is the case on the testimony of another. Indeed, he thinks, this is really what faith essentially is. For Aquinas, faith is believing God. And, though he holds that one might reasonably disbelieve what some people tell us, he takes it that one has no reason for disbelieving God. The content of Christian faith, he says, is taught by God. So its source is reliable and its content true. 'Faith', he asserts, 'assents to anything only because it is revealed by God, and so faith rests upon the divine truth itself' (ST 2a2ae, 1,1; cf. DV XIV, 8). Those with faith, he adds, are 'learners with God as their teacher' (ST 2a2ae, 2,3).

And how do people get taught by God? In the same way, Aquinas answers, that they get taught in general – by someone telling them something. And here he understands 'someone' and 'telling' in a literal sense. People have declared that God has 'spoken' to them since they have enjoyed some extraordinary 'religious' experience. For Aquinas, however, God has spoken to everyone, and has done so just as we speak to each other: by being a talking human being. In other words, Aquinas's account of the virtue of faith is utterly dependent on his belief in the Incarnation. As we have seen (cf. Chapter 16), he takes Christ to be 'the first and chief teacher of the faith' (ST 3a, 7,7). And Aquinas thinks that Christ is able to be such precisely because he is God, from which Aquinas takes it that Christ had no faith (cf. ST 3a, 7,3). Someone with faith, he thinks, believes and does not know. But since Christ is God, says Aquinas, he knew as God knows and is therefore in a position to teach with authority.

Yet, how does Aquinas know this? The answer, of course, is that he does not claim to do so. Instead, he turns to the life and work of Christ as recorded in the gospels, and he believes both that Christ is God and that what he teaches is true. One might expect him to hold that faith is a virtue since Christ is evidently God and since his teaching cannot, therefore, be sensibly rejected. Yet that is not his view. Since Aquinas maintains that the divinity of Christ is not provable or demonstrable, he thinks that it can be intelligibly denied. And he is of the same opinion when it comes to all that he deems to be part of the content of faith. Making a sharp distinction between faith and knowledge, Aquinas is clear that assent to the truths of faith is not a matter of intellectual coercion, as, for example, when one cannot but conclude that, if all cats are carnivores and if Smokey is a cat, then Smokey is a carnivore.

In fact, says Aquinas, faith is really midway between knowing, on the one hand, and entertaining a supposition or opinion, on the other. Suppose I know that such and such is the case. Then, Aquinas reasons, I am certain of it, and my certainty is shown in how I talk and behave. Yet I might only conjecture or postulate that such and such is the case. And here Aquinas would say that I lack certainty because I lack knowledge, and that this too will show itself in how I speak and act. He means that, while my certainty 'that p' will lead me unhesitatingly to assert 'that p', my surmising or supposing 'that p' will not. And, with these points in mind, Aquinas concludes that faith is like knowledge since those who have it display a degree of conviction which is not to be found in those with suppositions, opinions, conjectures, and the like; and also that faith is like conjecture, and so on, since those who have it lack the insight or understanding which knowledge comprises. 'Among acts of the intellect', says Aquinas, some include a firm assent without pondering, as when people think about what they know . . . Other mental acts are marked by a pondering that is inconclusive, lacking firm assent . . . The act of believing, however, is firmly attached to one alternative, and, in this respect, the believer is in the same state of mind as one who has knowledge or understanding. Yet the knowledge of believers is not completed by a clear seeing, and, in this respect, they are like people having a doubt, a suspicion, or an opinion. (ST 2a2ae, 2,1)

Yet why should faith, so understood, be thought of as taking us beyond that of which we are naturally capable? If I tell you that I had eggs for breakfast and if you firmly believe me just because I am telling you, then you would seem to have something like what Aquinas has in mind when he speaks about faith. And your doing so is hardly remarkable. Yet, for Aquinas there *is* something remarkable when it comes to those with faith. For he thinks that they entertain truths which cannot be known by human reason (and are therefore in possession of what is divinely revealed).

According to Aquinas, the object of faith is God (cf. ST 2a2ae, 1,1). For him, the faithful believe God, just as you might believe me. Yet you can believe me only by believing what I say. Your believing me involves you in accepting what I assert. It has propositional content. If you believe me, then, on my say-so, you believe that such and such is or is not the case. And, with this point in mind, Aquinas insists that those with faith believe what can be stated propositionally (cf. ST 2a2ae, 2,6 and DV XIV, 11). In fact, he says, they believe (even if only implicitly) what is professed in texts like the Apostles' Creed. They believe *that* God is Father, Son, and Spirit, *that* Christ is God incarnate, and so on.

Yet Aquinas does not think that those with faith have a privileged understanding of God. In his view, they take to be true what they do not comprehend. And, on his account, the Christian creeds do not supply a picture of God. Rather, he says, they provide guidelines for thinking and behaving. If I (with no medical knowledge) am told that I have cancer and if I believe the doctor who tells me so, then I am in possession of a truth on which I shall, inevitably, reflect and act. According to Aquinas, it is something like this with those who have faith. His view is that the faithful possess what they cannot acquire by their own efforts: truths about God, and truths about themselves which are bound up with what God has revealed of himself.

Yet, cannot believers come to have faith for reasons which are naturally explicable? Aquinas thinks that someone might come to proclaim the Christian faith only because of what nature can accomplish. He does not put it in quite these terms, but he thinks that if, for example, you brainwash me so that I end up reciting the Apostles' Creed, then there is a natural explanation for what is going on with me, just as there would be if you wired me to a machine which made me mouth the words 'Jesus is God Incarnate'. For Aquinas, however, faith is not explicable (or, at least, not fully explicable) in naturalistic terms since it is voluntary, and since only God can bring it about that one *voluntarily* subscribes to the truths of faith. Knowledge, he thinks, compels assent, while what is believed in faith does not. 'To be imperfect as knowledge', he says, 'is of the very essence of faith' (ST Ia2ae, 67,3).

So faith, Aquinas concludes, is voluntary (cf. ST 2a2ae, 2,1 and DV XIV, 2). And if it is voluntary, then its source is divine, not created. As we have seen, Aquinas takes human freedom to derive from God. When it comes to faith, his position is that this also derives from God. Yet faith, he maintains, differs from some human choosing since it results in assent to what is true of God and is, therefore, perfective of the one who has it. Faith is a virtue, says Aquinas, since it leads us into truth and, therefore, is good for us (cf. ST 2a2ae, 4,5). It is theological, or 'supernatural', since what it leads us to is God's work in us, both when it comes to what is believed (this not being knowable by human reason) and with respect to its cause.

Aquinas, however, does not want to say that the virtue of faith simply consists in merely believing the truths of the Christian religion. He distinguishes between 'formed' faith (the genuine article) and 'unformed' faith, which he takes to be anything but a virtue. Suppose that I take no pleasure in my belief in Christian doctrine. Suppose that I despise what God is as Christians take him to be on the basis of revelation. In that case, Aquinas thinks, there is belief, but it is dead since it does not lead to a willing acceptance of what God is all about (cf. ST 2a2ae, 5,2 and DV XIV, 6). Or, as Aquinas also says, the virtue of faith is inseparable from the virtue of charity. To have faith, he holds, is to be drawn to the ultimate good, which is nothing less than God. And, he reasons, one cannot be so drawn if one is not, all along, somehow in love with what God essentially is. Since Aquinas takes God to be essentially loving, he naturally concludes that those with faith must love as God loves. They must, he says, want the divine good, which is 'the proper object of charity' (ST 2a2ae, 4,3).

HOPE

Before he turns explicitly to the virtue of charity, however, Aquinas always speaks first about the theological virtue of hope, which, for him, is unintelligible apart from faith (just as faith is unintelligible apart from charity). And that is so because of the way in which he contrasts faith and knowledge. Faith, he thinks, is not a matter of seeing, and those who have it must therefore hope and not know. Faith, says Aquinas, 'gives rise to hope', and hope's object is 'eternal beatitude' and 'the divine assistance . . . both of which are made manifest to us by faith' (ST 2a2ae, 17,7). The difference between faith and hope, he thinks, lies only in the fact that hope is for what is future to us ('eternal beatitude').

And why is it virtuous? Because, says Aquinas, it is a matter of trusting God. A virtue, he argues, makes its possessor good and his or her activity sound. And hope, he thinks, does just this since it keeps us in tune with God and with what he has revealed, and since God is our ultimate good (cf. ST 2a2ae, 17,1 and SG III, 153). One might say that there is nothing especially unusual about hope since most of us hope for lots of things. And one might wonder why Aquinas takes it to be something to which nature cannot lead us. For him, however, the theological virtue of hope is not just any old looking forward to what one does not possess: it is a looking forward to what only God can provide. And it springs from faith, which, Aquinas consistently insists, is not explicable as is something produced by created causes. Indeed, Aquinas says, the object of hope is nothing less than God. 'We should', he argues, 'hope for nothing less from God than his very self' (ST 2a2ae, 17,2).

When you come to think of it, this is quite an extraordinary thing for someone like Aquinas to claim. For, in speaking as he does, he does not mean that we should hope to be around God and to benefit from him, as, for example, members of a British Cabinet might be thought to be around and to benefit from a Prime Minister. Aquinas hopes to share in what God is by nature, and we have now seen how different he takes this to be when set beside what is created. This is what makes his teaching on hope so remarkable. And this, of course, is why he holds that the virtue of hope depends on the virtue of faith. It is also why he thinks that there is no hope and no faith without charity.

CHARITY

Important though he takes faith and hope to be, Aquinas also regards them as dispensable or undesirable. For our destiny, he thinks, is not to be eternally faithful and hopeful: it is to share God's life, in which faith and hope have no place. 'Hope will pass away in heaven', he says, 'just as faith will, and so neither of them is found in the blessed' (ST 2a2ae, 18,2; cf. Ia2ae, 67,4). Here, of course, Aquinas is echoing the teaching of St Paul (cf. 1 Corinthians 13:8–13). On Aquinas's account, we need faith and hope only as means to an end. But this is not how he views charity. For him, charity reflects what God essentially is, and so it is not to be discarded or grown out of as we come to a perfect union with him. Charity, Aquinas says, is loving as God loves. It takes us up into what God is as Father, Son, and Spirit. It raises us to the state of loving God as he loves himself, which Aquinas takes to mean that those with charity are loved *by* God as he loves himself.

But how does God love himself? According to Aquinas, he does so by eternally willing, always being at rest in, and ever delighting in absolute goodness for its own sake, not as a means to an end (cf. SG I, 90–91). And this, says Aquinas, is what charity is. It is nothing less than loving God for the goodness that he is. Yet Aquinas also holds that charity is a matter of God loving us. For he thinks that its existence in us is loved by God since God is essentially charity (cf. ST 2a2ae, 23,2 and SG IV, 21) and cannot fail to delight in the loving of God for the goodness that he is. In Aquinas's view, those with charity resemble what God is, and so they are loved by God and share in God's life.

Aquinas sometimes makes this point by saying that charity is friendship (*amicitia*) with God. In his view (as in Aristotle's), friendship involves loving others and, therefore, willing good for them, *for their own sake*. 'If what we will is our own good,' he says, 'it is a love not of friendship but of desire' (ST 2a2ae, 23,1). So friendship, for Aquinas, has a selflessness about it. It is loving others as they love themselves. Yet he holds that it is also reciprocal. He takes friends to be those who return each other's friendship. 'Good will alone', he argues, 'is not enough for friendship, for this requires a mutual loving; it is only with a friend that a friend is friendly. But such reciprocal good will is based on something in common' (ST 2a2ae, 23,1). For Aquinas, true friends have a common project. They are in tune with each other when it comes to what they want. They share a common will or goal. They are of one mind, and live and work together accordingly. And this, Aquinas insists, is exactly what is there when people have charity. For they love what God loves, and God loves them precisely because they do so. According to Aquinas, those with the virtue of charity have (albeit imperfectly) entered into what God is essentially. They are, in a sense, God's equals. Hence, for example, when he quotes Christ as saying 'No longer do I call you servants' (John 15:15), Aquinas bluntly asserts that these words 'can only be explained in terms of charity, which is, therefore, friendship' (ST 2a2ae, 23,1).

And how does this virtue show itself in those who have it? Aquinas's central answer is: by living as the gospels tell us that Christ lived and taught us to live. For him, it is really as simple as that, though he has a lot to say (much more than I can summarize here) when it comes to interpreting the teaching of Christ as recorded in the gospels. So, for example, he takes those with charity to be people who act or would want to act in accordance with what we find endorsed in the Sermon on the Mount (Matthew 5–7). He takes them to thirst for righteousness, to be peacemakers, to respect their neighbours, to place God before everything else . . . and so on.

One should also notice that he takes them to be concerned with themselves. Aquinas takes charity to include loving other people as we love ourselves. But we cannot do that if we do not love ourselves. So Aquinas concludes that charity encompasses self-love as well. It sounds odd, he admits, to speak of *amicitia* with oneself. Yet Aquinas thinks that being friends with God means loving what God loves, which includes ourselves. It even includes our bodies. 'Our bodily nature,' says Aquinas, 'far from issuing from an evil principle . . . is from God. We can therefore use it for God's service . . . Accordingly, with the same love of charity by which we love God, we also ought to love our body' (ST 2a2ae, 25,5). In the name of Christianity, people have sometimes urged that we should despise our bodies and revile what we are as physical things, with physical needs and tastes. For Aquinas, however, such a view is far too simplistic. 'Material creatures', he observes, 'are by nature good' (ST Ia, 65,2). So he finds nothing intrinsically wrong in cherishing what is material, and he thinks that it might be charitable to do so. Someone seeking death for its own sake would, he maintains, be making a big mistake.

But why should charity be thought to take us beyond what we can achieve simply as human beings? Why should it be something which only God can bring about? I have friends whom I love. So do you, I presume. There is surely nothing surprising in the fact that there is friendship. So, why does Aquinas think that we are not naturally capable of charity?

Because he holds that people with the virtue of charity are acting as those who have faith and because they are, therefore, enjoying a union with God which he might never have offered to people. As we have seen, Aquinas denies that faith is naturally explicable. We have it (if we have it) because God, and nothing else, causes us to have it, because God acts in us to make us believers. And the virtue of charity is not, Aquinas thinks, something which has to be there if it is true that human beings are there. In the twentieth century some theologians spent a lot of time worrying about whether God could have created people not destined for union with him. They especially felt that there could be no such thing as 'pure' human nature, considered in the abstract and without reference to beatitude. Well, Aquinas also holds that people are made for God (cf. ST Ia2ae, 109,3), but he does not think that they need to be beatified in order to be human. He holds that beatitude, the fruit of charity, is a gift to people, not a natural possession or something naturally acquirable. Charity, Aquinas observes, 'is our friendship for God arising from our sharing in eternal happiness, which is not a matter of natural goods but of gifts of grace . . . Consequently, charity is beyond the resources of nature and, therefore, cannot be something natural, nor acquired by natural powers, since no effect transcends its own cause' (ST 2a2ae, 24,2).

We have charity, says Aquinas, because of the work of God in us. Specifically, we have it by means of the Holy Spirit, 'who is the love of the Father and the Son' (*ibid.*). Virtues like those acknowledged by Aristotle can, Aquinas thinks, lead us to live well in the created world. But only virtues instilled by God can lead us to share in his life. As Aquinas sometimes puts it, they represent the arrival of a 'New Law', superseding the commands and injunctions found in the Old Testament, including ritual and judicial precepts (which Aquinas calls the 'Old Law').

The purpose of any law, says Aquinas, lies 'in establishing friendship, either between people, or between people and God' (ST Ia2ae, 99,2), and the Old Law did this to some extent. Yet it was very much a matter of external rules and regulations. The New Law, however, is 'instilled in our hearts'. It has its effect 'not only by indicating to us what we should do, but also by helping us to accomplish it' (ST Ia2ae, 106,1). According to Aquinas, the New Law 'consists chiefly in the grace of the Holy Spirit, which is shown forth by faith working through love . . . People become receivers of this grace through God's Son made human, whose humanity grace filled first and thence flowed forth to us' (ST Ia2ae, 108,1). To a large extent, Aquinas takes 'faith working through love' to be shown in how we act towards each other. But he also takes it to be shown in how we behave as individuals coming to God face to face and on our own, so to speak. For, as we shall see in the next chapter, Aquinas thinks that we can, in charity, address God personally and share in his love by ritual which, though resembling that envisaged in the Old Testament, also greatly exceeds it because of God's action in it.

20

Prayer and Sacraments

Aquinas seems to have liked having a regular rhythm to his day. Our sources for his life tell us that he went to Confession each morning. Then he said Mass and attended another Mass. Afterwards, his time was normally devoted to reading, writing, teaching, and praying. In the evening he attended the Office of Compline, asking God for 'a quiet night and a perfect end'. It all sounds very devout. Yet Aquinas clearly was devout. He always prayed before writing, and he prayed when he ran into any kind of difficulty. He was a rigorous and original thinker, but he did not see his relationship with God as a merely intellectual matter, as consisting, for instance, only in what he wrote and argued about God. Theologians frequently insist that faith must be a matter of personal engagement between believers and God rather than something theoretical. And that was also Aquinas's view. He thought that Christians need to live as though they really believe what they preach.

How can they do so? For Aquinas, they can do so primarily by imitating Christ, by living according to his teaching and precepts, and, if need be, by being prepared to die for them. In other words, Christians can exhibit the virtues of faith, hope, and charity. But Aquinas thinks that they can also do more: that they can practise the virtue of religion (*religio*). They can, for example, worship God and occupy themselves with rituals intended to honour him and him alone (cf. ST 2a2ae, 84 and ST 2a2ae, 81,7). Aquinas concedes that worship can lead to excess when it ends up amounting to superstition and obsession with externals (cf. ST 2a2ae, 93,2). Yet he holds that God should be worshipped since he has given us much (cf. ST 2a2ae, 80,1) and since 'he infinitely surpasses all things and exceeds them in every way' (ST 2a2ae, 81,4). Aquinas also thinks that it is appropriate for people to express their faith in religious rites and ceremonies since people are bodily beings who therefore fittingly express themselves in bodily ways (cf. ST 2a2ae, 81,7). With an eye on texts such as John 4:24 ('God is spirit, and those who worship him must worship him in spirit and truth'), Aquinas agrees that the virtue of religion is 'interior' since it consists in people acknowledging and wanting God and what he is about. Yet, he adds, 'in order to be united to God, the human mind needs to be guided by the sensible world'. 'In divine worship', says Aquinas, 'it is necessary to make use of corporeal things . . . so that our minds may be aroused to the spiritual acts which join us to God' (ST 2a2ae, 81,7). According to Aquinas, those with faith, hope, and charity are not living a 'real' life in a 'spiritual' world and a 'pseudo-life' in a physical one. They are 'ensouled bodies' whose destiny lies in their resurrection (cf. Chapter 11 above).

With a special eye on these facts, Aquinas thinks that those with an interest in the virtue of religion should especially pay attention to prayer and to the celebration of the Christian sacraments. Why? Because he thinks that prayer is one of the most effective ways in which we can put our belief in God into practice on a day-to-day basis, and because he is convinced that people can benefit from the work of Christ by actions and gestures which bring humanity and divinity together as they were brought together when God became a man. According to Aquinas, in addition to faith, hope, and charity, prayer and the Christian sacraments are ways in which God lives in us and in which we, in this life, live in God.

AQUINAS ON PRAYER

The word in Aquinas's writings which is most properly translated as 'prayer' is *oratio*. Although in classical Latin this word meant 'speech', early Latin-speaking Christians used it in the sense of the classical term *precatio*, which meant 'petition'. And this usage survived well into the middle of the twelfth century, which is hardly surprising in view of what we find in the New Testament. According to the gospels, when Jesus taught his disciples how to pray, he gave them the 'Our Father', which is a string of requests or petitions (cf. Matthew 6:7 ff.; Luke 11:2 ff.). And, when urging his disciples to pray, he told them to ask for things (Luke 11:5 ff. and 18:1 ff.).

By the time of Aquinas, however, the picture had become rather blurred, as it seems to be today. In 1 Thessalonians 5:17 one is told to 'pray without ceasing'. And in 1 Timothy 2:1 we read: 'I urge that supplications, prayers, intercessions, and thanksgiving be made for all people'.

Texts such as these were taken by some medieval writers and their prede-
cessors to imply that prayer must be more than a matter of petition and
that petition should be thought of as a low-grade or elementary stage in
prayer. Such seems to have been the view of, for example, John Cassian
(c. 360–435), St Bernard of Clairvaux (1090–1153), and William of
St Thierry (c. 1085–1148).

In his *Commentary on the Sentences*, Aquinas offers a complicated and
indecisive discussion of parts of prayer and kinds of prayer (cf. SL
4,15,4). By the time he is writing the *Summa theologiae*, however, he has
a definite and clear view to offer. In that work prayer is petition, without
qualification or decoration and without any suggestion that petition is an
inferior kind of prayer. It is asking for things from God. And, considered
as such, says Aquinas, it falls within God's providence. Why? Because, in
his view, it is the way in which God wills to get certain things done.
Divine providence, he writes:

> does not merely arrange what effects are to occur; it also arranges the
> causes of these effects and the relationships between them. And among
> other causes, some things are caused by human acts. So human beings
> have to do certain things, not so as to change God's plan by their acts,
> but in order to bring about certain effects by their acts, according to the
> pattern planned by God. The same thing applies also to natural causes.
> Similarly in the case of prayer we do not pray in order to change God's
> plan, but in order to obtain by our prayers those things which God
> planned to bring about by means of prayers, in order, as Gregory says,
> that our prayers should entitle us to receive what almighty God planned
> from all eternity to give us. (ST 2a2ae, 83,2)

That quotation gives one the core of Aquinas's teaching on prayer. But its
sense needs to be explained. And, perhaps, what is first and most
important to stress is that Aquinas thinks of prayer as a thoroughly com-
monplace practice. Many accounts of prayer suggest that it is a technique
which has to be learned (perhaps from a guru or spiritual 'master'). For
Aquinas, however, exactly the opposite is true. On his account, prayer has
nothing to do with methods and skills. Nor is it the preserve of an élite
whose members are 'experts' in prayer. For Aquinas, prayer is an instance
of something with which we are perfectly well acquainted quite apart
from any religious concerns we may have: the practice of trying to get
what we need from those who are able to help us. It is an act of practical
reason (cf. Chapter 12 above). It is a matter of recognizing what we need
and trying to acquire it in an intelligent way. So Aquinas insists that prayer

should include asking for specific things, including what we need in order to live (i.e. temporal goods). It is, he says, 'lawful to pray for whatever it is lawful to desire. And it is lawful to desire temporal things, not as an end in themselves or as our primary object, but as supports which help us on our way towards beatitude, inasmuch as they serve to sustain our bodily life and play an instrumental role in our virtuous deeds' (ST 2a2ae, 83,6).

But does it make sense to conceive of prayer as asking for things from God? Critics of petitionary prayer have denied that it does, for a number of reasons. They have said, for example, that its practice is inconsistent with belief in a God who is both omniscient and good. For, if God is omniscient, he knows what we want or need without us having to tell him. And, if he is good, he will give us what we want or need without being asked. It has also been held that the practice of petitionary prayer is improper since, if God is immutable, he cannot be changed by anything that we might say or do. Some authors have even complained that those who engage in petitionary prayer are subscribing to a form of magic, that they are absurdly trying to manipulate or control God in some way.

Aquinas is conscious of the fact that objections such as those just mentioned might be brought against those who pray. 'On the face of it', he writes, 'it is not appropriate to pray' since:

(1) Prayer seems to be needed to give information about what we want from the person we are asking for something. But 'Your Father knows that you need all these things' (Matthew 6:32). So it is not appropriate to pray to God. (2) Prayer is a way in which we change the mind of the person to whom we are praying, so that he will do what is being asked of him. But God's mind cannot be changed or deflected . . . (3) It is more generous to give something without waiting to be asked than it is to give something to someone who asks for it . . . But God is extremely generous. So it is apparently not appropriate that we should pray to God. (ST 2a2ae, 83,2)

Yet, as we might expect, Aquinas does not find the objections unanswerable. In praying, he replies, we are not trying to inform God of anything. We are acknowledging our needs and the fact that he can help us. And prayer should not be thought of as an attempt to effect a change in God. We aim to get by our prayers what he has planned to give us. 'Our prayer', says Aquinas, 'is not designed to change God's plan; the purpose of prayer is to obtain by our entreaties what God has already planned' (ST 2a2ae, 83,2; cf. SG III, 95)

Aquinas agrees that God gives much without being asked, but he also thinks that God wants to give us some things because we ask him to do so, so that we may be confident in going to him and so that we might recognize him as the source of all good. God, says Aquinas, 'gives us many things out of sheer generosity. The reason why he wants to give us some things in response to our petition is that it is profitable for us to acquire a certain confidence in running to him and to recognize that he is the source of all that is good for us' (ST 2a2ae, 83,2). According to Aquinas, prayer is a means by which people are able to relate to God as to a friend. Friends, we find, aim to satisfy each other's needs. And they are able to do this because they can express their needs to each other. In the same way, so Aquinas suggests, people can express their needs to God, who can therefore bring it about, not just that certain goods come to pass, but that certain goods come to pass as desired by people (cf. SG 3,95).

One might reply that, if the will of God is unchangeable, our prayers can make no difference to anything. But that, says Aquinas, would be a foolish objection. 'To claim that we should not pray in order to obtain anything from God, on the ground that the ordering of providence is immutable', he argues, 'is like saying that we should not walk in order to arrive at some place and that we should not eat in order to be fed, all of which is patently absurd' (SG 3,96). According to Aquinas, the fact that God exists changelessly and works in everything does not mean that rain does not make things wet or that food does not nourish. By the same token, he reasons, the fact that God exists changelessly and works in everything does not mean that my prayer cannot be a cause of something coming about by virtue of God's will. If I do not pray for anything, then nothing that occurs can be thought of as an answer to my prayer. But, Aquinas contends, if I pray for something and if what I pray for occurs, its occurrence can be called an answer to my prayer. He thinks that, though nothing can cause God to will what he has not willed from eternity, God may will from eternity that things should come about in accordance with my prayers and, therefore, as answers to them.

AQUINAS ON SACRAMENTS

In Aquinas's view, all grace derives from Christ as the Son of God in whom the fullness of grace (the divine life) is present (cf. ST 3a, 7 and 8). And it is natural that Aquinas should say this since he takes Christ to be God drawing us to share in the life of the Trinity. It is significant, however, that he should emphasize the fact, as he certainly does. On his account, God does not need to be incarnate in order to confer grace on people. So, why does he believe it important to stress that grace derives from Christ? The answer lies in the fact that Aquinas firmly believes that God brings us to himself as creatures of flesh and blood. He thinks that, in the end, we are drawn into the life of God by someone like ourselves, by someone living a human life in our material world. And he believes that this is where sacraments enter into the picture.

Following the teaching of Peter Lombard (finally ratified by the Council of Trent), Aquinas acknowledges seven sacraments (baptism, confirmation, penance, the Eucharist, priestly ordination, marriage, and the anointing of the sick). And he says that sacraments help us to participate in the business of the Incarnation as creatures living in space and time. According to Aquinas, Christ did not simply teach us about God. He *was* God. And his life was nothing less than God with us inviting us to be with him and to be like him. And the sacraments are means by which we, after the death and resurrection of Christ, can participate in all of that. Christ was a physical, historical individual, and Aquinas believes that his life was the final revelation and expression in history of God's love for us. But what about people living after Christ? According to Aquinas, because of the sacraments they are no worse off than those who met Christ personally and accepted all that he stood for and embodied. By virtue of the sacraments, says Aquinas, people directly share in what was going on in the Incarnation. For him, sacraments are means by which we may benefit from what God was doing in the life, death, and resurrection of God the Word incarnate.

Aquinas maintains that Christians should not think of God as distant or remote. He holds that they should recognize God to be always present. He also thinks that they should receive and live out God's revelation of himself in Christ, and that they should do so in physical, bodily, everyday behaviour. In Aquinas's view, Christians are those who do things which truly constitute a history of love between them and God. And, as surely as the history of love between people includes declaring love, making love, talking together, eating together, giving presents, and celebrating anniversaries, so, says Aquinas, the history of love between Christians and God includes celebrating the sacraments. For Aquinas, these are natural and obvious aids by which Christians can be what they are meant to be. They are ways through which Christians join themselves to and benefit from what God was doing in the life, death, and resurrection of God the incarnate Word. They 'constitute certain sensible signs of invisible things by which people are sanctified' (ST 3a, 61,3).

The notion that sacraments are signs is one that Aquinas inherits from St Augustine, according to whom a sacrament is always a 'sign' (*signum*) of some sacred 'thing' (*res*) (cf. *De doctrina Christiana*, 2). According to Augustine, sacraments are rites which image or reflect what is not observable to the senses. They employ what is material (as, for example, baptism makes use of water), but they signify what is not material. Indeed, says Augustine, they *effect* what is not material, for they actually bring people closer to God and do not just symbolize some eternal truth about God and human beings. For Augustine, sacraments confer grace and can be thought of as an extension of Christ's saving work. They signify, and actually are, means by which God acts in us to bring us to himself. And this is how Aquinas thinks of sacraments. For him, they are ways in which the Incarnation (a physical reality) can have an effect in us by virtue of rites and ceremonies (also physical realities). Hence it is that, turning to the question 'Are the sacraments necessary for the salvation of human beings?', Aquinas answers 'Yes'.

First, he says, people are helped by sacraments in a way appropriate to their manner of knowing since human beings achieve knowledge of spiritual and intelligible things through their 'experience of physical and sensible realities' (cf. Chapters 5 and 11). It is, Aquinas reasons, 'characteristic of divine providence that it provides for each being in a manner corresponding to its own particular way of functioning. Hence it is appropriate that in bestowing certain aids to salvation upon us the divine wisdom should make use of certain physical and sensible signs called the sacraments' (ST 3a, 61,1). Aquinas thinks that it belongs to human nature to use signs, to express the transcendent not in itself but through what it transcends, through using natural things as pointing beyond themselves.

Second, Aquinas continues, people are captivated by physical objects and processes and need to be helped by means of them. 'For if they were to be confronted with spiritual realities pure and unalloyed, their minds, absorbed as they are in physical things, would be incapable of accepting them' (ST 3a, 61,1). Aquinas thinks that our preoccupation with material things is a root cause of sin, and he regards it as appropriate that we should be cured of sin through material things. In this way, he suggests, we can be helped to achieve a humble and realistic picture of ourselves. And, he adds, we can indulge our interest in physical things. 'In our activities', says Aquinas, 'we are particularly prone to involve ourselves with physical things. Lest, therefore, it should be too hard for us totally to dispense with physical actions, we were given certain physical practices to observe in the sacraments' (ST 3a, 61,1).

So Aquinas argues that sacraments are good because they harmonize with the symbolic life that is natural to human beings, they keep us realistically aware of our bodily nature and its limitations, and they are fun. But it is also important to note that, in Aquinas's teaching, Christ is the first sacrament, the primary sign and cause of God's life in us. His physical life and death are, says Aquinas, actual means by which God brings his work of creation to completion. According to Aquinas, people are brought to share in God's life by means of Christ's life and death. And, so Aquinas adds, the same can be said with respect to the sacraments. In Aquinas's view, Christ is effective in the life of the Church considered as sacramental. Just like the life, death, and resurrection of Christ, the sacraments of the Church are physical signs and genuine causes of grace. They are symbols which make real what they symbolize. Through them we are united to God even in this life. Through them we become sharers in the divine nature.

So Aquinas's basic position on the sacraments is that they are the final historical realization of what God is as Creator and as incarnate sanctifier. Aquinas is prepared to accept that there were sacraments of a kind before the Incarnation. He calls them 'sacraments of the Old Law' and identifies them with the rituals legislated for in the Old Testament. They were, he says, 'certain sensible signs of invisible things by which people are sanctified' (ST 3a, 61,3). For Aquinas, however, the important sacraments are 'the sacraments of the New Law', by which he means the Christian sacraments. For he holds that these were instituted by Christ and that they are his chosen way of joining us to him as the eternal Word of the Father (ST 3a, 60,5).

Aquinas thinks it important to stress that we use natural symbols when celebrating the sacraments (i.e. words, objects, and ceremonies which one can easily, or naturally, think of as imaging or reflecting what is happening as sacraments are celebrated). For Aquinas, sacraments are sacred signs because they are, to begin with, ordinary and intelligible human signs and symbols. Yet he also insists that the final and indispensable warrant for celebrating the sacraments as we do lies in the fact that we are doing what Christ told us to do. We might make use of all sorts of natural symbols to celebrate and to signify all sorts of things. According to Aquinas, however, sacraments are not just natural symbols used in accordance with our tastes and inclinations. They show us what God does as choosing to draw us to him. So they belong to the realm of revelation, and we need God to instruct us when it comes to them.

One might argue that any object or ritual can be a means of grace. One might also hold that some human authority (e.g. religious leaders) can determine whether an object or ritual can be a means of grace. But this is not Aquinas's view. His line is that things in nature do not by themselves have intrinsic power to sanctify (he does not view sacraments in magical terms). He also thinks that the occurrence of sanctification cannot be determined by any human decision. Whether a physical process involving physical objects is actually a means by which people are taken up into God's plan to lead them to himself depends, he thinks, on whether God is actually leading people to himself by that physical process or those physical objects. And whether or not he is doing that, says Aquinas, is ultimately to be gleaned only from what, in the person of Christ, he tells us about his activity.

For Aquinas, sacraments are language in which God speaks to us. And Aquinas holds that God must be allowed to talk in his own words and must not have ours forced into his mouth. Since 'human sanctification lies under the power of God who sanctifies', says Aquinas, 'it is not for people to decide by their own judgement which materials are to be chosen for them to be sanctified by. This, rather, is something which should be determined by divine institution' (ST 3a, 60,5). Not surprisingly, therefore, Aquinas compares the sacraments with Scripture. He says that God communicates spiritual realities to us through sensible signs in the sacraments and through verbal images in Scripture (ST 3a, 60,5).

And what does Aquinas take God to be telling us with respect to the celebration of sacraments? One thing he takes him to be saying is that Christians should not regard themselves as lone individuals separate from other human beings. For Aquinas, the sacraments, with their ritual and physical elements, bring people to God as a body or collection. They knit people together with each other as well as with God. They are, as Aquinas significantly calls them, 'the sacraments of the Church' (cf. Introduction to ST 3a, 60).

Even before Aquinas gives the reasons noted above for sacraments being necessary, he quotes from St Augustine to assert that 'it is impossible to unite people within a religion of any name, whether true or false, unless they are kept together by means of some system of symbols or sacraments in which they all share'. 'It is necessary for human salvation', says Aquinas, 'that people should be united in the name of the one true religion' (ST 3a, 61,1). According to Aquinas, good sacramental theology is also good ecclesiology. It is not an account of what individual people are *on their own*: it is concerned with what people are *together* as members of Christ's body, which Aquinas calls 'the Church'.

Indeed, he holds, the sacraments *constitute* the Church since this is the body of people who celebrate the sacraments *together* and who therefore share in God's life insofar as is possible this side of the grave. Aquinas frequently uses the word *sacramenta* (sacraments) by itself. But this is always an abbreviation for him. His full phrase is either *ecclesiae sacramenta* (the sacraments of the Church) or *fidei sacramenta* (signs pertaining to the Church, or signs of faith). The post-Tridentine tradition of sacramental thinking was content to describe a sacrament as an 'outward sign of inward grace', a sign of the sanctification going on in individuals. But Aquinas's view is much more comprehensive and much less individualistic than this. For him, every sacrament symbolizes not merely something in me or in you but a whole sweep of salvation history, past, present, and future. A sacrament, for him, is a symbol on at least three levels. It reaches back into the past to link with the life of Christ. It points to what is going on in the present, the sanctification of human beings. And it is prophetic of the future kingdom of God. In Aquinas's view, to understand a sacramental sign is to see in it all these facets.

Aquinas, of course, is aware of some fairly standard objections to the celebration of sacraments and to the claim that we need to celebrate them (cf. ST 3a, 61,1). For example, he notes the suggestion that mere bodily practices can have little relevance to human salvation. Here he is thinking of the way in which New Testament authors almost unanimously warn people away from a religion of minute and cultic practices so as to point them to what John's gospel calls the worship of the Father 'in spirit and truth' (John 4:23 f.). Aquinas also notes the teaching that the grace of Christ is sufficient for us (cf. 2 Corinthians 12:9). In the light of this teaching, he asks, should we not conclude that sacraments are unnecessary, that they belong to a religion of 'works', a religion of the kind castigated by St Paul in texts like his letter to the Romans, a religion of slavery rather than a religion of freedom? Aquinas also wonders whether we should not also conclude that to erect a sacramental system is to deny the sufficiency of what Christ has achieved by his life, death, and resurrection. Either what Christ did is enough, or it is not. If it is, then there is no need for prescribed sacramental practices. So, why bother with them?

But Aquinas denies that sacraments are irrelevant or unimportant. Why? Because to regard sacraments as superfluous is to look at the matter from the point of view of what God does rather than from the perspective of human need. In Aquinas's view, if what God does is something that he does for *people*, then we have to look at the sort of thing people are. And, Aquinas thinks, it is what we know of people that makes sense of sacraments.

According to Aquinas, it is obvious that Christian perfection is not a matter of rubrical observance. And he takes it as obvious that Christ's grace *is* sufficient for us and that there is nothing we can do to add to his way of making God present to us. But he also thinks that the sacraments are physical activities considered as symbolic or meaningful. They are means by which God can express what he is for us and we can express what we think of him. And though Aquinas believes that all grace comes through Christ, he also thinks that it comes to us as human beings in a human way and that the sacraments of the Church are examples of how this is so. Aquinas has no doubt that we are saved by Christ and by Christ alone. In his view, however, the sacraments have their value precisely because of this. For Aquinas thinks that it is through them that Christ's work is brought to bear on us.

In other words, Aquinas's approach to the sacraments is another aspect of his view that people can come to God only as limited, bodily individuals. Do we have an immediate and direct knowledge of God? As we have seen, Aquinas thinks that we do not (cf. Chapter 5). For him, our knowledge of God in this life must proceed on the basis of what we can observe in the physical world that God has made. Can we know about the inner life of God by our own efforts? Or can we determine what God is for us by reflecting on our knowledge of God's character? As we have also now seen, Aquinas's answer to this question is again negative. For him, God must reveal what his life essentially is, just as he must tell us whether or not he chooses to invite us to share it. And this pattern of thinking is what we find when turning to Aquinas on sacraments, just as we find it when turning to what he says on the life and work of Christ.

The course that Christ's life took was not, for Aquinas, the only way in which God could have united himself with people. But it was, he says, a fitting way given what people are like. And the notion of what people are like is what chiefly governs his teaching on the sacraments. He looks for the sacraments to pass away, together with faith and hope. But he also recognizes that we presently live as human agents with human tendencies and needs. And he thinks of the sacraments as God's way of meeting us considered as such. Religion and the worship of God, he insists, is not for God's sake: it is for our sake, as is the Incarnation. For Aquinas, God has no need of us and is unaffected by what we do and by what we are. He is not even affected by becoming a man. According to Aquinas, however, God *has* become a man and has, therefore, made use of what is human, or humanly understandable, to draw us to him. And Aquinas holds that God is doing the same when it comes to the Christian sacraments.

21

Aquinas's Achievement

Is Aquinas worth reading today? Philosophers and theologians have often disagreed with him over details. And many of their criticisms may be thoroughly justified. Indeed, it would be surprising if this were not the case since even the greatest thinkers make mistakes. Nonetheless, Aquinas has some important things to teach us, both from the perspective of philosophy and from that of theology. In my exposition of his thinking, and in keeping with the intention of the series to which this book belongs, I have aimed to be sympathetic. It should be evident why I take Aquinas to be significant. Yet it might be worthwhile for me to venture an explicit assessment of the value of his writings and ideas. To do so in a short concluding chapter may, of course, seem inadequate since Aquinas is such a voluminous author and clearly an intellectual giant (as even his critics normally concede). But there are some additional points I would like to make. And here, I think, is the best place to make them.

FAITH AND REASON

If asked to say in a sentence what Aquinas's greatest achievement was, I would reply that he showed the need for theology to be married to philosophy. Medieval theologians often called philosophy the 'female slave'or 'handmaiden' (*ancilla*) of theology. In doing so, however, they were usually not disparaging it. People who could afford maid-servants in the Middle Ages recognized their need of them. They relied on them as people today rely on doctors, nurses, firefighters, and the police ('public servants' as they are sometimes called). And this is how Aquinas relies on philosophy. He does not think that it should have the last word when it comes to what is true and important, but neither does he think that we can seriously engage with what is true and important without it. And in this he is surely right.

Many contemporary theologians seem to take a different view. Why? A common reply can be summarized in the slogan 'Faith is not answerable to limited human reasoning'. For some theologians, the message of Christianity comes as a challenge to philosophical reflection, not as something with which to bed down. The idea here is that God's revelation (the subject matter of theology) is not a product of human intellectual pondering. And it stands in judgement over philosophy since it tells us what we cannot discern for ourselves and reminds us of the serious difference between God and creatures. On this account, the job of the theologian is to listen to the word of God, not to argue with it from a perspective which does not accept it at the outset. St Paul says: 'Has not God made foolish the wisdom of the world? For since, in the wisdom of God, the world did not know God through wisdom, it pleased God through the folly of what we preach to save those who believe. For Jews demand signs and Greeks seek wisdom, but we preach Christ crucified, a stumbling block to Jews and folly to Gentiles' (1 Corinthians 1:20–23). These words, and others in Scripture, have led many to suppose that philosophical reflection is strictly irrelevant when it comes to Christianity.

Yet there is no reason to suppose that Aquinas disagrees with St Paul when it comes to wisdom and folly. And there is no reason to suppose that he would be unsympathetic to the theological case against philosophy just noted. St Paul refers to people who hold that it is foolish to be a Christian; and he holds that they are wrong. Yet the same can be said of Aquinas. St Paul does not cite instances of people claiming that Christianity is folly: but Aquinas does. He cites many arguments offered by those convinced that Christians are misguided – and his conclusion regarding them is thoroughly Pauline. True wisdom, he thinks, lies in the Christian revelation given in Scripture, which he takes to govern all sensible reflection on God and Christianity. Only ignorance of Aquinas's writings could lead one to castigate him for thinking that philosophy is superior to revelation.

But Aquinas does not believe that philosophy is irrelevant from the viewpoint of theology. As we have seen, he is no hard rationalist. He does not hold that Christians should abandon their religion if they cannot establish its truth on philosophical grounds (cf. Chapter 5). And he is convinced that much Christian teaching cannot be shown to be true by philosophical means (cf. Chapters 16–19). But he is equally convinced that Christians can only benefit from good philosophical reflection. And that is surely what he has to believe if he is to be taken seriously as a Christian thinker. For Christian teaching can hardly be important if it is esoteric, self-enclosed, and unconnected with what we can know to be true. It must surely engage with life and the world as we can understand them even apart from revelation. It must link up with and answer questions that we naturally ask. This seems to be the biblical understanding of Christianity, just as it seems to be the way in which the greatest theologians have understood it. And this is the tradition in which Aquinas stands. In his own day, as in ours, there were some who took a different view. These people held that there is Christian truth and philosophical truth and that both are true even when they contradict each other. But truth cannot contradict truth. And Aquinas's greatest achievement lies in his attempts to explore the implications of this fact with an eye on Christian doctrine. He rightly thought that Christian theologians cannot teach truly about God and people if they do not pay attention to what, if anything, can be known about them. For how could they do so if what they say ignores or conflicts with what we can know of God and people?

Yet Aquinas also rightly thought that Christian theologians need philosophical reflection even when it comes to what God has revealed. You might suppose that, as long as you start with, say, the Bible and the Councils of the Church, you cannot go wrong. But you might, of course, go *terribly* wrong. People who start with true premises can reason very badly on the basis of them and thus go from truth to error. Being right at the outset does not guarantee that one will be teaching correctly as one continues. But how is one to determine whether true premises are being used to erroneous effect? As far as I can see, the only possible answer is 'clear and rigorous philosophical thinking'. Serious theological reflection on Christian truth can never distance itself from philosophy.

One might reasonably reply that 'philosophy' is not easily definable and that people we now call philosophers have taught many different and conflicting things, some of which are plainly incompatible with Christian doctrine. But philosophers are typically people who try to think clearly: they typically seek to argue on the basis of reason. Confronted by an argument, they are fond of asking whether its premises entail its conclusion. They also have a habit of trying to evaluate premises. 'Does it make sense to say this?' 'Is it unreasonable to believe that?' These are just the sort of questions which one can expect a philosopher to raise, and they are ones which theologians ignore at their peril even if it is true that they are expounding a teaching which is not based on human reasoning. To ignore them is effectively to say that theologians can rightly say anything that they like. Aquinas saw this point very clearly, and I take this to be a reason why contemporary theologians and those interested in theology should pay some attention to him.

One might say that they need not do so since the Bible speaks for itself and needs no philosopher to interpret and expound it. But the Bible does not speak for itself, and it does need interpreters. It tells us, for instance, that God created the heavens and the earth and that he is also an eagle hovering over a nest, someone who can speak to a person face to face, a woman in childbirth, a case of dry rot, and spirit without body. Are we to take all of these statements literally? If not, why not? And which are to be taken literally? The Bible, as such, cannot answer such questions about itself. Instead, it poses a problem: and who is to solve the problem? The interpreters of biblical texts have to be us. And we cannot interpret in a vacuum. We have, in effect, to think about them philosophically, as Aquinas did. His philosophical views differ strikingly from those of many other philosophers. So I am obviously not saying that those who read the Bible should take account of all that philosophers have written and that this is what Aquinas thought; but I am saying that readers of the Bible cannot avoid taking positions on a number of philosophical issues, whether explicitly or implicitly. And I am suggesting that Aquinas, more than many Christian thinkers, was aware of this fact, which is much to his credit.

THE CONCEPT OF GOD

If asked to say in a sentence what Aquinas's second greatest achievement was, I would reply that he gives us a solid and reasoned antidote to idolatry. I take idolatry to be the worship of a creature. And I say that Aquinas provides an antidote to it since I take him to have successfully shown that what many have taken to be God, and therefore to be worshipped, is not God at all. In particular, I take him to have shown that much that is currently offered as an account of God is grounded on a premise which is fundamentally idolatrous. This is the premise 'God is a person' as construed in the light of the philosophy of Descartes.

As I noted in Chapter 11, Descartes maintains that people (persons) are immaterial thinking substances contingently connected with bodies. They entertain thoughts. They reason. They have beliefs. They go from one intellectual state to another. And, though essentially immaterial, they have effects in the world of matter. According to Descartes, I am a disembodied mind, yet I can get things done in the material world. But is Descartes right in thinking like this? It seems to me, as it does to many others, that his account of what people are has been blown to pieces by texts such as

Wittgenstein's *Philosophical Investigations* (Oxford, 1958). Curiously, however, Descartes' account of people seems to have been taken to heart by many contemporary theologians and philosophers of religion. For we often find them saying or presuming that God is more or less what Descartes takes people to be: a person without a body who invisibly thinks and wills and lives a life as our contemporary. Some of them have told us that he is causally affected by what happens in the world. Many have insisted that he is temporal and mutable. Some have suggested that God might have lapses of memory or that we can imagine what it is like to be God by introspection and by thinking of ourselves as acting in the world.

But is such a view remotely credible? Is it credible even on the supposition that Descartes is absolutely right in what he says of people? Surely, it is not. Or perhaps I should say that it is evidently wrong if considered as an account of what Christians mean, or ought to mean, by 'God'. As well as describing God in all sorts of concrete ways, biblical authors continually insist that God is incomparable since he is the Lord of heaven and earth, the Creator of the universe, the one who, as St Paul puts it, 'calls into existence the things that do not exist' (Romans 4:17). The notion of God as a Cartesian disembodied person is just incompatible with the Bible when taken as a whole. It is far too anthropomorphic.

Biblical authors certainly speak of God in anthropomorphic terms. But they also heavily qualify their anthromorphisms. In general, the biblical God cannot sensibly be thought of as just one more thing to list in an account of the things that there are. If one person plus another person equals two things, or if one cat plus one dog equals two things, then God plus a creature cannot. A much more subtle account than the 'person without a body' one is needed if we are to do justice to biblical texts. In particular, we need an account of God which never loses sight of the fact that, if there is a Creator, then something effects the difference between there being something and nothing. In one tone of voice, we need to speak of God as if he could be thought of as being like something in the world, something we could in principle understand. But, in another tone of voice, we need to say something which pulls in a different direction. We need to say that God is the source of everything we know and understand.

Yet all of that is precisely what Aquinas thinks. As we have seen, his theology and philosophy (or his philosophical theology) are overshadowed by the question 'How come anything at all?' And he is acutely aware of ways in which God as Creator must differ from creatures. He is anxious to give an account of positive ways in which people speak of God. Yet he is profoundly sensitive to the dangers of idolatry. And on this basis he reflects about God to very good effect. Or so I think. His teaching as I described it in Chapters 7 to 10 seems to me a model of what Christian (not to mention Jewish and Islamic) talk of God should be. Many who have read Aquinas on the existence and nature of God have come away unimpressed. Some have felt that Aquinas is not truly biblical in what he says of God. Others have found things of which to complain in the details of his arguments. It seems to me, however, that only a superficial reading of Scripture could lead one to describe Aquinas's 'doctrine' of God as unbiblical. And, I would suggest, if his approach to God is not fundamentally correct, then there is no God – or none worth believing in and worshipping. All that Aquinas says of God springs from his conviction that Scripture is revelation and that the Christian Church teaches truly. But this did not prevent him from asking whether what Scripture and the Church say about God is subject to independent support. My view is that Aquinas talks a great deal of sense in following up this question and in seeking to answer it. I also suggest that, in doing so, he offers an account of God which faithfully represents both the Bible and the Christian tradition based on it.

AQUINAS AND CHRISTIAN THEOLOGY

Yet perhaps that conclusion is mistaken given some other things that theologians have said in recent years. Here I am especially thinking of two lines of criticism that have been levelled against Aquinas. According to the first, his theology is outdated since it heavily depends on an approach to Scripture that no theologian can take seriously today. Why? Because, so the argument goes, much of it erroneously presupposes that we can read the New Testament as a substantially reliable account of what Jesus of Nazareth said and did. According to the second line of criticism, Aquinas's theology has been superseded by Trinitarian insights that Aquinas lacks. Why? Because, so it has often been argued, Aquinas mistakenly writes as though the Trinity primarily concerns God in himself rather than what the Trinity is for us. Aquinas's formal discussion of the Trinity in the *Summa theologiae* (ST Ia, 27–32) comes as part of an account of what God essentially is. But, it has been said, that way of proceeding gives a distorted impression of the truth since it downplays the fact that God, for Christians, is first and foremost Father, Son, and Spirit as revealed to us in history.

The first of these criticisms is thoroughly understandable when one thinks of what many twentieth-century New Testament scholars have written. For these have often been very sceptical when it comes to the historicity of the gospel narratives. According to some scholars, we cannot read these narratives as even *intending* to be historical. According to others, we are unable to determine what is historical in them. Fans of Aquinas have commonly written about him without any serious reference to the literature of which I now speak. Insofar as they have criticized Aquinas, they have tended to raise philosophical objections to his teaching. But doubts about the historicity of the gospels, to the extent that they are well grounded, strike at Aquinas's thinking just as much as any well-grounded philosophical argument.

They do so rather more, in fact. Aquinas does not believe in God just because of philosophical arguments: he starts from a position of faith. But faith in what? As we saw in Chapters 16–20, Aquinas's faith rests heavily on what he takes to be the teachings of Christ. And, if it can be shown that we really have no access to them, Aquinas's theological system would be seriously undermined. Some have said that the Christian Gospel is not about historical facts. And Aquinas can be taken to be on their side at one level. He does not, for instance, think that Christian doctrines can be proved or successfully refuted by anything that an historian might produce. But he takes the teaching of Christ to give us the only possible warrant we could have for believing in doctrines such as those of the Incarnation and the Trinity. Aquinas believes that human reflection can throw a lot of light on what these doctrines mean and imply. His bottom line, however, is that they come to us from Christ as reported in Scripture. So justified scepticism when it comes to what is often called 'the problem of the historical Jesus' would be very damaging to the core of his teaching.

But is there such a justified scepticism? Has it been shown that Aquinas was wrong to suppose that the gospels provide a generally reliable record of the teachings of Jesus? I am not qualified to enter into debates about the historicity of the gospels. But, to judge by the recent writings of New Testament specialists, it seems premature to conclude that the gospels do not give us an account of Christ's teaching comparable to that which Aquinas took them to give.

A helpful survey of recent work on 'the historical Jesus' is Mark Allan Powell's *Jesus as a Figure in History* (Louisville, Kentucky, 1998). Powell traces the history of scepticism when it comes to the gospel narratives. And he pays special attention to what some of the currently most prominent biblical scholars are saying about it. And, if Powell's account is accurate, then at least this much is clear: it is definitely not the case that Aquinas's approach to the New Testament is one which no theologian can take seriously today. Those who think that it is untenable normally do so because they believe that biblical scholarship has shown the gospels to be historically unreliable. But such a belief does not square with what contemporary biblical scholars seem to be saying. And, even if it did, it would not therefore follow that Aquinas is wrong in his reading of the gospels.

Biblical scholars might not think of themselves as philosophers, but they give reasons for their conclusions and, in this sense, are doing philosophy. Are their reasons good ones insofar as they are employed to conclude that someone like Aquinas is wrong when it comes to what he takes Jesus to have taught? This is not a question which can quickly be answered simply by attending to what might or might not be attributable to Jesus given the usual methods of historical investigation. Suppose Jesus was divine. What could an historian, as an historian, do to determine what Jesus is or is not likely to have said? The answer is, surely, 'Little'. To suggest that we can know what God is likely to say or do seems absurd – apart from a revelation from God concerning his intentions.

What, though, of the objection to Aquinas that focuses on the significance of the Trinity? It has often been levelled against him by contemporary theologians. I have to say, however, that it seems to me a thoroughly misguided objection. For anyone who reads Aquinas as a whole ought to be able to see that he clearly emphasizes that the Trinity is for people and that human destiny is to be thought of in Trinitarian terms. Critics of Aquinas on the Trinity sometimes report him as thinking of the Trinity as somewhat unrelated to us and as located elsewhere than in what is sometimes referred to as 'the economy of salvation'. But this objection attacks Aquinas simply by ignoring what he says.

Aquinas does teach (at least by implication) that the Trinity would exist whether or not there were people. But, as a Christian theologian, he could hardly say otherwise since to do so would be to allege that the existence of God depends on that of people. Nonetheless, when he reflects in detail on the life of the Trinity, most of what he has to say concerns how God works for the benefit of people through the Incarnation and the sending of the Holy Spirit. Before he turns to the Trinity, considered as our salvation, he regularly (and not just in the *Summa theologiae*) talks about what can be said of it as part of an account of what God is eternally. But why should he not do that? Indeed, one might add, it is surely important that he does so. For talk about the Trinity and human salvation must presuppose some understanding of the Trinity in itself and with no reference to people. And that understanding is not going to be achieved by reflection on what the Trinity does but might not have done.

One might reply, of course, that there can be no question of any 'does but might not have done' when it comes to the Trinity. For, should it not be said that God just *is* a Trinity that offers itself to people in 'the economy of salvation'? But Aquinas does not think otherwise. As we saw in Chapter 10, his God is immutable and cannot, therefore, be sensibly thought of as creating and saving as an afterthought. God's act of creating is not, for Aquinas, a reaction to circumstances. And salvation is not, for example, an originally unplanned rescue operation.

On Aquinas's account, 'the economy of salvation' springs from what God changelessly is. But what *cannot* be true of the Trinitarian God? According to Aquinas, it cannot be true that the Trinity needs creatures to be what it is as God. Nor can it be true that anything outside it could compel it to make and to elevate creatures. So Aquinas thinks, and in my view correctly, that there is nothing improper in considering what the Trinity might be said to be apart from creatures. If Aquinas's teaching on the Trinity extended only to what he has to say about the Father, the Son, and the Spirit in eternity, it might be reasonable to accuse him of a somewhat unChristian Trinitarianism. But it does not. His teaching on the Trinity also includes the Incarnation. And it is much in evidence in what he has to say about the theological virtues and the Christian sacraments.

Critics of Aquinas on the Trinity have sometimes accused him of structuring his writings in a way that shows his Trinitarian thinking to be fundamentally unChristian. They have said that he emphasized a 'tract' approach to theology, one tract being 'On God' (*De Deo Uno*) and another being 'On the Trinity' (*De Deo Trino*). In doing so, it has been suggested, Aquinas encouraged the view that God's unity precedes his triunity and that the Trinitarian life of God is somehow added on to the divine unity. But Aquinas never wrote tracts with titles like *De Deo Uno* and *De Deo Trino*. Such things are the products of theologians living long after him, and there is no reason to suppose that Aquinas would have approved of them. His own approach is different. Since he takes the divine nature to be common to each person of the Trinity, Aquinas sees no problem in asking what divinity amounts to without simultaneously engaging in Trinitarian theology. There can be no doubt, however, that the Trinity lies fairly and squarely at the centre of his thinking when that is taken as a whole.

Does this mean that Aquinas is a good theologian? That depends on what you take a good theologian to be. Some current theologians hold that the doctrinal positions which Aquinas expounded, explored, and defended have been somehow shown to be basically false. In their view, the business of theology now is to salvage what one can from 2,000 years of

Christian error. And, if they are right, then Aquinas is of limited theological interest today. But are they right?

I can hardly begin to comment on that question here. Still, it is at least worth noting that Aquinas's doctrinal commitments remain those of many theologians and religious believers today. It is also worth stressing that Aquinas is very sensitive to objections which might be raised against these commitments. Modern theologians anxious to lead us beyond Christian doctrine as traditionally accepted by Councils of the Church and the like ('revisionists' as they sometimes call themselves) are commonly concerned to do so on philosophical grounds. They typically think that it is, for example, unreasonable to suppose that a man could be God or that God could be three in one. Aquinas thought otherwise: and he defended himself on philosophical as well as theological grounds. Did he do so well? Readers can begin to judge for themselves by returning, for instance, to what I report him as arguing in Chapters 16 and 17. My own view is that he defended himself very well and that 'revisionist' theologians need to engage with his arguments. For this reason, I take him to be very much a theologian of contemporary relevance.

AQUINAS AND PHILOSOPHY

Is Aquinas also of contemporary philosophical relevance? As I explained in Chapter 1, many philosophers think that he is. But philosophers are no less subject to error than theologians and the rest of us. So the fact that many philosophers now take him seriously proves nothing by itself. Whether or not Aquinas is philosophically important today can be determined only by detailed discussions of his arguments. I have attempted to explain what some of them amount to so as to bring out their strengths. At this point, therefore, I shall simply make a few general observations when it comes to Aquinas and philosophy, observations which you might like to consider as you reflect on his writings for yourself.

The first is that Aquinas raises some very good questions. It has been said that philosophy begins in wonder. And, if that is true, then Aquinas is a typical philosopher, for he is continually moving from query to query. Since some of his disciples have presented his writings as comprising a cut-and-dried system in which all truth is to be found and all important problems are solved, Aquinas is often taken to be concerned only to lay down answers. But his questions are as numerous as his answers. And he does not always take his answers to be definitive. This is, perhaps, especially clear when it comes to his most radical and presiding question: how come anything at all? In raising this question, Aquinas is taking wonder to its limit. But his efforts to respond to it are, as we have seen, largely attempts to note what the answer to the question cannot be.

Aquinas is famous for having a 'doctrine' of God. Yet one might equally say that he is a kind of agnostic, though not in the usual sense of the word as employed with respect to God. The theistic agnostic typically says 'We do not know, and the universe is a mysterious riddle.' And this is not Aquinas's view exactly. Yet he does want to say that the universe is a riddle and that we do not understand what the answer to it is. He gives the name 'God' to the answer, and he thinks that, if there were no God, there would be no mysterious universe and nobody to be mystified. But he does not take this conclusion as putting an end to further questions: he takes it as an invitation to ask many more. His arguments for the existence of God are arguments to show that there are real questions to which we do not and cannot know the answer. And it is worth emphasizing that, in following them up, Aquinas exhibits great intellectual modesty and politeness. Philosophers can be astonishingly intolerant of those who do not agree with them. The same is true of theologians, and sometimes to a greater degree. Yet Aquinas is never intolerant as he writes. Perhaps because he is unusually sensitive to the mystery of God, he is reticent and painstaking when it comes to noting and responding to objections to his own opinions. Whether or not his arguments and conclusions are correct, his manner of discussing alternative ones is a model that many would do well to imitate.

And many might also do well to refrain from thinking of Aquinas's philosophy as 'medieval' rather than 'modern'. The word 'medieval' is often used pejoratively so as to signify the equivalent of 'benighted' or 'unenlightened'. Philosophers who use the word in this way are usually supposing that medieval philosophy belongs to a dark age of thought in which nothing of philosophical importance was said – and a lot of philosophers really do think this. Hence, for example, many university departments of philosophy ignore medieval philosophy. They provide courses on ancient Greek philosophy (normally confined to a study of Plato and Aristotle, though there were many other ancient Greek philosophers). Then they jump to Descartes, and to 'modern philosophy', as if nothing of philosophical interest happened in between. But medieval philosophers have a lot of interest to say, and Aquinas is an especially notable example. With an eye on a contrast between 'medieval' and 'modern', it is worth stressing that what he argues often foreshadows much that we find in the writings of 'modern' philosophers.

His teaching on the topic of mind and body is one example since it bears fruitful comparison with what Wittgenstein says; and Aquinas is comparable to Wittgenstein in other ways. A famous British philosopher once claimed that similarities between them allow us to speak of a 'marriage' between Wittgenstein and Aquinas. A somewhat less famous philosopher sensibly replied that an announcement of the marriage would be premature. Yet Wittgenstein and Aquinas have similar things to say even apart from their interest in philosophy of mind. Take, for example, their approach to the question of reasonable belief. Largely under the influence of Descartes, legions of philosophers have claimed that knowledge is prior to belief and must, therefore, be treated more seriously. But this is not Wittgenstein's view. And, as we have seen, it is not that of Aquinas. Then again, consider some ways in which Wittgenstein and Aquinas might be compared as philosophers of religion. For Wittgenstein, if God exists, he is beyond human comprehension, and belief in him (and religious belief in general) should not be confused with some kind of empirical or scientific hypothesis. In his *Lectures on Religious Belief* (Oxford, 1970) Wittgenstein additionally insists that belief in Christianity cannot rest on historical grounds. Yet these are all theses which Aquinas, in his own way, also defends. If Wittgenstein on religious belief is 'modern' as opposed to 'medieval', then so is Aquinas.

CONCLUSION

But slogans and labels make for sloppy thinking, and they are of little value when it comes to talking good philosophy and theology. Aquinas does not go in for them at all; instead, he raises a lot of questions. And he tries to deal with them in detail and with special attention to what might be said in favour of conflicting answers. The only way to evaluate his thinking is to pay close attention to his arguments. I have tried to give you an account of some of them, one which has aimed to be more than a bald summary. But the intricacies of Aquinas's thinking need to be taken seriously and approached accordingly. In short, those with an interest in Aquinas need to read him carefully and at length; and then they need to think about what they have read. If this book encourages readers to embark on such an enterprise, I should be delighted. The reward will match the effort. For Aquinas was an outstanding Christian thinker.

Chronological List of Aquinas's Writings

Works sometimes ascribed to Aquinas may well be texts of which he was not the author in any sense. What follows is a list of Aquinas's writings with respect to which there is not too much scholarly controversy concerning their authenticity. They are cited by the Latin titles commonly used for them, together with English translations of these. But note that we cannot always be sure of the titles which Aquinas gave to his writings (notably, in the case of the *Summa theologiae* and the *Summa contra Gentiles*). Within each category below, works are cited in roughly chronological order of composition, though in some cases this order is uncertain. For detailed discussions concerning the dating of Aquinas's writings, see Jean-Pierre Torrell, *Saint Thomas Aquinas: The Person and His Work* (Washington, DC, 1996).

GENERAL THEOLOGICAL TREATISES

Scriptum super libros Sententiarum (*Commentary on the* Sentences *of Peter Lombard*: c. 1252–57).

Summa contra Gentiles, sometimes referred to as *Summa contra Gentes* (*Summary against the Pagans* [sc. people neither Jewish or Christian]: c. 1259–65).

Summa theologiae, sometimes referred to as *Summa theologica* (*Summary of Theology*: c. 1265–73).

Compendium theologiae (*Compendium of Theology*: c. 1265–73).

DISPUTED QUESTIONS

Quaestiones disputatae De veritate (*Disputed Questions on Truth*: c. 1256–59).

Quaestiones disputatae De potentia (*Disputed Questions on the Power [of God]*: c. 1265–66).

Quaestio disputata De anima (*Disputed Question on the Soul*: c. 1265–66).

Quaestio disputata De spiritualibus creaturis (*Disputed Question on Spiritual Creatures*: c. 1267–68).

Questiones disputatae De Malo (*Disputed Questions on Evil*: c. 1266–70).

Quaestiones disputatae De virtutibus (*Disputed Questions on the Virtues*: c. 1271–72).

Quaestio disputata De unione verbi incarnati (*Disputed Question on the Union of the Incarnate Word*: c. 1271–72).

Quaestiones de quodlibet I–XII (*Quodlibetal Questions I–XII* [concerning a very large range of topics]: c. 1252–56 and c. 1268–72).

BIBLICAL COMMENTARIES

Expositio super Isaiam ad litteram (*Commentary on Isaiah*: c. 1248–54).

Super Ieremiam et Threnos (*Commentaries on Jeremiah and Lamentations*: c. 1248–52).

Expositio super Job ad litteram (*Commentary on Job/Literal Exposition on Job*: c. 1261–65).

Catena aurea (*The Golden Chain*: c. 1262–64 [commentary on the Gospels drawing on quotations from the Church Fathers]).

Lectura super Matthaeum (*Commentary on Matthew*: c. 1269–70).

Lectura super Ioannem (*Commentary on John*: c. 1270–72).

Expositio et Lectura super Epistolas Pauli Apostoli (*Commentaries on the Letters of St Paul*: dating very difficult to establish, possibly 1265–73).

Postilla super Psalmos (*Commentary on the Psalms*: c. 1273).

COMMENTARIES ON ARISTOTLE

Sententia Libri De anima (*Commentary on Aristotle's* On the Soul: 1267–68).

Sententia Libri De Sensu et sensato (*Commentary on Aristotle's* On Sense [*and* On Memory]: c. 1268–69).

Sententia super Physicam (*Commentary on Aristotle's* Physics: c. 1268–69).

Sententia super Meteora (*Commentary on Aristotle's* Meteorology: c. 1268–70).

Sententia Libri Politicorum (*Commentary on Aristotle's* Politics: c. 1269–72).

Expositio Libri Peri hermeneias (*Commentary on Aristotle's* On Interpretation [*De Interpretatione*]: c. 1270–71).

Expositio Libri Posteriorum (*Commentary on Aristotle's* Posterior Analytics: c. 1270–72).

Sententia Libri Ethicorum (*Commentary on Aristotle's* Nichomachean Ethics: 1271–72).

Sententia super Metaphysicam (*Commentary on Aristotle's* Metaphysics: c. 1270–72).

Sententia super librum De caelo et mundo (*Commentary on Aristotle's* On the Heavens: c. 1272–73).

Sententia super libros De generatione et corruptione (*Commentary on Aristotle's* On Generation and Corruption: c. 1272–73).

OTHER COMMENTARIES

Expositio super librum Boethii De trinitate (*Commentary on Boethius's* De Trinitate: c. 1257–59).

Expositio in librum Boethii De hebdomadibus (*Commentary on Boethius's* Hebdomads [actually, Boethius's third theological tractate]: c. 1257–59).

Expositio super Dionysium De divinis nominibus (*Commentary on [Pseudo-] Dionysius's* The Divine Names: c. 1261–68).

Expositio super librum De causis (*Commentary on the Book of Causes*: c. 1272).

POLEMICAL WRITINGS

Contra impugnantes Dei cultum et religionem (*Against those who Impugn the Cult of God and Religion*: 1256).

De perfectione spiritualis vitae (*On the Perfection of the Spiritual Life*: 1269–70).

De unitate intellectus contra Averroistas (*On the Unicity of the Intellect Against the Averroists*: 1270).

Contra doctrinam retrahentium a religione homines a religionis ingressu [commonly referred to as *Contra retrahentes*] (*Against the teachings of those who prevent men entering the religious life*: 1271).

De aeterntate mundi (*On the Eternity of the World*: c. 1271).

TREATISES AND OTHER WORKS ON ASSORTED TOPICS

De ente et essentia (*On Being and Essence*: c. 1252–56).

De principiis naturae (*On the Principles of Nature*: c. 1252–56, possibly earlier).

De regno ad regem Cypri (*On Kingship, to the King of Cyprus*: c. 1267).

De substantiis separatis (*On Separate Substances*: c. 1271).

Contra errores Graecorum (*Against the Errors of the Greeks*: c .1263–64).

De mixtione elementorum (*On the Mixture of Elements*: c. 1270).

LITURGICAL AND RELATED WORKS

Collationes in decem praecepta (*Homilies on the Ten Commandments*: c. 1261–73).

Officium de festo Corporis Christi (*Office for the Feast of Corpus Christi*: c. 1264).

Hymn *Adoro Te* (commonly referred to by its Latin title: date unknown).

Collationes in orationem dominicam, in Symbolorum Apostolorum, in salutatem angelicam (*Homilies on the Lord's Prayer, the Apostles' Creed, and the Angelic Greeting*: c. 1268–73).

Index

There are many concrete illustrations of the ideas expressed in the text and the author makes particular reference to his cat Smokey who recurs throughout. The most significant illustrations are indexed under 'analogies'.